THE TURKEY COOKBOOK

THE
TURKEY
COOKBOOK

Rick Rodgers

A John Boswell Associates/King Hill Productions Book

HarperPerennial
A Division of HarperCollins*Publishers*

FIRST EDITION

Designed by Karen Savary

Library of Congress Cataloging-in-Publication Data

Rodgers, Rick, 1953–
    The turkey cookbook / Rick Rodgers. — 1st Perennial Library ed.
      p. cm.
    ISBN 0-06-055278-6
    ISBN 0-06-096558-4 (pbk.)
    1. Cookery (Turkey) I. Title.
  TX750.5.T87R63 1990   89-46113
  641.6′6592—dc20

---

90 91 92 93 94 CGI/HC 10 9 8 7 6 5 4 3 2 1
90 91 92 93 94 CGI/HC 10 9 8 7 6 5 4 3 2 1 (pbk.)

Acknowledgments

A special thank-you to my friends at Perdue Farms for generously supplying their excellent turkey products for recipe-testing purposes. Chris Whaley and Stephanie Burton in Salisbury, Maryland, were particularly helpful. Anne Salisbury and Nancy Plumaker at R.C. Auletta, Perdue's public relations representatives in New York City, supplied me with much information and support.

Thanks to Teresa Farney of the National Turkey Federation for providing statistics and facts. Mary Kemmamer, of the National Wild Turkey Federation, and I had a long talk about wild turkey hunting and cooking that I incorporated into my wild turkey tips. Ariane Daugin of D'Artagnan and I also "talked turkey," but particularly about farm-raised organic and wild turkeys, of which she is an excellent purveyor. Thanks also to Lisa Readie and the Barbecue Industry Council.

Many people were generous with recipes and inspirations. Some are food professionals; all are great cooks and most are great friends: Bruce Aidells, Harriet Bell, Paul and Julie Buhtanic, Steve Butz, Joseph Costanzo, George Germon, Beulah Hesen, Johanne Killeen, Elizabeth Menicou, and Eleanor Rodgers.

Diane Kniss is an invaluable friend, in or out of the kitchen. She's been priceless to me for years, but her help on this project cannot be measured, only deeply appreciated. Other friends who tested recipes and washed dishes include Steve Evasew and Nancy Swiezy, both excellent chefs and caterers in their own right. Cynthia and Steven Stahl's family, from great-grandmother Ardelle to newcomer Jackson, were also indefatigable testers and eaters. Patrick Fisher is my best friend and a great typist.

Susan Wyler, my compatriot and editor, is to be thanked for being one of the two most fateful phone calls of 1989.

Contents

Introduction

THE NEW TURKEY

No less a patriot than Benjamin Franklin was a great fan of turkey: "I wish the eagle had not been chosen as the representative of our country. He is a bird of bad moral character. . . . The turkey is a much more respectable bird, and withal a true original native of America." It is said that Franklin even lobbied for the turkey to be featured on our national seal.

While it never made official status, the large bird remains a glorious part of America's folklore and a well-established staple on holiday tables. The new turkey choices, however—ground turkey, turkey cutlets, turkey sausages, and boned turkey roasts, to name just a few of turkey's modern guises—are causing a lot of excitement these days. With easy-to-prepare, reasonably priced cuts so accessible in supermarkets throughout the country, cooks are reaching for turkey as a light alternative to red meat and as a welcome change from the omnipresent chicken and high-priced veal.

As a result of developing these recipes, I've learned that turkey is amazingly versatile—as shown by such diverse dishes as Guadalajara Grilled Drumsticks; Turkey, Pasta, and Vegetable Salad with Spicy Peanut Dressing; and Sweet-and-Sour Baked Turkey Cutlets—but it is so low in fat (and cholesterol) that it requires its own cooking temperatures and techniques.

You can't just make a one-to-one substitution of ground turkey for ground beef or turkey cutlets for veal scallops. In flavor and texture, turkey makes a fine alternative, but to remain tender and juicy, it should be prepared according to its own standards. That's what is offered here. *The Turkey Cookbook* explains how to cook all the turkey cuts you'll encounter to their best advantage, in the most delicious and sometimes surprising ways.

This brand-new collection of recipes was inspired by seasonings and cooking styles from all over the world. There are Buffalo Turkey Wings with Blue Cheese Dip and Turkey Drumsticks Osso Buco–Style. There's easy Pennsylvania Dutch Turkey Noodle Supper for everyday meals and Red, White, and Green Turkey Lasagne for company. Turkey cutlets rival veal scallopini in delicate taste and speedy preparation, and I've included a large group of these recipes—such as Turkey and Mushroom Stroganoff and Chicken-Fried Turkey Steaks with Ranch-House Milk Gravy—to get you out of the kitchen in record time.

Kids love ground turkey, especially when it is served between toasted hamburger buns in the guise of Sloppy Toms or over pasta, as in Turkey and Tomato Pasta Sauce Presto. It makes fabulous meat loaves, and if you like comfort food, you've got to try Farmer's Turkey Potpie with Mashed Potato Crust.

Of course, a big bird is still one of the easiest foods to cook up for a crowd, and I have certainly not neglected the pièce de résistance that graces every Thanksgiving table: whole roast turkey. I'll let you in on the most sure-fire way I know to create the juiciest, crispiest, most succulent turkey ever. Both traditional and new ways with turkeys are outlined, from Perfect Roast Turkey with Gorgeous Giblet Gravy to Wild Turkey with Glazed Chestnut Stuffing and even a Texas Turkey, roasted split in half for speedier results.

What is Thanksgiving without a groaning board of side dishes? In Chapter 9 you can select from a cornucopia of stuffings and other fixings to enliven any turkey dinner. Gingery Lemon-Cranberry Chutney, Oyster and Sausage Gumbo Dressing, Scalloped Sweet Potatoes with Streusel Topping, and Rick's Melt-in-Your-Mouth Corn Bread are just a few.

And what is roast turkey without leftovers? You'll buy the biggest turkey you can find just so you can turn leftovers into Turkey and Corn Croquettes with Fresh Tomato Salsa, Cheesy Tomato and Turkey Bake, or Turkey, Bacon, and Tomato Club Sandwiches. You may even find yourself resorting to roasting or poaching a whole or half turkey breast just for meat to recycle into one of these exciting recipes.

While *The Turkey Cookbook* is full of everyday recipes, in Chapter 7 you will find recipes that are reserved for those special glitzy affairs that warrant a little extra time and attention. Daube of Turkey, Turkey and Wild Mushroom Risotto, Galantine of Turkey, and Turkey Company Casserole with Zucchini and Potatoes make a show-off out of the humble bird. And when the weather is warm, and you're entertaining outdoors, do not neglect turkey on the grill. Imagine what a hit Spice-Rubbed Smoked Turkey with Bourbon Soppin' Sauce or Turkey Thigh and Summer Vegetable Kebabs will make at your next picnic.

ALL ABOUT TURKEY

Types of Turkeys

TOMS AND HENS: Just as there are two basic kinds of people, there are two basic kinds of turkeys—male and female. Female hens are raised to weigh 8 to 16 pounds. Male toms, bred to give the high yield of white breast meat that so many Americans favor, weigh 14 to 26 pounds.

There is no difference in tenderness or moistness between hens and toms. In choosing, your only consideration should be how many people you are serving. I allow a minimum of 1 pound of uncooked turkey per person. Of course, appetites vary and people do tend to stuff themselves when that big bird is on the table, so if you want to have healthy leftovers, add an extra ¼ pound per person.

You may notice that both toms and hens are almost always labeled "young" turkeys. The term refers to the fact that even the oldest tom on the market is only 5½ months old. More mature stewing turkeys are only available to the food service industry.

FRESH TURKEY: Whether it's a tom or a hen, a fresh turkey is always my first choice. The taste is full and natural, and I can do without the long defrosting ritual, which invariably leads to a loss of flavorful juices. Choose a Grade A bird, with clean white skin free of bruises or tears. Store in the coldest part of the refrigerator, at around 40 degrees, and use within two days of purchase.

Be sure you are, in fact, buying a fresh, not thawed, turkey. Many butcher shops buy their turkeys fresh and then deep-freeze them at the market to fit inventory schedules. If your turkey package is marked "fresh," but the turkey inside is hard and frosty, have a little talk with the butcher. To be sure you get the fresh turkey of your choice, order up to 2 weeks in advance around holiday seasons.

FROZEN TURKEY: Many people prefer the convenience of buying a frozen turkey, especially at the supermarket or during the weekend before Thanksgiving, when there is a run on the bird. All frozen turkeys can be delicious if thawed and cooked properly. Here are some helpful tips:

▶ For best results, use frozen, uncooked turkeys within 6 months of purchase.

▶ Never defrost turkey at room temperature.

▶ For best results, defrost turkey in the refrigerator. Allow a full 24-hour period *for each 5 pounds* of turkey.

▶ If you are in a hurry, defrost the turkey in a sink full of cold water, changing the water and turning the turkey often. Allow 30 minutes for each pound of turkey. Never add warm water to speed thawing.

I don't like to use the microwave to defrost turkey, and most microwaves won't hold a turkey larger than 12 pounds. If you must use this method for speed, follow the directions in your model's instruction booklet and turn the turkey often for even penetration of the microwaves.

SELF-BASTING TURKEYS: These turkeys, fresh or frozen, have been injected with a solution of broth, fat, and/or flavorings. Self-basting birds are juicy, but I find these additions can mask the sweet, natural taste of an unadulterated, perfectly roasted turkey. One could compare it to the choice between a country ham and one that has been water-injected and canned. Both have their place.

ORGANIC FREE-RANGE TURKEY: Farm raised in a relatively spacious environment that gives them room in which to run around and scratch, these turkeys develop more muscle, which makes them a bit tougher, but also more flavorful. Organic turkey feed is natural and free of antibiotics. (By the way, hormones have been outlawed in the entire poultry industry since the late 1950s.) While organic turkeys are raised with integrity and have good flavor and a texture that is somewhat firmer than that of ordinary fresh turkeys, they are significantly more expensive, and whether or not the subtle difference is worth it is highly subjective. Look for organic, free-range turkeys in better butcher shops or at farmers' markets. They can also be mail-ordered from D'Artagnan, 399 St. Paul Avenue, Jersey City, New Jersey 07306; 800-327-8246; 201-792-0748.

KOSHER TURKEYS: Kosher turkeys are raised and slaughtered according to strict Jewish dietary laws. They are raised free-range in a fashion similar to organic turkeys and are fed antibiotic-free feed. Some people feel that the method of slaughter, in which all the blood is immediately drained from the body, leads to a fresher, cleaner taste. Many kosher poultry products are frozen, so care must be taken in defrosting and cooking the turkeys in order to ensure that the extra money used to purchase a kosher bird is well spent.

FARM-RAISED WILD TURKEYS: This sounds like an anachronism, but most of the wild turkey you buy to eat—actually a different variety from ordinary Thanksgiving turkey—is raised in a domestic environment—organically and free-range. Add to these expensive procedures the law of supply and demand, and you have one costly, but great-tasting bird.

Comparing the flavor of wild turkey to regular turkey is like comparing sourdough bread to plain bread: both are delicious, but there is a depth of flavor in one that some people appreciate and others find too strong. The white meat is actually quite similar to ordinary turkey, but the succulent dark meat has a distinctive taste all its own. If you've never savored a wild turkey and you like slightly gamey meats, do try one for an important occasion.

Do not be alarmed if the skin is off-white and freckled. Wild turkeys have dark pigmentation. Regular domesticated turkeys are bred with all white feathers so no color will show on the skin after plucking.

I roast farm-raised wild turkeys the same way as the Thanksgiving variety, making sure to baste often, since wild turkeys are quite lean. They have a characteristic humped breast bone and less of a meat-to-bone ratio than other turkeys, so it is necessary to allow a full 1¼ pounds per person. Store-bought wild turkeys are rarely larger than 8 to 10 pounds.

Wild turkeys are available in some butcher shops, often on special order. Two reliable mail-order sources are D'Artagnan (800-327-8246; 201-792-0748) for the East Coast and the Midwest, and Durham-Night Bird Game and Poultry Company (415-873-5035), 650 San Mateo Avenue, San Bruno, California 94066.

WILD WILD TURKEYS: Strict game laws have done a good job protecting this once nearly extinct bird, and they have made a fantastic comeback in many states, including New York, Pennsylvania, and Massachusetts. Free-roaming wild turkeys are smart, fast flying, and well protected by their heavy armor of dark feathers. There are plenty of game cookbooks that deal with hunters' cuisine. The recipes in this book were developed specifically for the farm-raised wild turkey. However, I will share some general tips for roasting a bagged wild turkey.

These birds get plenty of exercise, so they have very little fat, and their legs, thighs, and wings can be extremely tough. A tenderizing soak in a wine marinade is a good idea. Since the white meat remains more uniform, and there is no way of knowing for sure how tough (or tender) the dark meat will be until after cooking, most of my hunter friends recommend cooking them separately. Roast the breast and prepare the dark meat as a confit, soup, or stew to serve as a separate course or the next day. If you do roast the bird whole and the dark meat turns out to be exceedingly tough, chop or grind it and turn it into hash or meatballs. When roasting, be sure to baste the turkey often with marinade, melted butter, or broth. Covering the breast with a few strips of blanched bacon also discourages dryness.

For specifics on roasting a whole turkey, see Chapter 1.

The New Turkey

What's revolutionary about turkey today is not so much the different varieties available as it is the different cuts. If you don't need a whole turkey, sometimes you can buy a half or a quartered very small bird. If you only like white meat, there are breasts—half, whole, bone in, or boned and tied into a turkey breast roast. There are cutlets—skinless, boneless slices of lean meat that can be pounded into thin scallopini that cook in less than 10 minutes. There are extra-thick and meaty turkey steaks and delicate tenderloins.

If you prefer dark meat, there are turkey drumsticks, turkey thighs, and turkey wings. There is ground turkey, which is proving itself immensely popular because of its versatility and ability to stand in for ground red meat. All these cuts (and methods of cooking them) are discussed at length at the beginning of the appropriate chapters.

There is also smoked turkey, which makes a great substitute for smoked chicken or ham. And there are prepared turkey products—turkey Italian-style sausage, turkey kielbasa, and turkey lunch meats, for example—readily available at supermarkets.

As a Manhattan caterer, I incorporated turkey into my menus to support my clients' health-conscious eating standards. Instead of serving turkey only in the form of an occasional holiday roast, I began offering Turkey Salad with Asparagus, Mushrooms, and Hazelnuts on the buffet at a spring wedding; Moroccan Turkey and Spice Mini-turnovers as an elegant hors d'oeuvre at a French embassy reception; Lucky's Turkey Pizza with Tomato Sauce, Olives, and Jalapeños at outdoor summer events; and even Chunky Turkey Chili at an office party. Whether your menu is upscale and elegant or down-home and simple, remember, turkey is no longer a once-a-year bird.

THE TURKEY COOKBOOK

CHAPTER ONE

The Big Bird:
Cooking a Whole Turkey

I f it's time for a big roast turkey, but you don't want to serve the same old meal, this chapter will help you out. In addition to Perfect Roast Turkey, the best traditional bird you can present, there is a Middle Eastern–inspired Roast Turkey with Pomegranate Sauce; Italian Lemon-Rosemary Turkey with Roasted Potatoes and Garlic; Spanish Turkey with Ham, Raisins, Olives, and Sherry; and spicy Texas Turkey with Chili-Onion Rub, to name just a few of the choices.

Here is some general information on how to roast any turkey to perfection.

PREPARING TURKEY FOR ROASTING

When you first bring the bird home from market, if it is wrapped, leave it in its plastic wrapping. These are specially devised by producers to preserve the meat. When you're ready to cook the turkey, begin by cleaning the bird well. Remove the giblets from both the neck and body cavities. Rinse the turkey thoroughly inside and out under cold running water until there is no trace of blood. Wipe the inside of the turkey well and pat the outside dry with paper towels. Dry skin crisps much better when it is roasted.

If you're planning to stuff the turkey, do so just before roasting. For everything you'll ever want to know about stuffing, see Chapter 9.

Trussing the bird is easy, especially if you do it my way, which requires no needle, string, or fancy sewing. Simply secure the neck skin to the back with a wooden toothpick or a small metal skewer. Tuck the wings akimbo behind the turkey's shoulders; this gives the bird a solid foundation to rest on and protects the wing tips from burning. (If you insist on an old-fashioned look, tie the wings to the turkey's side with kitchen string and shield the wing tips with aluminum foil.)

Many turkeys come with a metal or heatproof plastic clip located near the tail vent. This is called a "hock lock," and it should be used to secure the ends of the drumsticks in place. Some turkeys have a ring cut into the skin near the vent to provide the same service. If your turkey has no hock lock, simply tie the ends of the drumsticks together with white kitchen string.

ROASTING THE TURKEY

The primary goal of roasting any whole turkey is to assure juicy, tender meat with crisp, golden-brown skin. What makes this harder than it sounds is that different parts of the turkey are done at different times. The white meat breast, which is cooked through at 165 to 170 degrees, will be done well before the dark meat legs and thighs, which must reach 180 degrees. (Even the instant pop-up thermometers that come with some turkeys can't solve this problem, because they must be calibrated for one temperature or the other.) By the time the dark meat is done, the white meat will be overcooked and beginning to dry out.

There are two easy procedures I recommend to keep the entire turkey moist and tender: tenting the breast with foil and basting. Loosely covering the top of the turkey with aluminum foil creates a moist-heat environment in that area, which prevents drying out. The foil is removed during the last hour of roasting to allow the skin to brown nicely. Do not tent the *entire* bird, or it will taste steamed.

Basting—which also helps keep the bird moist, facilitates the crisping of the skin, and creates flavorful pan juices for gravy—should be done every 15 to 20 minutes. (The only alternative to this constant attention is the Cheesecloth Basting Method, page 6.) Melted butter, dry white wine, turkey stock or chicken broth, apple or orange juice—or any combination of the above—can be used. A bulb baster or long-handled brush are helpful for basting so you can reach all over the bird quickly. Lift up the foil tent to baste the entire breast well, but do not linger, or the oven temperature will drop and may throw off your timing.

Choose a large, shallow roasting pan with sides no higher than 2 inches. I know many people (including myself formerly) use a deep, dark-blue speckled enamel roasting pan, but I find that the height cuts down on heat circulation, and the bird doesn't brown as well. *Always* put the turkey on a roasting rack inside the pan to raise it out of the drippings and allow the hot air to circulate underneath.

To be sure the turkey is roasted to optimum temperature, a meat thermometer should be inserted in the thickest part of the thigh near the body, parallel to, but not touching, the thigh bone. Or use an instant-reading thermometer to test the bird often during the last hour of the estimated roasting time. If your turkey comes with a pop-up thermometer, use it as a signal to tell if the bird is done, and double-check with a standard meat thermometer.

Long, slow roasting at 325 degrees yields the best results. The meat will not shrink as much as at a higher temperature, more juices will be retained, and the drippings will not burn as easily. Estimate roasting times as follows:

Hens (8 to 16 pounds): 20 to 25 minutes per pound
Toms (16 pounds and up): 15 to 20 minutes per pound

Turkey roasting times are always approximate, as maddening as that can be, because of several factors:

▶ Varying conformations of turkeys
▶ Differences in oven temperatures (Hint: Always use an oven thermometer to guarantee accuracy.)
▶ Sporadic heat loss from opening the oven door
▶ Exact temperature of the turkey when it goes into the oven

I always estimate on the long side, because if the turkey is done early, it can sit in a warm spot, loosely covered with foil, and hold its heat for at least 1 hour without getting cold. If your meat thermometer suddenly alerts you that the turkey is in danger of overcooking, remove it from the oven immediately and set it in a cool, well-ventilated place to stop the cooking process as quickly as possible.

▶ *Never* cook a turkey overnight at very low temperatures.

▶ *Never* partially cook a turkey one day, refrigerate it, and try to complete the cooking the next day.

Both these methods are unsafe.

HOW TO TELL WHEN THE TURKEY IS DONE

▶ The meat thermometer, inserted in the meatiest part of the thigh, not touching bone, reads 180 degrees.

▶ The thigh and drumstick feel tender when pressed with a finger (protected from the heat with a folded paper towel). Don't cook until the drumstick "jiggles" in its socket, or the bird may well be overcooked.

▶ The turkey has suddenly released a lot of juices into the bottom of the pan.

▶ If the thigh is pierced with a fork or the tip of a knife, the juices run clear yellow with no trace of pink.

SERVING THE TURKEY

Garnishing

Even if you don't own a huge heirloom-quality serving platter, it's easy to present a whole roast turkey with style. A large wooden carving board has often served in place of fine china at my house. Curly, dark green kale makes an attractive bed to cradle the mahogany bird. Sometimes I'll surround the turkey with tiny ears of colorful dried Indian corn, small gourds, or bouquets of fresh herbs. Clusters of grapes, miniature Lady apples and Seckle pears, which are all in season throughout autumn and winter, are beautiful decorations.

Carving

Let the roast turkey stand at room temperature for at least 20 minutes before carving. The brief cooling period allows the hot juices to be drawn back into the meat and makes carving much neater. Use this time to make your gravy and to get all the side dishes on the table. Remove any stuffing from the turkey and serve it separately.

Carving is simple if you have a long, thin, very sharp knife. An electric knife is a great investment, even if you only use it on holidays. Think of the turkey in terms of human anatomy—i.e., the leg is connected to the thigh; the turkey's wing is its arm, which connects to the shoulder joint, and so on. Here's my step-by-step technique for carving a whole bird.

1. Remove the drumsticks and thighs on both sides by pulling each leg away from the body and cutting through the skin to reach the meat and expose the ball joint. Sever the thigh at the hip joint where it meets the body. Separate the drumsticks from the thighs at the connecting joint.
2. To allow more people to enjoy the dark meat, tilt each drumstick, holding it from the foot end, and cut downward around the bone to slice the meat. Holding the thigh with a long carving fork, carve away the meat parallel to the bone.
3. Cut off the wings at the shoulder joints.
4. Hold the breast firmly with a fork. One side at a time, make a deep horizontal base cut parallel to the table down near the wing; then cut down along the breast to carve it into thin slices, as you would a ham. Every slice will stop at the parallel base cut.

If you still feel shy about carving, present the whole roast bird in all its burnished glory. Then vanish into the kitchen and divvy up the meat where no one's looking.

Storing Leftovers

After dinner, try to get any leftover turkey or stuffing into the refrigerator within 2 hours of serving. Never leave leftovers out overnight.

Always refrigerate stuffing separately. Cut away any remaining meat from the carcass and wrap it tightly with aluminum foil. Refrigerate at 40 degrees or below and serve within 2 or 3 days. Frozen leftovers should be used within 3 months.

▶*Cheesecloth Basting Method* Here's an alternative method of basting preferred by some cooks to the attentive, loving basting that I think produces the best turkey. If you wish to try the cheese-cloth method, follow these directions. Cut a double thickness of cheesecloth large enough to drape completely over the entire turkey (not just the breast) with an extra 2 inches all the way around. You may need two overlapping pieces. Rinse the cheese-cloth well under cold running water and squeeze dry. Dip the cheesecloth in about 1/3 cup vegetable oil or melted butter and drape the soaked cloth over the entire bird; in this case there is no need to rub the bird with butter beforehand. Be sure that the excess cheesecloth is touching the bottom of the inside of the roasting pan. Pour 1 cup of water into the bottom of the pan. The cheesecloth will act as a wick, soaking up the pan drippings and distributing them over the bird. Be sure that the pan drip-pings do not boil away; add additional water to the bottom of the pan, if necessary.

Perfect Roast Turkey with Gorgeous Giblet Gravy

Here are my detailed instructions on how to roast the crispiest, juiciest, tastiest turkey you have ever dreamed of carrying to a dining room table. Roasting the turkey *unstuffed* cuts the cooking time by up to an hour, and the aromatic vegetables and herbs used instead add a lovely fragrance to the bird. If you choose this method, simply bake your favorite stuffing in a pan on the side.

Makes 16 to 20 servings

1 fresh tom turkey (18 pounds), neck and giblets reserved, liver and excess fat removed
1¼ teaspoons salt
¾ teaspoon freshly ground pepper
1 medium onion, chopped
1 medium carrot, chopped
1 medium celery rib, chopped
¼ cup chopped fresh parsley
2 tablespoons chopped fresh rosemary, or 1 teaspoon dried

2 tablespoons chopped fresh sage, or 1 teaspoon dried
2 tablespoons chopped fresh thyme, or 1 teaspoon dried
1 stick unsalted butter, softened
1 cup dry white wine or water
3 cups Homemade Turkey Stock (see page 246), or 1½ cups canned chicken broth mixed with 1½ cups water
¼ cup all-purpose flour

1. Rinse the turkey well, inside and out, under cold running water. Using lots of paper towels, wipe out the inside of the turkey and pat the outside completely dry.

2. Rub the cavity well with ½ teaspoon salt and ¼ teaspoon pepper. In a medium bowl, combine the onion, carrot, celery, parsley, rosemary, sage, and thyme; toss to mix. Loosely stuff the turkey's body and neck cavities with the vegetable-herb mixture. Cover the large body cavity with a small piece of aluminum foil to enclose the vegetables.

3. Using a thin metal skewer or wooden toothpicks, pin the neck skin to the turkey's back. Fold the wings akimbo behind the back. (Alternatively, if you prefer a classic look, tie the turkey wings to the sides of the breast with a loop of kitchen string.) Place the drumsticks in the hock lock, or tie them together with a piece of kitchen string. Rub the entire exterior of the turkey with the softened butter, then season the turkey all over with the remaining ¾ teaspoon salt and ½ teaspoon pepper.

(continued)

4. Preheat the oven to 325 degrees. Place the turkey on a rack in a large, shallow flameproof roasting pan, about 2 inches deep. Pour the wine into the bottom of the roasting pan. Loosely cover the turkey breast with aluminum foil.

5. Roast the turkey, basting quickly every 20 minutes with the pan drippings, for 4½ to 6 hours, allowing 15 to 20 minutes per pound, until a meat thermometer inserted in the meatiest part of the thigh, not touching a bone, registers 180 degrees. If at any point the drippings threaten to burn, add ½ cup water to the pan. About 1 hour before the turkey is done, remove the foil to allow the skin to brown. If the turkey begins to brown too deeply, loosely cover the area with aluminum foil. For more hints on when the turkey is done, see page 4. Remove the turkey to a carving board. Loosely cover with aluminum foil and let stand 20 minutes before carving. (The turkey will stay warm for at least 1 hour.)

6. While the turkey is roasting, prepare the giblets. Trim the heart and gizzard. In a medium saucepan, bring the trimmed giblets and stock to a boil over moderate heat. Reduce the heat to a simmer, cover, and cook until the giblets are very tender, about 1¼ hours. Remove the giblets, reserving the stock, and chop finely. Set the chopped giblets aside.

7. While the turkey is standing, make the gravy. Pour the pan drippings into a 1-quart glass measuring cup and let stand 5 minutes. Skim off the clear yellow fat that rises to the top, transferring the fat to a small bowl. Add enough of the reserved stock to the drippings to measure 4 cups total cooking liquid. Set the roasting pan over two burners on top of the stove over moderately low heat. Add ¼ cup of the reserved fat. Sprinkle in the flour and cook, whisking often, for 2 minutes. Whisk in the cooking liquid and bring to a boil, scraping up the brown bits from the bottom of the pan. Reduce to a simmer, add the giblets, and cook, whisking often, for 3 minutes. Season with additional salt and pepper to taste. Pour the gravy into a warmed sauceboat and serve with the turkey.

▶ *Approximately 45 million whole turkeys are consumed every Thanksgiving.*

Texas Turkey with Chili-Onion Rub

This is a different, very interesting approach to roasting a big bird. The turkey is split in two and rubbed with an eye-opening paste of onions, garlic, and spices. Each half is roasted on separate baking sheets. This dramatically reduces the cooking time, but not the flavor.

Makes 8 to 12 servings

1 hen turkey (10 pounds), neck, giblets, and excess fat removed
2 garlic cloves, crushed
1 jalapeño pepper, quartered and seeded

1 medium onion, quartered
1 stick unsalted butter, softened
2 to 3 tablespoons chili powder
1 teaspoon salt

1. Rinse the turkey well, inside and out, under cold running water. Pat dry with paper towels. Using a heavy cleaver or a large sharp knife, cut the turkey into two halves: Cut down both sides of the backbone through the ribs and discard the backbone. Open the turkey out like a book and cut down the center of the turkey through the breastbone. Place each turkey half, skin side up, on a large baking sheet.

2. In a food processor, with the machine on, drop the garlic cloves and jalapeño pepper through the feed tube to mince. Add the onion and pulse until finely chopped. Add the butter, chili powder, and salt; process until smooth. Spread the spiced butter over the turkey skin. Let the turkey stand for 1 hour at room temperature. (For fuller flavor, cover each turkey half well with plastic wrap and refrigerate overnight. Remove the turkey from the refrigerator 1 hour before roasting.)

3. Preheat the oven to 350 degrees. Loosely cover the turkey halves with aluminum foil and bake on the top and bottom shelves of the oven, basting often with the pan drippings, for 2¼ to 2¾ hours, allowing about 15 minutes per pound, until the thigh registers 180 degrees. Switch the positions of the baking sheets halfway through the baking period. About 45 minutes before the end of the roasting time, remove the foil to allow the skin to brown.

4. Remove the turkey to a carving board. Loosely cover with aluminum foil and let stand 10 to 15 minutes before carving.

Roast Turkey with Rich Pork and Fruit Stuffing, Lombardy Style

This ornate stuffing's treasure chest of ingredients—pork, chestnuts, prunes, pears, apples, rosemary, and nutmeg—reveals its Renaissance Italian origin. You will probably have leftover stuffing, which should be roasted alongside the turkey. It is sumptuous, exquisite, and *rich!*

Makes 10 to 14 servings

1 hen turkey (12 pounds), neck, giblets, and excess fat removed
1 stick unsalted butter, softened
1 large onion, finely chopped
1 pound ground pork
1 pound chestnuts, roasted, peeled, and coarsely chopped (see page 37)
2 medium green apples, cored and finely chopped
2 medium ripe pears, cored and finely chopped

½ cup finely chopped pitted prunes
2 large eggs, lightly beaten
¼ cup grated Parmesan cheese
2¾ teaspoons salt
1 tablespoon chopped fresh rosemary, or 1 teaspoon dried
¾ teaspoon freshly ground pepper
¼ teaspoon freshly grated nutmeg
2 cups dry white wine

1. Preheat the oven to 325 degrees. Rinse the turkey well, inside and out, under cold running water. Pat dry with paper towels.

2. In a medium skillet, melt 3 tablespoons butter over moderate heat. Add the onion and cook, stirring occasionally, about 5 minutes, until golden.

3. In a large bowl, combine the cooked onion with the ground pork, chestnuts, apples, pears, prunes, eggs, Parmesan, 2 teaspoons of the salt, rosemary, ½ teaspoon pepper, and the nutmeg; mix well. Loosely fill the large body cavity with the pork and fruit stuffing. Cover the exposed stuffing with a small piece of aluminum foil. Place any remaining stuffing in a lightly oiled 1-quart baking dish, cover with aluminum foil, and refrigerate.

4. Using a thin metal skewer or wooden toothpicks, pin the turkey's neck skin to the back. Fold the turkey's wings akimbo behind the back. Place the drumsticks in the hock lock or tie them together with kitchen string. Rub the turkey all over with the remaining 5 tablespoons butter. Season the turkey with the remaining ¾ teaspoon salt and ¼ teaspoon pepper. Place

the turkey on a rack in a large, shallow flameproof roasting pan. Pour 1 cup of the wine into the bottom of the pan. Loosely cover the turkey breast with aluminum foil.

5. Roast the turkey, basting often with the pan drippings, for 4 to 5 hours, allowing 20 to 25 minutes per pound, until the thigh meat registers 180 degrees. If at any point the drippings threaten to burn, add ½ cup water to the pan. About 1 hour before the end of the roasting time, remove the aluminum foil from the breast to allow the skin to brown and bake the reserved stuffing until a meat thermometer inserted in the center reads 165 degrees, about 1 hour. Remove the turkey to a carving board. Loosely cover with aluminum foil and let stand 20 minutes before carving.

6. While the turkey is standing, make the sauce. Pour all of the pan drippings into a 1-quart glass measuring cup or a medium bowl and let stand 5 minutes. Skim off the clear yellow fat that rises to the top. Set the roasting pan on top of the stove on two burners over moderately high heat. Add the pan drippings and the remaining 1 cup of wine. Bring to a boil, scraping up the brown bits on the bottom of the pan with a wooden spoon. Cook until evaporated to 1½ cups, about 5 minutes. Season with additional salt and pepper to taste. Pour the sauce into a warmed sauceboat and serve with the turkey and stuffing.

▶ *The legend goes that when the red man acted as hunting scout for the white man, the white man always chose the choice game, such as the turkey, for himself. The Indian naturally became distrustful of the settlers, and to "talk turkey" came to mean talking honestly at the beginning of a business deal.*

Spanish Turkey with Ham, Raisins, Olives, and Sherry

The Spanish are ingenious at creating inspired culinary combinations. While the individual ingredients in this robust stuffing may seem disparate, they blend together beautifully. Sherry adds a redolent nutty character to the bird and to the sauce.

Makes 12 to 16 servings

1 hen turkey (14 pounds), neck, giblets, and excess fat removed
¾ cup raisins
1½ cups dry sherry
5 cups fresh bread crumbs
½ pound smoked ham, such as prosciutto, Serrano, or Black Forest, cut into ½-inch cubes
1 cup slivered almonds, toasted (see page 229)
½ cup pimiento-stuffed green olives, coarsely chopped
2 large eggs, lightly beaten
1½ teaspoons salt
¾ teaspoon freshly ground pepper
¼ teaspoon ground cinnamon
6 tablespoons unsalted butter, softened
About 2 cups Homemade Turkey Stock (see page 246), or 1 cup canned chicken broth mixed with 1 cup water

1. Preheat the oven to 325 degrees. Rinse the turkey well, inside and out, under cold running water. Pat dry with paper towels.

2. In a small nonreactive saucepan, combine the raisins and ½ cup of the sherry. Bring to a simmer over low heat; remove from the heat.

3. In a large bowl, combine the bread crumbs, the raisins with their liquid, the ham, almonds, olives, eggs, ¾ teaspoon of the salt, ½ teaspoon of the pepper, and the cinnamon; mix well. Loosely place the stuffing in both the turkey's neck and body cavities. Cover the exposed stuffing in the large cavity with a small piece of aluminum foil. Using a thin metal skewer or wooden toothpicks, pin the neck skin to the turkey's back. Fold the wings akimbo behind the back. Place the drumsticks in the hock lock or tie together with kitchen string. Rub the turkey all over with the softened butter. Season with the remaining ¾ teaspoon salt and ¼ teaspoon pepper. Place the turkey on a rack in a large, shallow flameproof roasting pan. Loosely cover the turkey breast with aluminum foil.

4. Roast the turkey, basting often with the remaining 1 cup sherry and then the pan drippings, for 4½ to 5¾ hours, allowing 20 to 25 minutes per pound, until the thigh meat registers 180 degrees. If at any point the drippings threaten to burn, add ½ cup water to the pan. About 1 hour before the end of the roasting time, remove the foil over the turkey's breast to allow the skin to brown. Remove the turkey to a carving board. Loosely cover with aluminum foil and let stand 20 minutes before carving.

5. While the turkey is standing, make the sauce. Pour all of the pan drippings into a 1-quart glass measuring cup or a medium bowl and let stand 5 minutes. Skim off the clear yellow fat that rises to the top. Set the roasting pan on top of the stove on two burners over moderately high heat. Add the defatted pan drippings and the stock. Bring to a boil, scraping up the brown bits on the bottom of the pan with a wooden spoon. Boil until reduced to 2 cups, about 8 minutes. Season with additional salt and pepper to taste. Pour the sauce into a warmed sauceboat and serve with the turkey and stuffing.

Bayou Roast Turkey with Dirty Rice Dressing

All of the flavors of Cajun Country—onions, green peppers, garlic, sausage, and an explosion of spices—come into play here. The turkey is bathed with a zippy butter baste that encourages a crisp, highly seasoned skin. The rice dressing, cooked separately, is called "dirty" because of the earthy color acquired by the unrestrained addition of browned ground sausage and turkey giblets.

Makes 8 to 12 servings

1 hen turkey (12 pounds),
    neck, giblets, and excess fat
    removed, giblets reserved for
    dressing
1½ teaspoons salt
½ teaspoon freshly ground black
    pepper
1 medium onion, chopped
1 medium green bell pepper,
    chopped
1 medium celery rib with leaves,
    chopped
1 garlic clove, chopped
1 stick unsalted butter

1 teaspoon paprika, preferably
    Hungarian sweet
¾ teaspoon dried thyme
¾ teaspoon dried oregano
¼ teaspoon onion powder
¼ teaspoon cayenne pepper
1 bay leaf, crumbled
Dirty Rice Dressing (recipe follows)
About 2½ cups Homemade Turkey
    Stock (see page 246), or 1¼ cups
    canned chicken broth mixed with
    1¼ cups water
3 tablespoons all-purpose flour
⅓ cup chopped fresh parsley

1. Preheat the oven to 325 degrees. Rinse the turkey well, inside and out, under cold running water. Pat dry with paper towels. Season the body cavity of the turkey with ½ teaspoon of the salt and ¼ teaspoon of the black pepper. Place the chopped onion, bell pepper, celery, and garlic in the cavity. (If you prefer to stuff the bird with Dirty Rice Dressing, omit the chopped onion, bell pepper, celery, and garlic. Loosely stuff the turkey's neck and body cavities with the dressing, placing any remaining stuffing in a 1½-quart covered buttered baking dish. Cover the exposed dressing in the large cavity with a small piece of aluminum foil.)

2. Using a thin metal skewer or wooden toothpick, pin the neck skin to the turkey's back. Fold the wings akimbo behind the back. Place the drumsticks in the hock lock, or tie together with kitchen string. Loosely cover the turkey

breast with aluminum foil. Place the turkey on a rack in a large, shallow flameproof roasting pan.

3. In a small saucepan, melt the butter. Stir in the paprika, thyme, oregano, onion powder, cayenne, bay leaf, and the remaining 1 teaspoon salt and ¼ teaspoon black pepper.

4. Roast the turkey, basting often with the melted butter mixture, for 4 to 5 hours, allowing 20 to 25 minutes per pound, until the thigh meat registers 180 degrees. About 1 hour before the end of the roasting time, remove the foil to allow the skin to brown. Remove the turkey to a carving board. Loosely cover with aluminum foil and let stand at least 20 minutes before carving.

5. Meanwhile, pour all of the pan drippings into a 1-quart glass measuring cup or a medium bowl and let stand 5 minutes. Skim off the clear yellow fat that rises to the top and reserve 3 tablespoons. Add enough of the stock to the pan drippings to make 3 cups total liquid. Set the roasting pan on top of the stove on two burners over moderately low heat. Add the reserved turkey fat and cook until hot, about 30 seconds. Whisk in the flour and cook, whisking constantly, for 1 minute. Whisk in the turkey liquid, scraping up the browned bits on the bottom of the pan, and bring to a boil. Reduce the heat to a simmer and cook, whisking often, for 3 minutes. Stir in the chopped parsley. Season the gravy with additional salt and pepper to taste. Pour the gravy into a warmed sauceboat and serve with the turkey and dressing.

Dirty Rice Dressing

Makes about 8 cups

1 pound smoked turkey kielbasa, pork kielbasa, or andouille (see Note)
Turkey gizzard, heart, and liver, trimmed
4 tablespoons unsalted butter
2 medium onions, chopped
2 medium celery ribs with leaves, chopped
1 medium green bell pepper, chopped
2 garlic cloves, minced
1 teaspoon paprika

½ teaspoon dried thyme
½ teaspoon dried oregano
¼ teaspoon cayenne pepper
¼ teaspoon freshly ground black pepper
2 cups long-grain rice
About 1¾ cups Homemade Turkey Stock (see page 246), or 1 cup canned chicken broth mixed with ¾ cup water
2¼ cups water
Salt

1. Remove the casings from the sausage. Slice the sausage into ½-inch-thick rounds. In a food processor fitted with the metal blade, process the sausage, gizzard, heart, and liver until finely ground. In a large saucepan, melt the butter. Add the ground meats and cook over moderately high heat, stirring occasionally, until the meat juices are evaporated and the mixture is beginning to stick to the bottom of the pan, about 10 minutes.

2. Add the onions, celery, bell pepper, and garlic. Cook, stirring often, until the vegetables are softened, about 5 minutes. Stir in the paprika, thyme, oregano, cayenne, and black pepper. Add the rice, stock, and water. Bring to a boil, reduce the heat to low, cover tightly, and simmer until the liquid is absorbed and the rice is tender, about 30 minutes. Season with salt to taste, but you probably will find the sausage has salted the dressing enough. Either bake separately in a preheated 350-degree oven, covered, until heated through, about 30 minutes, or use to stuff a turkey.

Note: Smoked turkey kielbasa and pork andouille are available by mail order from Aidells's Sausage Company, 1575 Minnesota Street, San Francisco, California 94107, 415-285-6660.

Moroccan Roast Turkey
with Couscous and Vegetable Dressing

Alive with myriad spices, this is a knockout centerpiece to reserve for a large group of friends who all enjoy food with a kick to it. I created the Couscous and Vegetable Dressing to go with this turkey, but serve the dressing on the side only, please, because as a stuffing, the couscous overcooks and becomes mushy. I like to serve an eggplant-and-tomato dish as a side vegetable.

Makes 8 to 10 servings

1 hen turkey (12 pounds), neck, giblets, and excess fat removed
½ cup fresh orange juice
¼ fresh lemon juice
1½ sticks unsalted butter, softened
1 tablespoon plus 1 teaspoon paprika, preferably Hungarian sweet
2 teaspoons ground coriander
1½ teaspoons ground cumin
1 teaspoon ground ginger
¾ teaspoon salt

¼ teaspoon cayenne pepper
2 garlic cloves, crushed
2 large onions, sliced
About 2¼ cups Homemade Turkey Stock (see page 246), or 1¼ cups canned chicken broth mixed with 1 cup water
Harissa, sambal oolek, or hot pepper sauce, to taste (see Note)
Conscous and Vegetable Dressing (recipe follows)

1. Rinse the turkey well, inside and out, under cold running water. Pat dry with paper towels. In a large bowl, combine the orange juice and lemon juice. Place the turkey in the bowl, baste inside and out with the juice mixture, and let stand at room temperature, turning once or twice, for 1 hour. Remove the turkey from the bowl and drain it; reserve and refrigerate the juices. Pat the turkey dry with paper towels.

2. In a medium bowl, combine the butter with the paprika, coriander, cumin, ginger, salt, cayenne, and garlic; blend well. Rub the spiced butter all over the turkey, inside and out. Let the turkey stand for at least 2 hours, or overnight, at room temperature, covered loosely with plastic wrap and refrigerated.

3. Preheat the oven to 325 degrees. Place the sliced onions in the turkey's body cavity. Using a thin metal skewer or wooden toothpicks, pin the neck

(continued)

skin to the turkey's back. Fold the wings akimbo behind the back. Place the legs in the hock lock or tie them together with kitchen string. Place the turkey on a rack in a large, shallow flameproof roasting pan.

4. Roast the turkey, basting often with the reserved juices, and then the pan drippings, for 4 to 5 hours, allowing 20 to 25 minutes per pound, until the thigh meat registers 180 degrees. About 1 hour before the end of the roasting time, remove the foil to allow the skin to brown. Remove the turkey to a carving board. Loosely cover with aluminum foil and let stand for at least 20 minutes before carving.

5. Meanwhile, pour all of the pan drippings into a 1-quart glass measuring cup or a medium bowl and let stand 5 minutes. Skim off the clear yellow fat that rises to the top. Add enough of the turkey stock to the pan drippings to make 3 cups total liquid. Set the roasting pan on top of the stove on two burners over moderate heat. Pour in the turkey liquid and bring to a boil, scraping up the brown bits from the bottom of the pan with a wooden spoon. Season with salt and harissa or hot pepper sauce to taste. (The sauce should be thin and spicy.) Pour the sauce into a warmed sauceboat; use to moisten the turkey and the couscous dressing, served alongside.

> *Note:* Harissa *is a very hot Moroccan blend of chilies, garlic, and spices and is available at Middle Eastern groceries.* Sambal oolek *is a similar Indonesian chili paste, available by mail order from Dean and Deluca, 800-221-7714; 212-431-1691.*

Couscous and Vegetable Dressing

If you are unfamiliar with couscous, you're in for a treat. Couscous—tiny grains of pasta that cook up tender and tasty—is the national dish of Morocco.

Makes about 10 cups

1 cup raisins
6 cups Homemade Turkey Stock (see
    page 246), or 3 cups canned chicken
    broth mixed with 3 cups water
2½ cups water
6 tablespoons unsalted butter
2 teaspoons mint
1 teaspoon salt
½ teaspoon ground turmeric

½ teaspoon ground cinnamon
½ teaspoon ground cumin
¼ teaspoon cayenne pepper
4 small carrots, cut into ¼-inch dice
2 medium zucchini, cut into ¼-inch
    dice
2 packages (10 ounces each) couscous
4 scallions, thinly sliced
½ cup slivered blanched almonds

1. Put raisins in a bowl. Add enough hot water to cover by 1 inch. Let stand until plumped and softened, 30 to 60 minutes; drain.

2. In a large saucepan, bring the stock, water, butter, mint, salt, turmeric, cinnamon, cumin, and cayenne to a boil over high heat. Add the diced carrots and zucchini and cook for 1 minute. Stir in the couscous, cover tightly, and remove from the heat. Let the couscous stand for about 5 minutes, or until all the liquid is absorbed.

3. Fluff the couscous with a fork. Stir in the plumped raisins, scallions, and almonds. Transfer to a warmed serving dish.

> *Note: The couscous dressing can be prepared up to 4 hours ahead. After step 2, transfer the cooked couscous to a roasting pan and let cool, occasionally raking the couscous with your fingers and breaking up any lumps. Cover and refrigerate for up to 6 hours. To reheat, bake, covered, in a 350-degree oven, stirring occasionally, until heated through, about 30 minutes.*

Roast Turkey with Pomegranate Sauce

Pomegranates are one of autumn's treats, and they are popular in many cultures as a cooking ingredient as well as a fruit. The tiny red seeds are festive looking, and their tangy-sweet taste complements turkey meat beautifully. The rice, pine nut, and giblet stuffing provides a simple foil.

Makes 10 to 14 servings

1 hen turkey (12 pounds), neck and excess fat removed, heart, liver, and gizzard reserved
2 sticks plus 2 tablespoons unsalted butter, softened
3 medium onions, finely chopped
3 cups long-grain rice
⅔ cup pine nuts
3 cups canned chicken broth mixed with 3 cups water

2 teaspoons salt
¾ teaspoon freshly ground pepper
½ cup chopped fresh parsley
About 4 cups Homemade Turkey Stock (see page 246), or 2 cups canned chicken broth mixed with 2 cups water
3 medium pomegranates
¼ cup all-purpose flour

1. Rinse the turkey well, inside and out, under cold running water. Pat dry with paper towels. Trim the reserved heart, liver, and gizzard; mince and set aside. In a large saucepan, melt 1 stick of the butter over moderate heat. Add the onions and minced giblets; cook, stirring often, until the onion is softened and the giblets have lost their raw look, about 3 minutes. Add the rice and pine nuts, and cook, stirring, until the rice turns opaque, about 2 minutes. Add the chicken broth, water, 1½ teaspoons of the salt, and ½ teaspoon of the pepper. Bring to a boil, reduce heat to low, cover, and simmer until the rice has absorbed all of the liquid, 20 to 25 minutes. Remove the rice from the heat and stir in the parsley. Let the rice stuffing cool.

2. Preheat the oven to 325 degrees. Fill the neck and body cavities loosely with the rice stuffing. Cover the exposed stuffing in the large cavity with a small piece of aluminum foil. With a thin metal skewer or wooden toothpicks, pin the turkey's neck skin to its back. Fold the turkey's wings akimbo behind the back. Place the drumsticks in the hock lock or tie together with kitchen string. Rub the turkey with 6 tablespoons of the butter. Season with the remaining ½ teaspoon salt and ¼ teaspoon pepper. Place on a rack in a

large, shallow flameproof roasting pan. Pour 1 cup of the turkey stock into the bottom of the pan. Loosely cover the breast with aluminum foil.

3. Roast the turkey, basting often with the pan drippings, for 4 to 5 hours, allowing 20 to 25 minutes per pound, until the thigh meat registers 180 degrees. If at any point the drippings threaten to burn, add ½ cup water to the pan.

4. Meanwhile, cut open the pomegranates. Remove and reserve 1 cup of the seeds; squeeze the juice from the remainder (see page 20). About 1 hour before the turkey is done, remove the foil and continue basting, using the pomegranate juice in addition to the pan drippings. Remove the turkey to a carving board. Loosely cover with foil, and let stand 20 minutes before carving.

5. Meanwhile, pour all of the pan drippings into a 1-quart glass measuring cup and let stand 5 minutes. Skim off the clear yellow fat that rises to the top. Add enough turkey stock to make 4 cups total liquid. Set the roasting pan on top of the stove on two burners over moderately low heat. Add the remaining 4 tablespoons of butter and melt. Whisk in the flour and cook, whisking constantly, for 1 minute. Whisk in the turkey liquid and bring to a boil, scraping up the brown bits from the bottom of the pan. Reduce the heat to a simmer and cook, whisking often, for 3 minutes. Stir in the reserved pomegranate seeds and cook for 30 seconds. Season with additional salt and pepper to taste. Pour the sauce into a warmed sauceboat and serve with the turkey and rice stuffing.

> ▶ *Here's an easy way to remove the seeds and juice from a pomegranate. Submerge the pomegranate completely in a large bowl filled with cold water. Using a small sharp knife, score the pomegranate into quarters through the blossom end, cutting only about ¼ inch deep. Pull the pomegranate apart under the water. Loosen the seeds from the pith with your fingers. The seeds will sink to the bottom, and the pith will float to the top. Skim off the pith, discard the skin, and drain the seeds. To juice a pomegranate, place the seeds in a fine-meshed strainer set over a small bowl and press on the seeds with the back of a wooden spoon to extract the juice.*

Roast Turkey with Fragrant Rice Stuffing

Some of the most intoxicating aromas in the world waft through a kitchen where Indian food is being prepared. Here, I've made an exotically scented rice stuffing laced with cardamom, cinnamon, and ginger and bolstered with cashews and coconut. The stuffing is especially good if made with Indian basmati rice, which has a special character all its own. Served with Gingery Lemon-Cranberry Chutney (page 230), the whole dish is richly spiced without being fiery hot.

Makes 10 to 14 servings

1 hen turkey (12 pounds), neck, giblets, and excess fat removed
2 medium limes, cut in half
1 stick plus 5 tablespoons unsalted butter, softened
1 medium onion, finely chopped
2 cups basmati or long-grain rice (see Note)
1 teaspoon ground cardamom
1 teaspoon ground ginger
½ teaspoon ground cinnamon
½ teaspoon freshly ground pepper
¼ teaspoon ground cloves

4 cups water
2 teaspoons salt
1 cup roasted cashews, rinsed briefly under warm water to remove salt
1 cup coconut flakes, rinsed under warm water and squeezed dry to remove sugar
3 medium scallions, chopped
3 tablespoons all-purpose flour
About 4 cups Homemade Turkey Stock (see page 246), or 2 cups canned chicken broth mixed with 2 cups water

1. Rinse the turkey well, inside and out, under cold running water. Pat dry with paper towels. Place the turkey in a large bowl. Rub the turkey, inside and out, with the lime halves, and squeeze the lime juice over the turkey. Let the turkey stand at room temperature for 1 hour.

2. Preheat the oven to 325 degrees. In a large saucepan, melt 4 tablespoons of the butter over moderate heat. Add the onion and cook, stirring often, until onion is softened, about 3 minutes. Add the rice and cook, stirring, until the rice turns opaque, about 2 minutes. Add the cardamom, ginger, cinnamon, ¼ teaspoon of the pepper, and cloves; stir until very fragrant, about 1 minute. Add the water and 1½ teaspoons of the salt. Bring to a boil. Reduce the heat to low, cover, and simmer until the rice has absorbed all the liquid, 20 to 25 minutes. Remove the rice from the heat; stir in the cashews, coconut, and scallions. Let the rice stuffing cool.

3. Spoon the rice stuffing loosely into the turkey's neck and body cavities. Using a thin metal skewer or wooden toothpicks, pin the turkey's neck skin to its back. Cover the exposed stuffing in the large cavity with a small piece of aluminum foil. Fold the turkey's wings akimbo behind the back. Place the drumsticks in the hock lock or tie together with kitchen string. Rub the turkey with 6 tablespoons of the remaining butter. Sprinkle the remaining ½ teaspoon salt and ¼ teaspoon pepper all over the skin. Place the turkey on a rack in a large, shallow flameproof roasting pan. Pour 1 cup of the turkey stock over the turkey. Loosely cover the breast with aluminum foil.

4. Roast the turkey, basting often with the pan drippings, for 4 to 5 hours, allowing 20 to 25 minutes per pound, until the thigh meat registers 180 degrees. If at any point the drippings threaten to burn, add ½ cup water to the pan. About 1 hour before the turkey is done, remove the foil to allow the skin to brown. Remove the turkey to a carving board. Loosely cover with foil, and let stand 20 minutes before carving.

5. While the turkey is standing, make the sauce. Pour all of the pan drippings into a 1-quart glass measuring cup and let stand 5 minutes. Skim off the clear yellow fat that rises to the top. Add enough stock to make 3 cups total liquid. Set the roasting pan on top of the stove on two burners over moderately low heat. Add the remaining 3 tablespoons butter and melt. Whisk in the flour and cook, whisking constantly, for 1 minute. Whisk in the turkey liquid and bring to a boil, scraping up the brown bits from the bottom of the pan. Reduce the heat to a simmer and cook, whisking often, for 3 minutes. Season with additional salt and pepper to taste. Pour the sauce into a warmed sauceboat and serve with the turkey and stuffing.

Note: Basmati rice is available at Indian groceries and by mail order from Dean and Deluca, 560 Broadway, New York, New York 10012, 800-221-7714; 212-431-1691.

Steve's Sausage-Stuffed Roast Turkey
with Rosemary-Wine Sauce

No, not sausage stuffing, but a big tom turkey stuffed and roasted with sweet Italian sausages! My friend, playwright Steve Butz, is famous for his Thanksgiving bashes, where each year he usually creates a new pièce de résistance. But this was so good, he says, guests have actually insisted on its return appearance for the last four years. Try it, and you'll see what they're raving about.

Makes 16 to 18 servings

1 tom turkey (18 pounds), neck, giblets, and excess fat removed
1 teaspoon salt
½ teaspoon freshly ground pepper
20 sweet Italian pork sausages (about 3½ pounds; see Note)
2 tablespoons olive oil
1 tablespoon dried rosemary, crumbled

2 cups hearty dry red wine, such as Zinfandel
About 2 cups Homemade Turkey Stock (see page 246), or 1 cup canned chicken broth mixed with 1 cup water
4 tablespoons unsalted butter
¼ cup all-purpose flour

1. Preheat the oven to 325 degrees. Rinse the turkey well, inside and out, under cold running water. Pat dry with paper towels. Season the inside of the turkey with ½ teaspoon of the salt and ¼ teaspoon of the pepper. Using a thin metal skewer or wooden toothpicks, pin the turkey's neck skin to its back. Prick the sausages all over with a fork. Place 4 of the sausages inside the turkey's large body cavity. Cover the exposed sausage with a small piece of aluminum foil. Fold the turkey's wings akimbo behind the back. Place the drumsticks in the hock lock or tie them together with kitchen string. Brush the turkey all over with the olive oil; sprinkle with the remaining ½ teaspoon salt and ¼ teaspoon pepper and 1 teaspoon of the rosemary.

2. Split 2 sausages lengthwise, almost all the way through, and open them like a book. Using wooden toothpicks, secure them on each side of the turkey's breast. Place the turkey on a rack in a large, shallow flameproof roasting pan. Pour 1 cup of the red wine into the bottom of the pan. Arrange the remaining 14 sausages in the pan around the turkey. Loosely cover the breast with aluminum foil.

3. Roast the turkey, basting often with the pan drippings, for 4½ to 6 hours, allowing 15 to 20 minutes per pound, until the thigh meat registers 180 degrees. About 1 hour before the end of the roasting time, remove and discard the aluminum foil and the sausages on the breast.

4. Remove the turkey to a carving board. Loosely cover with foil and let stand 20 minutes before carving. Transfer the browned sausages around the turkey to a serving dish, cover, and keep warm. Coarsely chop the pale, steamed sausages inside the turkey and set aside.

5. Meanwhile, pour all of the pan drippings into a 1-quart glass measuring cup or a medium bowl and let stand 5 minutes. Skim off the clear yellow fat that rises to the top. Add the remaining red wine and enough stock to make 4 cups total liquid. Set the roasting pan on top of the stove on two burners over moderately low heat. Add the butter and melt. Whisk in the flour and cook, whisking constantly, for 1 minute. Whisk in the turkey liquid, scraping up the brown bits from the bottom of the pan, and bring to a boil. Add the remaining 2 teaspoons rosemary and the chopped sausages. Reduce the heat to a simmer and cook, whisking often, for 3 minutes. Season with additional salt and pepper to taste. Pour the sauce into a warmed sauceboat and serve with the turkey surrounded by the browned sausages.

Note: Turkey Italian-style sausages, with their very low fat content, do not take well to this long roasting period, so use pork sausages here.

Italian Lemon-Rosemary Turkey with Roasted Potatoes and Garlic

Lemon, garlic, and rosemary have always been a popular trio in my kitchen, especially with poultry. This is an Italian turkey, scented from the inside by being stuffed with whole lemons and a head of garlic. Rosemary branches and bay leaves, slipped under the skin, not only flavor the meat, but show through after roasting and make for a visually interesting presentation. Potato wedges are baked alongside, basted with the mouth-watering drippings from the roast.

Makes 10 to 14 servings

1 hen turkey (12 pounds), neck, giblets, and excess fat removed
2 teaspoons salt
¾ teaspoon freshly ground pepper
2 small lemons, rinsed
1 bunch fresh rosemary, or 2 tablespoons dried rosemary, crumbled
6 bay leaves
3 large heads of garlic

¼ cup plus 2 tablespoons olive oil
1½ cups dry white wine
7 medium baking potatoes, peeled and cut lengthwise into eighths
About 1 cup Homemade Turkey Stock (see page 246), or ½ cup canned chicken broth mixed with ½ cup water
3 tablespoons cold butter, cut into pieces

1. Preheat the oven to 325 degrees. Rinse the turkey well, inside and out, under cold running water. Pat dry with paper towels. Season the turkey, inside and out, with 1 teaspoon of the salt and ¼ teaspoon of the pepper.

2. Pierce the lemons all over with a needle or a round toothpick. Slip your fingers underneath the skin on both sides of the breast, starting at the large end near the tail vent. (This is easy to do if you make a small incision in the membrane that separates the skin from the meat, and work your fingers in at that point. Slip in 2 large rosemary sprigs or 1 tablespoon of the dried rosemary and 3 bay leaves on each side of the breast, arranging them in a decorative pattern. Cut 1 garlic head in half crosswise and rub the turkey with it inside and out. Place the garlic halves, pierced lemons, and remaining rosemary in the body cavity. Cover the exposed stuffing with a small piece of aluminum foil. Using a thin metal skewer or wooden toothpicks, pin the turkey's neck skin to its back. Fold the wings akimbo behind the back. Place the drumsticks in the hock lock or tie together with kitchen string. Place

the turkey on a rack in a large, shallow flameproof roasting pan. Brush the turkey completely with 2 tablespoons of the olive oil. Loosely cover the turkey breast with aluminum foil.

3. Roast the turkey, basting every 20 minutes with 1 cup of the white wine, and then with the pan drippings, for 2 hours.

4. Meanwhile, bring a large saucepan of lightly salted water to a boil. Cook the potato wedges for 4 minutes. Drain, rinse with cold running water, and pat completely dry with paper towels. Separate the cloves of 2 heads of garlic, but do not peel. In a large bowl, toss the potatoes with the unpeeled garlic cloves and the remaining 4 tablespoons olive oil, 1 teaspoon salt, and 1⁄2 teaspoon pepper.

5. After roasting the turkey for 2 hours, arrange the potatoes and garlic cloves around the bird and continue roasting, basting the potatoes often with the pan drippings, for 2 to 3 hours, until the thigh meat registers 180 degrees. (This is a total roasting time of 4 to 5 hours, allowing 20 to 25 minutes per pound of turkey.) Remove the turkey to a carving board. Loosely cover with aluminum foil and let stand for at least 20 minutes before carving. Transfer the potatoes to a heatproof serving dish, cover loosely with foil, and keep warm in the turned-off oven. (If the potatoes and garlic are tender before the turkey is done, remove with a slotted spoon to a serving dish, cover, and keep warm. If the potatoes are not tender when the turkey is done, transfer to a baking dish, increase the oven temperature to 375 degrees, and continue baking while the turkey is standing.)

6. Meanwhile, pour all of the pan drippings and cavity juices into a 1-quart glass measuring cup or a medium bowl and let stand for 5 minutes. Skim off the clear yellow fat that rises to the top. Add enough of the stock to make 2 cups total liquid. Set the roasting pan on top of the stove on two burners over moderately high heat. Add the remaining 1⁄2 cup of white wine and bring to a boil, scraping up the brown bits from the bottom with a wooden spoon. Boil until the wine has evaporated by half, about 1 minute. Add the turkey liquid and boil for 1 minute, to reduce slightly. Off heat, whisk in the butter, 1 tablespoon at a time, and season with additional salt and pepper to taste. Pour the sauce into a warmed sauceboat. (There will be just a few spoonfuls of the light sauce for each person.)

7. Remove and discard the lemons, garlic, and rosemary from the turkey cavity. Serve the turkey immediately with the roasted potatoes and garlic and the sauce.

Sweet-and-Sour Glazed Turkey Chinoise

I have drawn from a wok-full of Chinese cooking tricks to create this gorgeous bird. The Chinese liquid seasoning mixture flavors the bird from the inside out as it marinates overnight and as it roasts. And the cranberry glaze, reminiscent of plum sauce, turns this turkey a blazing mahogany color. Serve with your favorite rice dressing on the side.

Makes 16 to 20 servings

1 tom turkey (18 pounds), neck, excess fat, and giblets removed
¼ cup plus 3 tablespoons vegetable oil
5 scallions, thinly sliced
¼ cup coarsely chopped fresh ginger
4 garlic cloves, crushed
¼ cup low-sodium soy sauce
2 tablespoons dry sherry or Chinese rice wine

3½ cups Homemade Turkey Stock (see page 246), or 2 cups canned chicken broth mixed with 1½ cups water
2 tablespoons brown sugar
2 cinnamon sticks
¼ teaspoon fennel seeds
¼ teaspoon crushed hot pepper flakes
1 large orange, quartered
Sweet-and-Sour Glaze (recipe follows)
¼ cup cornstarch
Salt and freshly ground pepper

1. Rinse the turkey inside and out under cold running water. Pat dry with paper towels. In a large skillet, heat 3 tablespoons of the oil. Add the scallions, chopped ginger, and garlic. Cook over moderately high heat, stirring occasionally, until the mixture is fragrant, about 30 seconds. Add the soy sauce, dry sherry, ½ cup of the stock, the brown sugar, cinnamon sticks, fennel, and hot pepper. Simmer over low heat for 3 to 5 minutes. Pour into a heatproof bowl and let cool.

2. Place the quartered orange in the turkey's large body cavity and pour in the cooled soy-sauce mixture. With metal or wooden skewers and kitchen string, tightly lace the opening closed. Fold the wings akimbo behind the back to hold the neck skin in place. Place the drumsticks in the hock lock or tie them together with kitchen string. Set the turkey on a lightly oiled rack in a large, shallow roasting pan and refrigerate, loosely covered, overnight. Let stand at room temperature for 1 hour before roasting. Season with salt and pepper.

3. Preheat the oven to 325 degrees. Roast the turkey, basting often with

the remaining ¼ cup vegetable oil, and then the pan drippings, for 4½ to 6 hours, allowing 15 to 20 minutes per pound, until the thigh meat registers 180 degrees. During the last hour of the estimated roasting time, baste the turkey every 15 minutes with Sweet-and-Sour Glaze. If the glaze begins to scorch, tent the turkey loosely with aluminum foil. Remove the turkey to a carving board. Loosely cover with aluminum foil and let stand 15 to 20 minutes before carving.

4. Meanwhile, make the sauce. Pour all the pan drippings into a 1-quart glass measuring cup or a medium bowl and let stand for 5 minutes. Skim off the clear yellow fat that rises to the top. Add enough of the remaining stock to the pan drippings to measure 4 cups total liquid. Dissolve the cornstarch in ¼ cup cold water.

5. Set the roasting pan on top of the stove over two burners. Pour in the turkey liquid and the dissolved cornstarch. Bring to a boil over moderate heat, scraping up the brown bits from the bottom and sides of the pan with a wooden spoon. Reduce the heat and simmer for 2 minutes, stirring occasionally. Season the sauce with additional salt and pepper to taste. Pour into a warm sauceboat.

6. Remove the string and skewers from the turkey. With a bulb baster, remove and discard as much of the liquid seasoning from the body cavity as possible. Carve the turkey and serve with the sauce.

Sweet-and-Sour Glaze

Makes about 2 cups

1 can (16 ounces) cranberry
   sauce
2 tablespoons light brown
   sugar

2 tablespoons raspberry or cider
   vinegar
1 tablespoon grated fresh ginger
¼ teaspoon cayenne pepper

In a medium nonreactive saucepan, combine the cranberry sauce, brown sugar, vinegar, ginger, and cayenne. Cook over low heat, stirring often, until the cranberry sauce has melted. Set the glaze aside at room temperature. If it cools and becomes too solid, reheat gently until viscous.

Roast Turkey with Greek Stuffing and Lemon Sauce

The Greeks have a word for it: *avgolemono*, a golden soup or sauce made of a rich, lemon-spiked broth thickened with eggs. It is the perfect foil for the delectable stuffing of ground turkey, rice, currants, and pine nuts.

Makes 10 to 14 servings

2 cups water
⅔ cup lemon juice
1 stick plus 3 tablespoons unsalted
   butter, softened
1 teaspoon salt
1 cup long-grain rice
½ cup pine nuts
1½ pounds ground turkey
4 medium scallions, chopped
2 tablespoons chopped fresh dill, or
   1½ teaspoons dried

½ teaspoon freshly ground pepper
½ cup currants
1 hen turkey (12 pounds), neck,
   giblets, and excess fat removed
1 medium lemon, halved
About 3 cups Homemade Turkey
   Stock (see page 246), or 1½ cups
   canned chicken broth mixed with
   1½ cups water
2 tablespoons all-purpose flour
3 large eggs, at room temperature

1. In a medium saucepan, bring the water, ⅓ cup of the lemon juice, 1 tablespoon of the butter, and ½ teaspoon of the salt to a boil over moderately high heat. Add the rice, reduce the heat to low, cover, and simmer until the rice has absorbed all of the liquid, about 20 minutes.

2. In a large skillet, toast the pine nuts over moderate heat, stirring often, until lightly browned, about 2 minutes. Transfer the pine nuts to a plate and reserve.

3. In the same skillet, melt 2 tablespoons of the butter over moderate heat. Add the ground turkey and cook, stirring and breaking up the meat with a wooden spoon, until it loses its pink color, about 3 minutes. Add the scallions, dill, and ¼ teaspoon of the pepper. Cook, stirring, for 1 minute. In a large bowl, combine the ground turkey with the rice, pine nuts, and currants.

4. Preheat the oven to 325 degrees. Rinse the turkey well, inside and out, under cold running water. Pat dry with paper towels. Rub the turkey inside and out with the lemon halves. Loosely fill the neck and body cavities with the rice stuffing. Using a thin metal skewer or wooden toothpicks, pin the

turkey's neck skin to its back. Cover the exposed stuffing in the large cavity with a small piece of aluminum foil. Fold the turkey's wings akimbo behind the back. Place the drumsticks in the hock lock or tie them together with kitchen string. Rub the turkey all over with 6 tablespoons of the butter. Season with the remaining ½ teaspoon salt and ¼ teaspoon pepper. Place the turkey on a rack in a large, shallow flameproof roasting pan. Pour 1 cup of the stock in the bottom of the pan. Loosely cover the breast with aluminum foil.

5. Roast the turkey, basting often with the pan drippings, for 4 to 5 hours, allowing 20 to 25 minutes per pound, until the thigh meat registers 180 degrees. If at any point the drippings threaten to burn, add ½ cup water to the pan. About 1 hour before the turkey is done, remove the aluminum foil. Remove the turkey to a carving board. Loosely cover with foil and let stand 20 minutes before carving.

6. Meanwhile, pour all the pan drippings into a 1-quart glass measuring cup or a medium bowl and let stand 5 minutes. Skim off the clear yellow fat that rises to the top. Add enough of the remaining stock to make 3 cups total liquid. Set the roasting pan on top of the stove on two burners over moderately low heat. Add the remaining 2 tablespoons of butter and melt. Whisk in the flour and cook, whisking constantly, for 1 minute. Whisk in the turkey liquid and remaining ⅓ cup lemon juice. Bring to a boil, scraping up the brown bits on the bottom of the pan. Reduce the heat to a simmer and cook, whisking often, about 3 minutes.

7. In a small bowl, beat the eggs well. Gradually whisk about ½ cup of the hot sauce into the eggs. Reduce the heat to very low and gradually whisk the egg mixture back into the remaining sauce. Cook, whisking constantly, until the sauce thickens slightly, about 1 minute; do not boil. Season with additional salt and pepper to taste. Pour the sauce into a warm sauceboat and serve with the turkey and rice stuffing.

Microcooked Whole Turkey

I must be honest and say that I far prefer whole turkey when roasted in a conventional oven. The microwave successfully braises and poaches some turkey dishes well, but for a crisp brown skin and perfect texture, I do it the old-fashioned way. However, if you are in a hurry or want to whip up a large amount of turkey that will be cut up and used in a big recipe, then the microwave can help you out. There are a number of things to keep in mind when microcooking turkey:

▶ It isn't necessary to brush browning liquids, such as soy sauce, onto the turkey skin when microcooking, since the lengthy cooking time will allow the skin to brown lightly, though it will not crisp.

▶ Most microwave ovens cannot handle a bird larger than 12 pounds.

▶ The turkey must be turned for even cooking. You should turn and rotate the turkey on both sides as well as its back and breast during the microcooking period. If your microwave has a carousel, you can turn it on the back and breast only.

▶ Don't salt the turkey until after cooking, because the microwaves are attracted to salt and could cause drying.

▶ Be sure to remove any metal hock locks or timing thermometers that the manufacturer may have placed on the turkey.

▶ This recipe was tested in a 700-watt microwave oven. If your microwave oven has lower wattage, increase your cooking times accordingly.

Makes 8 to 12 servings

1 hen turkey (10 pounds), giblets, neck, and excess fat removed
1 stick unsalted butter, softened
1 teaspoon paprika
1 medium onion, sliced
1 medium carrot, sliced
1 medium celery rib, sliced
¾ teaspoon poultry seasoning

½ teaspoon salt
About 2 cups Homemade Turkey Stock (see page 246), or 1 cup canned chicken broth mixed with 1 cup water
3 tablespoons all-purpose flour
Freshly ground pepper

1. Rinse the turkey well, inside and out, under cold running water. Pat dry with paper towels. Rub the turkey all over with 5 tablespoons of the butter and sprinkle with the paprika. In a medium bowl, combine the onion, carrot, celery, and poultry seasoning. Place the vegetables in the body cavity. (You may use your favorite stuffing in place of the vegetables. Stuffing does not affect microwave cooking time.) Tie the drumsticks together with kitchen twine. Place the turkey, breast-side down, on a microwave-proof rack and roasting pan. Tent the pan with wax paper.

2. Estimate the entire microcooking time, 1½ to 2 hours, allowing 9 to 12 minutes per pound. Microcook on High (100 percent) for the first 10 minutes. Reduce microwave oven setting to Medium (50 percent) and continue microcooking another 35 minutes, the halfway point of the estimated cooking time. Protecting your hand with wads of wax paper, turn the turkey breast-side up. Pour off the accumulated juices and reserve. Continue microcooking on Medium, covered with wax paper, until the entire estimated microcooking time is up, about 45 minutes. (If the turkey wing tips or breastbone start to overbrown, cover with small pieces of aluminum foil.) Remove the turkey from the microwave oven, cover with aluminum foil, and let stand for 20 minutes. Test for doneness after the standing time. The turkey is done when a meat thermometer inserted in the thickest part of the thigh, not touching a bone, reads 180 degrees. Season the turkey with the salt.

3. Combine all cooking juices in a 1-quart glass measuring cup or microwave-proof bowl and let stand for 5 minutes. Skim off the clear yellow fat that rises to the top. Add enough stock to measure 2½ cups. Microcook on High until boiling, about 3 minutes.

4. In a 1-quart glass measuring cup, cook the remaining 3 tablespoons butter on High until melted, about 2 minutes. Whisk in the flour and microcook on High until light brown, about 2 minutes. Whisk in the hot cooking liquid and microcook on High until thickened, about 2 minutes. Season with additional salt and pepper to taste. Pour the gravy into a warmed sauceboat and serve with the turkey.

Cider-Basted Wild Turkey with Roast Apples

Whenever you cook a wild turkey, keep it simple so the true flavor of the bird is complemented, and not masked, by your enhancements. Apples go beautifully with feathered game, so my wild turkey is basted with hard cider and surrounded by roasted apple halves. If you prefer to stuff this bird, use the Wild Rice, Cranberry, and Pecan Dressing on page 236 and omit the onion, green apple, and sage in step 1.

Makes 6 to 8 servings

1 wild turkey (8 pounds), neck, giblets, and wing tips removed
1 teaspoon salt
½ teaspoon freshly ground pepper
1 medium onion, sliced
1 medium green apple, such as Granny Smith, cored and sliced
1 tablespoon chopped fresh sage, or 1 teaspoon dried
1 stick plus 1 tablespoon unsalted butter, softened

2 cups hard cider, or 1 cup dry white wine and 1 cup sweet cider
½ cup plus 2 tablespoons applejack or Calvados
6 large baking apples, such as Rome or Golden Delicious, peeled, halved lengthwise, and cored
About 2 cups Wild Turkey Stock (see page 246), or 1 cup canned chicken broth mixed with 1 cup water
3 tablespoons all-purpose flour

1. Preheat the oven to 325 degrees. Rinse the turkey well, inside and out, under cold running water. Pat dry with paper towels. Season the inside of the turkey with ½ teaspoon of the salt and ¼ teaspoon of the pepper. Place the onion, sliced green apple, and sage in the body cavity. Cover the large cavity with a small piece of aluminum foil. Using a thin metal skewer or wooden toothpicks, pin the turkey's neck skin to its back. Fold the turkey's wings akimbo behind the back. Place the drumsticks in the hock lock or tie together with kitchen string.

2. Rub the turkey all over with 6 tablespoons of the softened butter. Season with the remaining ½ teaspoon salt and ¼ teaspoon pepper. Place the turkey on a rack in a large, shallow flameproof roasting pan. Combine the hard cider with ½ cup of the applejack; pour 1 cup of this mixture into the bottom of the pan. Loosely cover the turkey breast with aluminum foil.

3. Roast the turkey, basting often, first with the remaining cider mixture, then the pan drippings, for 2 hours. (If the liquid in the bottom of the pan

begins to boil away and the drippings are in danger of burning, add water as necessary.) Remove the aluminum foil and surround the turkey with the apple halves; baste the apples well with the pan drippings. Continue roasting, basting often, until the turkey tests done and the thigh meat registers 180 degrees, about 40 minutes to 1¼ hours. This is a total cooking time of 2¾ hours to 3¼ hours, allowing 20 to 25 minutes per pound. (If the apples are tender but not falling apart before the turkey is done, remove with a slotted spoon to a serving dish, cover, and keep warm. If the apples are not tender when the turkey is done, transfer them to a baking dish, increase the oven temperature to 375 degrees, and continue roasting until tender while the turkey is standing.) Remove the turkey to a carving board. Loosely cover with aluminum foil and let stand 20 minutes before carving.

4. Meanwhile, pour all of the pan drippings into a 1-quart glass measuring cup or a medium bowl, and let stand 5 minutes. Skim off the clear yellow fat that rises to the surface. Add enough of the stock to make 3½ cups total liquid. Add the remaining 2 tablespoons applejack. Set the roasting pan on top of the stove on two burners over moderately low heat. Add the remaining 3 tablespoons butter and melt. Whisk in the flour and cook, whisking constantly, for 1 minute. Whisk in the turkey liquid and bring to a boil, scraping up the brown bits from the bottom of the pan. Reduce the heat to a simmer and cook, whisking often, for 3 minutes. Season with additional salt and pepper to taste. Pour the gravy into a warmed sauceboat and serve with the turkey surrounded by the cooked apple halves.

> ▶ *Wild turkeys are available by special order from some first-class butchers or by mail order from D'Artagnan, 399 St. Paul Avenue, Jersey City, New Jersey 07306, 800-327-8246 or 201-792-0748, and Durham-Night Bird Game and Poultry Company, 650 San Mateo Avenue, San Bruno, California 94066, 415-873-5035.*

Wild Turkey with Glazed Chestnut Stuffing

One of the most incredible stuffings I've ever encountered, this autumnal mélange of vegetables is continuously basted inside the wild turkey as it roasts. By covering the bird with blanched bacon strips, you are adding needed extra fat to keep the lean bird moist—but this does *not* make the bird self-basting, so baste often. Thanks to Ariane Daugin at D'Artagnan for her technique of basting the bird with wild turkey stock.

Makes 6 to 8 servings

1 wild turkey (8 pounds), neck, giblets, and wing tips removed
3 tablespoons unsalted butter
1 large onion, chopped
3 medium carrots, cut into ½-inch dice
1 teaspoon sugar

3 pounds chestnuts, roasted and peeled
1 teaspoon salt
½ teaspoon freshly ground pepper
¼ cup Madeira wine
8 strips of bacon
About 6 cups Wild Turkey Stock (recipe follows)

1. Rinse the turkey well, inside and out, with cold running water. Pat dry with paper towels.

2. In a large skillet, melt the butter. Add the onion and carrots, and cook over moderate heat, stirring often, until the onion is well softened, about 5 minutes. Add the sugar, chestnuts, ½ teaspoon of the salt, and ¼ teaspoon of the pepper, and cook until the onion is lightly browned, 3 to 5 minutes longer. Add the Madeira and cook until the liquid is evaporated, about 1 minute. Set the stuffing aside.

3. In a medium saucepan, cover the bacon with cold water and bring to a simmer over moderate heat. Cook 5 minutes, drain, rinse well with cold water, and drain again.

4. Place the chestnut stuffing in the large body cavity of the turkey. Cover the exposed stuffing with a small piece of aluminum foil. Using a thin metal skewer or wooden toothpicks, pin the turkey's neck skin to its back. Fold the turkey's wings akimbo behind the back. Place the drumsticks in the hock lock or tie them together with kitchen string. Season with the remaining ½ teaspoon salt and ¼ teaspoon pepper. Place 6 of the bacon strips over

the turkey breast and 1 strip over each drumstick, and tie in place with kitchen string. Place the turkey on a rack in a large, shallow flameproof roasting pan. Pour 1 cup of the stock into the bottom of the pan. Loosely cover the turkey breast with aluminum foil.

5. Roast the turkey, basting first with another 1½ cups stock, then with the pan drippings, allowing 20 to 25 minutes per pound, until the thigh meat registers 180 degrees, 2¾ hours to 3¼ hours. If the liquid in the bottom of the pan begins to boil away and the drippings are in danger of burning, add additional water as necessary. About 1 hour before the end of the roasting time, remove the foil over the breast to allow the skin to brown. Remove the turkey to a carving board. Loosely cover with aluminum foil and let stand 20 minutes before carving.

6. While the turkey is standing, make the sauce. Pour all of the pan drippings into a 1-quart glass measuring cup and let stand for 5 minutes. Skim off the clear yellow fat that rises to the top. Add enough of the remaining stock (about 3½ cups) to the drippings to make 4 cups. Set the roasting pan on top of the stove on two burners over high heat. Add the turkey liquid and bring to a boil, scraping up the brown bits from on the bottom of the pan with a wooden spoon. Boil until the sauce is thickened and evaporated down to 1½ cups. Season with additional salt and pepper to taste. Pour the sauce into a warm sauceboat. Serve with the turkey and stuffing.

> ▶ *To roast and peel chestnuts, preheat the oven to 350 degrees. Make a deep X in the flatter side of each chestnut with a small sharp knife. Place in a single layer on a baking sheet and bake for about 35 minutes, until the outer skin is split and crisp. Peel off the shells and, using a sharp knife, pare off any remaining brown skin. To loosen the skins on stubborn, hard-to-peel chestnuts, reheat for an additional 5 or 10 minutes.*

Wild Turkey Stock

Makes about 6 cups

Neck, heart, gizzard, and wing tips
   from wild turkey
2 tablespoons vegetable oil
2 pounds regular turkey wings,
   chopped at joints
1 small onion, chopped
1 small carrot, chopped

1 small celery rib, chopped
7½ cups water
½ cup dry red wine, such as Zinfandel
4 sprigs of parsley
¼ teaspoon dried thyme
¼ teaspoon peppercorns
1 small bay leaf

1. Using a heavy meat cleaver or a large knife, chop the neck into 1-inch pieces. In a medium nonreactive saucepan, heat the oil. Add the neck pieces, giblets, wing tips, and chopped turkey wings. Cook over moderately high heat, turning often, until the pieces are browned all over, about 10 minutes. Using tongs, transfer the turkey to a plate and reserve.

2. Add the onion, carrot, and celery to the pan. Cook, stirring often, until lightly browned, about 6 minutes. Return the turkey to the saucepan. Add the water and red wine. Bring to a simmer, skimming off the foam. Reduce the heat to low and add the parsley, thyme, peppercorns, and bay leaf. Simmer for 2 to 3 hours.

3. Strain the stock into a medium bowl. Let stand 5 minutes and skim off the clear yellow fat that rises to the surface. (The stock can be made up to 2 days ahead of serving, cooled completely, covered, and refrigerated.)

CHAPTER TWO

Solving the Leftover Turkey Problem

Turkey sandwiches and turkey-vegetable soup, created over Thanksgiving weekend from the remains of the big bird, are almost as traditional as roast turkey itself. In fact, I know of one family that has made turkey sandwiches the entire raison d'être for their Thanksgiving roast turkey. Jettisoning what they consider to be the totally unnecessary trappings of sweet potatoes, cranberry sauce, and pumpkin pie, this mom serves the bird with sliced bread, gravy, mayonnaise, and mustard. (The preceding is a *true* story; only the names have been deleted to protect the innocent.)

I love hot dark-and-white-meat turkey sandwiches, made with *both* stuffing and bread, gilded with leftover gravy. In fact, I love turkey sandwiches so much, I often roast or braise a turkey breast (half or whole) just so I will have the fixings. Follow my lead, and don't hold off to try these delicious "leftovers" recipes only once a year.

Here are hints on how to treat leftover turkey like the treasure that it is.

▶ One pound of cooked turkey, cut into 1-inch cubes, equals 3 packed cups. Allow ½ to ¾ cup of cooked, cut-up leftover turkey per serving when making casseroles or salads.

▶ Cool cooked turkey just to room temperature before refrigerating. Do not cover and refrigerate steaming hot meat, as the steam will create a warm, moist, bacteria-friendly environment. To quick chill, refrigerate the turkey, uncovered, just until cold; wrap tightly in aluminum foil and return to the refrigerator.

▶ Carve the leftover meat from the carcass and refrigerate the meat and bones separately. After I am positive everyone has finished picking at the carcass, I chop it up for soup with a cleaver or heavy knife. Use refrigerated cooked turkey within 3 to 4 days. Use leftover gravy and stuffing within 2 days. Be sure to heat stuffing thoroughly before using and bring gravy to a boil.

▶ You can double-wrap the leftovers in aluminum foil, label, and freeze them. If desired, cut the meat into cubes, 1 inch or smaller, and freeze them in 1-pound packages, as most of these recipes call for that amount. The frozen cooked turkey, held at 0 degrees or under, is best when used within 1 month but can be frozen up to 3 months. The turkey will still be healthy to eat, but the texture and flavor will deteriorate.

▶ Make Basic Braised Turkey Breast or Bacon-Wrapped Turkey Roast with Shallot Sauce (see pages 93 and 89) to create leftovers without roasting a whole turkey. A 5-pound whole turkey breast will yield about 3 pounds or 8 cups cubed cooked turkey meat.

▶ The cooking liquid from Basic Braised Turkey Breast can be substituted for the Homemade Turkey Stock in any recipe in this book. Let it cool completely, cover, and refrigerate for up to 3 days, or freeze for up to 2 months.

Still carrying the turkey sandwich torch, two new sandwich ideas are presented here: Turkey, Bacon, and Tomato Club Sandwiches with Blue Cheese Mayonnaise and Toasted Turkey, Cheddar, and Apple Sandwiches, as well as a recipe for an old favorite, Monte Cristo Sandwiches. And while the Old-Fashioned Turkey Vegetable Soup is represented, you might want to try Pennsylvania Dutch Turkey Noodle Supper or Nonni's Turkey Vegetable Soup with Ricotta Dumplings. Also present are updated versions of American cooking classics, such as New Wave Turkey à la King, Hash Pancakes O'Brien, Tearoom Turkey Turnovers, Zippy Turkey Divan, Turkey and Corn Spoon Bread, and Luisa's Turkey Tettrazini. And if you haven't thought of turkey and pasta, you will be converted by the sophisticated Pasta Bow

Ties with Smoked Turkey, Sun-Dried Tomatoes, and Basil or the Cheesy Tomato and Turkey Bake.

One of the best ways to incorporate leftover turkey is in Mexican dishes, since the chilies add spark to the neutral turkey flavor. This chapter includes recipes for Turkey Tostadas Mañana, Turkey and Olive Enchiladas with Red Sauce, and Turkey Chilaquiles. Try turkey in your favorite burritos and tacos, too.

Except for the soups, which simmer with little attention, none of these recipes is time-consuming, since few of us want to take on any challenges after pulling off a large holiday dinner. Turkey is so tasty and so good for you, consider these recipes for your everyday repertoire all year long.

All-in-One Gravy Loaf

My favorite Thanksgiving foods—turkey, stuffing, and gravy—are all combined in this one.

Makes 4 to 6 servings

2 tablespoons unsalted butter
3 tablespoons finely chopped onion
1 small celery rib, finely chopped
1 cup turkey gravy, leftover or canned
3 cups chopped cooked turkey
　(about 1 pound)
1½ cups fresh bread crumbs

2 whole large eggs plus 1 egg yolk,
　lightly beaten
2 tablespoons chopped fresh
　parsley
1 teaspoon poultry seasoning
½ teaspoon salt
¼ teaspoon freshly ground pepper

1. Preheat the oven to 350 degrees. In a medium skillet, heat the butter. Add the onion and celery and cook over moderate heat, stirring often, until the vegetables are softened, about 3 minutes. Add the gravy and heat through.

2. In a large bowl, combine the gravy mixture with the cooked turkey, bread crumbs, lightly beaten eggs, parsley, poultry seasoning, salt, and pepper. Transfer the mixture to a lightly buttered 9-by-5-by-3-inch loaf pan. Place the loaf pan in a larger baking pan.

3. Place the baking pan with the loaf pan in the oven. Add enough hot water to the baking pan to reach 1 inch up the side of the loaf pan. Bake until a meat thermometer inserted in the center of the loaf reads 165 degrees, 1 to 1¼ hours. Let the loaf stand for 10 minutes before slicing.

Cheesy Tomato and Turkey Bake

All you do is boil up some tube-shaped pasta and toss it with leftover turkey, tomatoes, herbs, and cheese, without even bothering to simmer up a tomato sauce. Homespun, yes, but definitely satisfying.

Makes 6 to 8 servings

1 pound tubular pasta, such as elbow macaroni, cooked

2 cups cooked turkey, cut into 1-inch cubes (about 12 ounces)

1 can (35 ounces) Italian peeled tomatoes, drained and coarsely chopped

1 pint low-fat cottage cheese

1 cup grated sharp Cheddar cheese (about 4 ounces)

4 scallions, chopped

1 teaspoon dried marjoram

½ teaspoon salt

½ teaspoon freshly ground pepper

½ cup fresh bread crumbs

1 tablespoon unsalted butter, cut into tiny cubes

1. Preheat the oven to 350 degrees. In a lightly buttered 9-by-13-inch baking dish, toss together the cooked pasta, turkey, tomatoes, cottage cheese, Cheddar cheese, scallions, marjoram, salt, and pepper. Sprinkle the bread crumbs over the top and dot with the butter. (The casserole can be prepared up to 4 hours ahead, covered, and refrigerated.)

2. Bake until the casserole is bubbling and the top is lightly browned, about 30 minutes.

▶ *A baby turkey is called a* poult. *Turkeys gather in* flocks.

Lazy Day Turkey Potpie

A golden-brown pastry globe puffs up dramatically from the baking dish in this easy-as-pie main dish. I am normally a "from scratch" cook, but on the day after Thanksgiving I am more than willing to use such conveniences as frozen vegetables and puff pastry and even canned turkey gravy, if Thursday's homemade has disappeared.

Makes 4 to 6 servings

2 cups turkey gravy, canned or leftover
2 cups leftover cooked vegetables, such as carrots, peas, and baby onions, or 1 package (10 ounces) frozen mixed vegetables, defrosted

1 pound cooked turkey, cut into 1-inch cubes (about 3 cups)
1 tablespoon dry sherry (optional)
Salt and freshly ground pepper
1 sheet frozen puff pastry (about 8½ ounces), defrosted
1 large egg, well beaten

1. In a large saucepan, combine the gravy, vegetables, turkey, and sherry. Bring to a simmer and cook over moderately low heat, stirring often, until the turkey is heated through, about 5 minutes. Season with salt and pepper to taste. Place the stew in a round 2½-quart baking dish.

2. Preheat the oven to 400 degrees. On a lightly floured work surface, gently roll out the pastry, just to diminish the creases in the sheet. Turn the pastry over and, using a pastry brush, brush away any excess flour. Using a sharp knife, cut out a circle of pastry at least 1 inch larger than the diameter of the top of the baking dish. Brush the circle lightly with some of the beaten egg. Place the pastry circle tautly over the top of the baking dish, *egg side down*, pressing the edges of the pastry onto the sides of the dish to adhere. If desired, cut out decorations from the remaining scraps of pastry. Brush them on the undersides with beaten egg and arrange them on top of the pastry.

3. Bake for 15 to 20 minutes, until the pastry has puffed and is golden brown. Serve immediately.

Turkey and Corn Spoon Bread

Spoon bread is a soft, spoonable cornbread that is a well-known Southern side dish. With chunks of turkey and a topping of Cheddar cheese, it is an enjoyable brunch or supper dish that I serve warm with a bowl of Fresh Tomato Salsa (see page 57).

Makes 4 to 6 servings

1 can (15 ounces) creamed corn
½ cup yellow cornmeal
3 large eggs, separated, at room temperature
2 tablespoons unsalted butter, melted
1 scallion, chopped
1 jalapeño pepper, minced, or 2 tablespoons chopped canned green chilies (optional)

¼ teaspoon freshly ground pepper
1½ cups cooked turkey, cut into 1-inch cubes (about ½ pound)
¼ teaspoon salt
1 cup grated sharp Cheddar cheese (4 ounces)

1. Preheat the oven to 350 degrees. Lightly butter a 9-inch-square baking dish. In a medium bowl, mix together the creamed corn, cornmeal, egg yolks, butter, scallion, the optional chili, and pepper. Stir in the turkey.

2. Beat the egg whites with the salt until soft peaks form. Fold the beaten whites into the corn mixture. Pour the batter into the prepared baking dish and sprinkle the grated cheese over the top.

3. Bake until a toothpick inserted in the center of the spoon bread comes out clean, 30 to 35 minutes.

Quick Turkey Curry with Fruits and Nuts

When I roast a whole turkey, I am very disappointed if I don't have enough leftovers to make turkey curry, because I get so much flavor for so little effort. My recipe gets a special lift from apple, banana, and yogurt, and a pleasant crunch from toasted almonds. Served with basmati rice, it's a dish beyond compare.

Makes 4 servings

3 tablespoons unsalted butter
1 medium onion, chopped
1 medium tart green apple, such as Granny Smith, cored and chopped
2 garlic cloves, minced
2 tablespoons curry powder, preferably Madras brand
2 tablespoons all-purpose flour

1½ cups Homemade Turkey Stock (page 246) or canned chicken broth
1 pound cooked turkey, cut into 1-inch cubes (about 3 cups)
½ cup plain yogurt
1 medium banana, cut into ½-inch slices
½ cup toasted slivered blanched almonds

1. In a large skillet, melt the butter. Add the onion, apple, and garlic and cook over moderate heat, stirring often, until softened, about 3 minutes. Sprinkle with the curry powder and stir for 15 seconds. Sprinkle on the flour and cook, stirring, for 1 minute. Stir in the broth and bring to a simmer; reduce the heat to low and cook for 5 minutes.

2. Stir in the turkey and cook until heated through, about 2 minutes. Stir in the yogurt and banana and cook until heated through, about 30 seconds; do not boil. Transfer to a serving dish, sprinkle with the almonds, and serve immediately.

▶ *Whenever cooking with curry powder, be sure that it is cooked first, in a little fat, or toasted briefly in a dry pan. This "opens up" the flavors and eliminates any pasty taste.*

"Take It Easy" Turkey and Dumpling Casserole

Another variation on the leftover turkey, gravy, and vegetables theme. This time, packaged biscuit dough comes to the rescue. I always stir chopped herbs into the dough to give the dumplings a prettier appearance and additional flavor.

Makes 4 to 6 servings

2 cups turkey gravy, leftover or canned
2 cups leftover cooked vegetables (such as green beans and mushrooms, carrots, parsnips, or lima beans), or 1 package (10 ounces) frozen mixed vegetables, defrosted

1 pound cooked turkey, cut into 1-inch cubes (about 3 cups)
¼ teaspoon dried sage
¼ teaspoon dried thyme
Salt and freshly ground pepper
1 cup biscuit mix, such as Bisquick
⅓ cup milk
¼ cup finely chopped fresh parsley

1. In a medium saucepan, combine the gravy, vegetables, turkey, sage, and thyme. Bring to a simmer over moderately low heat. Season with salt and pepper to taste.

2. In a medium bowl, stir together the biscuit mix, milk, and parsley until smooth. Drop by teaspoonfuls on top of the simmering stew. Cover tightly, and cook for 10 minutes. Uncover and cook 10 minutes longer. Serve hot.

Pennsylvania Dutch Turkey Noodle Supper

Looking for a different way to make turkey soup? Try this twist on Pennsylvania Dutch "potpie." (In Amish country, a potpie is a noodle dish, not a baked savory pastry.) Homemade noodles are simmered in a golden-hued turkey, potato, and celery broth, giving proof to the old Amish saying, "Those that work hard eat hearty."

If you don't feel like making homemade noodles, skip steps 1 and 2 and add ½ pound dried egg noodles at the beginning of step 5 and boil about 10 minutes, until almost tender, before adding the turkey.

Makes 6 to 8 servings

2 cups all-purpose flour
1½ teaspoons salt
3 large eggs, at room temperature
4 quarts plus 3 tablespoons water
1 tablespoon vegetable oil
1 turkey carcass, chopped into large pieces
5 medium celery ribs, cut into ½-inch slices
1 medium onion, sliced

1 medium carrot, sliced
6 sprigs of parsley
¼ teaspoon peppercorns
4 medium boiling potatoes, scrubbed, unpeeled, cut into 1-inch pieces
¼ teaspoon crumbled saffron threads
1 pound cooked turkey, cut into 1-inch cubes (about 3 cups)
1 scallion, thinly sliced

1. In a food processor, pulse the flour and ½ teaspoon of the salt to combine. In a small bowl, mix together the eggs, 3 tablespoons of the water, and the oil. With the machine on, add the egg mixture through the feed tube in a steady stream. Process until the mixture forms a stiff ball of dough on top of the blade. (If the dough is too wet or too dry, the dough will not form a ball. Feel the dough, and if it is sticky and wet, add additional flour, 1 tablespoon at a time. If the dough is dry, add additional water, 1 teaspoon at a time.) To knead, process the dough continuously for 45 seconds. (To make the noodle dough by hand, combine the flour and salt in a medium bowl. Make a well in the center. Place the eggs, water, and oil in the well. With a fork, beat the liquids together, gradually stirring the dry ingredients into the well until the mixture forms a dough. Knead the dough in the bowl for 10 to 15 minutes, until smooth and firm.) Wrap the dough in plastic and let it rest for 30 minutes at room temperature.

2. On a lightly floured work surface, roll out the dough to a 15-by-20-inch rectangle about ⅛ inch thick. With a pastry brush, brush away any excess flour from the top of the dough, turn the dough over, and brush away excess flour again. With a pastry wheel or a sharp knife, cut the dough into 4-inch-long noodles, ½ inch wide. (The noodles can be prepared up to 1 day ahead, wrapped in a plastic bag, and refrigerated.)

3. In a large stockpot, combine the turkey carcass, 4 quarts water, 1 sliced celery rib, onion, and carrot; bring to a boil over moderately high heat, skimming off any foam that rises to the surface. Add the parsley, remaining 1 teaspoon salt, and the peppercorns. Reduce the heat to low and simmer for 2 hours. Strain the broth into a large saucepan.

4. Bring the turkey broth to a simmer over moderate heat. Add the remaining 4 celery ribs, the potatoes, and the saffron. Bring back to a boil, reduce the heat to low, and simmer until the potatoes are almost tender, about 20 minutes.

5. Increase the heat to high, so the soup returns to a boil. Gradually add the noodle strips and boil until tender, 3 to 5 minutes. Add the turkey and cook until the turkey is heated through, about 2 minutes. Serve, garnished with the scallion.

▶ *Philadelphia is Thanksgiving Town, U.S.A., home of*

▷ *Benjamin Franklin, who preferred the turkey to the eagle as the national bird.*

▷ *Sara Josepha Hale, whose Philadelphia-based magazine successfully influenced President Lincoln to declare a national Thanksgiving holiday;*

▷ *The first Thanksgiving Day parade, by Gimbel's in 1923.*

Turkey and Olive Enchiladas with Red Sauce

One of the many advantages of a California childhood is that I was raised on Mexican food. This recipe, which multiplies and freezes readily, has been the star attraction of many a Rodgers family gathering. While it is a *muy bueno* way to use leftovers, I have also poached a half turkey breast to get enough cooked meat for my filling, or fried up a couple of batches of Low-Fat Turkey Chorizo (see page 119).

Makes 6 servings, 2 enchiladas each

2 tablespoons olive oil
1 medium onion, finely chopped
1 garlic clove, minced
3 tablespoons chili powder
1 can (14 ounces) Italian peeled tomatoes, finely chopped, and their juice
1 can (16 ounces) tomato sauce
½ teaspoon ground cumin

¼ teaspoon dried oregano
¼ teaspoon sugar
1 pound cooked turkey, cut into 1-inch cubes (about 3 cups)
4 cups grated Muenster or Monterey jack cheese (1 pound)
1 can (8 ounces) pitted black olives, sliced
12 corn tortillas

1. Preheat the oven to 375 degrees. In a medium skillet, heat the olive oil. Add the onion and garlic, and cook over moderate heat, stirring often, until softened, about 3 minutes. Add the chili powder and cook, stirring, for 30 seconds. Add the chopped tomatoes, tomato sauce, cumin, oregano, and sugar. Bring to a simmer, reduce the heat to low, and cook, stirring often to prevent scorching, until slightly thickened, about 15 minutes. Remove the sauce from the heat and cool slightly.

2. In a large bowl, combine the turkey, 3 cups of the grated cheese, and the olives. Lightly oil a 9-by-13-inch baking dish. Spread about ½ cup of the sauce on the bottom of the baking dish. One at a time, place a tortilla in the skillet with the remaining warm sauce until softened, about 10 seconds. Using your fingers or kitchen tongs, transfer the tortilla to a plate. Place about ⅓ cup of the filling down the center of the tortilla, roll up, and transfer, seam side down, to the prepared baking dish. Pour the remaining sauce over the top of the enchiladas. Cover the baking dish with aluminum foil. (The enchiladas can be prepared up to 1 day ahead, covered, and refrigerated.)

3. Bake until the sauce is simmering, about 30 minutes. Remove the foil

and sprinkle the top of the enchiladas with the remaining 1 cup cheese. Continue baking until the cheese is melted, about 5 minutes. Let the enchiladas stand for 5 minutes before serving.

Turkey Chilaquiles

Chilaquiles (chee-lah-*kee*-lays) are another south-of-the-border dish I learned at the apron strings of our cook in Guadalajara. Once you get your hands on some *tomatillos* (Mexican green tomatoes), it is ridiculously easy to make. You can substitute 1¼ cups of store-bought green salsa for the homemade salsa in the recipe, as I have done many times. Portion sizes are a problem—I have seen an entire skillet of *chilaquiles*, supposedly serving 4, be devoured by 2 aficionados, so be forewarned.

Makes 2 to 4 servings

12 corn tortillas, torn into quarters
Vegetable oil, for frying
1¼ cups green taco sauce or Tomatillo Salsa (recipe follows)

1 cup Homemade Turkey Stock (page 246) or canned chicken broth
1 cup chopped cooked turkey meat
½ cup grated Muenster cheese

1. Preheat the oven to 200 degrees. Place the tortillas on a baking sheet and bake until they are dried out but not hard, about 20 minutes.

2. Heat 1 inch of vegetable oil in a large skillet over moderately high heat. Fry the tortilla pieces in batches without crowding, turning once, until crisp, about 45 seconds. Transfer with a slotted spoon to paper towels to drain.

3. In a large skillet, heat the green sauce and turkey stock over moderate heat until simmering. Add the fried tortilla pieces, a few at a time, pushing the tortillas under the sauce with a spoon. When all the tortilla pieces have been added, reduce the heat to low and simmer for 5 minutes. Sprinkle the turkey and cheese over the *chilaquiles* and simmer until the turkey is hot and the cheese is melted, about 5 minutes. Serve immediately from the skillet.

Tomatillo Salsa

Tomatillos, sometimes known as *tomates verdes*, are not unripened green tomatoes, but members of the gooseberry family. To use fresh tomatillos, remove the papery husks and cook gently in simmering water until tender but not breaking apart, about 10 minutes. About 14 small fresh tomatillos, approximately 14 ounces, will equal the amount of drained tomatillos in a 13-ounce can.

Makes about 2 cups

2 cans (13 ounces each) tomatillos, rinsed, drained, and chopped
¼ cup chopped onion
¼ cup chopped fresh cilantro

2 garlic cloves, minced
1 jalapeño pepper, minced
¼ teaspoon salt
Pinch of sugar
2 tablespoons olive oil

1. In a food processor or blender, puree all of the ingredients except the olive oil.

2. In a medium skillet, heat the olive oil. Add the tomatillo mixture and simmer over moderately low heat, stirring often, until slightly thickened, 3 to 5 minutes. If adding to the *chilaquiles*, you may use the salsa immediately. If using as a condiment, let it cool completely. (The salsa may be made up to 2 days ahead, covered, and refrigerated.)

Zippy Turkey Divan

Turkey Divan is probably the classic leftover turkey dish. It certainly was the first "day after" recipe I was taught. I now zing up the recipe with a spoonful of mustard and Cheddar cheese, as the original recipe is a little too bland for me. If you want, break your budget by substituting cooked artichoke hearts or asparagus spears for the broccoli. In proper luncheon rooms, where the genteel version of the entrée is regularly served, a side basket of toasted English muffins is *de rigueur*.

Makes 4 servings

1 bunch broccoli, cut into florets
4 tablespoons unsalted butter
¼ cup all-purpose flour
2 cups milk, regular or low-fat, heated
2 teaspoons Dijon mustard
¼ teaspoon salt
⅛ teaspoon cayenne pepper
8 thick slices cooked turkey breast
   (about 1 pound)
½ cup grated Cheddar cheese

1. Boil the broccoli in a large saucepan of lightly salted water until crisp-tender, 2 to 3 minutes. Drain, rinse under cold water, and drain well. Pat the broccoli dry with paper towels.

2. In a heavy medium saucepan, melt the butter over moderately low heat. Whisk in the flour and cook, stirring, for 2 minutes. (Do not let the mixture brown.) Whisk in the milk, bring to a boil, reduce the heat, and simmer, whisking often, until thick, about 2 minutes. Remove from heat and whisk in the mustard, salt, and cayenne.

3. Preheat the oven to 400 degrees. In a lightly buttered baking dish, spread a thin layer of the sauce. Top with the turkey slices, the broccoli, and the remaining sauce. Sprinkle the cheese over the top. Bake until the cheese has melted and the top is lightly browned, about 20 minutes.

Luisa's Turkey Tetrazzini

Luisa Tetrazzini, a turn-of-the-century opera star, was a big girl who, judging by this dish, must have loved substantial meals. It was created in her honor by a well-meaning fan. Turkey, mushrooms, and macaroni in a sherry cream sauce, topped with a crunchy layer of buttered bread crumbs, is just the thing to bolster you before singing for 4 hours. My version is shortened from the original, and the sauce can be made in the same period of time it takes to boil water for the pasta.

Makes 4 servings

½ pound cooked tubular pasta, such as ziti or penne
5 tablespoons unsalted butter
1 tablespoon minced shallot or scallion
¾ pound fresh mushrooms, sliced
¼ cup all-purpose flour
2 cups half-and-half or milk, regular or low-fat

2 tablespoons dry sherry
½ teaspoon salt
¼ teaspoon freshly ground pepper
⅔ cup freshly grated Parmesan cheese
3 cups coarsely chopped cooked turkey (about 1 pound)
½ cup fresh bread crumbs

1. In a large saucepan of boiling salted water, cook the pasta until tender but still firm, 10 to 12 minutes. Drain the pasta well, rinse under cold water, and set aside.

2. In a large skillet, melt 4 tablespoons of the butter. Add the shallot and cook over moderate heat until the shallot is softened, about 1 minute. Add the mushrooms and cook, stirring often, until the mushrooms begin to brown, about 5 minutes. Sprinkle on the flour and cook, stirring, for 1 minute. Stir in the milk, sherry, salt, and pepper. Bring to a simmer, reduce the heat to low, and cook until thickened, about 3 minutes. Remove the sauce from the heat and stir in ⅓ cup of the Parmesan cheese.

3. Preheat the oven to 400 degrees. In a lightly buttered 3-quart baking dish, combine the cooked pasta and half of the sauce. Stir the turkey into the remaining sauce and pour over the pasta. Sprinkle the top of the pasta with the bread crumbs and the remaining ⅓ cup Parmesan. Dot the top with the remaining 1 tablespoon butter, cut into tiny pieces. Bake until the top is golden brown and crusty, about 20 minutes.

Nutted Turkey-Swiss Soufflé

Soufflés are a fantastic way to utilize leftovers, and, for all their high-falutin' attitude, they are surprisingly easy to make. My secret? Don't overbeat your egg whites—if they are too stiff, they won't fold into the sauce and incorporate properly.

Makes 3 to 4 servings

2 tablespoons freshly grated Parmesan cheese or bread crumbs
3 tablespoons unsalted butter
1 scallion, minced
3 tablespoons flour
1 cup Homemade Turkey Stock (see page 246) or canned chicken broth
4 large egg yolks

¾ cup finely chopped cooked turkey, preferably white meat
½ cup grated Swiss cheese, preferably Gruyère
⅓ cup finely chopped walnuts
½ teaspoon salt
¼ teaspoon white pepper
¼ teaspoon freshly grated nutmeg
5 large egg whites

1. Lightly butter the inside of a 1-quart soufflé dish. Roll the Parmesan cheese or bread crumbs around the inside of the dish to coat the sides, tapping out any excess.

2. Preheat the oven to 400 degrees. In a heavy medium saucepan, melt the butter over moderately low heat. Add the scallion and cook for 30 seconds. Whisk in the flour and cook, stirring, for 2 minutes. Do not let the mixture brown. Whisk in the stock, bring to a boil, reduce the heat to low, and cook, whisking often, until very thick, about 2 minutes. Remove from the heat and whisk in the egg yolks. Add the turkey, Swiss cheese, and nuts. Season the sauce with the salt, white pepper, and nutmeg.

3. In a separate bowl, beat the egg whites until they form soft peaks. Stir one-quarter of the beaten egg whites into the sauce, then carefully fold in the remaining whites. Transfer the mixture to the prepared soufflé dish and place in the oven. Immediately reduce the oven temperature to 350 degrees and bake until the top is puffed and golden brown and a wooden skewer inserted in the side of the "puff" comes out clean, 30 to 35 minutes. Serve immediately.

Turkey and Corn Croquettes
with Fresh Tomato Salsa

Here's another recipe from our culinary past that has been slightly updated to fit today's tastes. No longer a bland "ladies lunch" food, these crunchy croquettes give you a creamy filling packed with bits of turkey, corn, and colorful sweet peppers. I suggest serving them with tomato salsa, fresh or bottled.

Makes 12 croquettes

3 tablespoons unsalted butter
1 scallion, minced
1 small red bell pepper, finely chopped
⅔ cup all-purpose flour
½ cup milk, regular or low-fat
½ cup canned chicken broth
¼ teaspoon salt
⅛ teaspoon cayenne pepper
2 large egg yolks, lightly beaten

1½ cups minced cooked turkey
  (about ½ pound)
½ cup fresh or defrosted frozen corn
  kernels
2 whole large eggs,
  lightly beaten
2 cups fresh bread crumbs
Vegetable oil, for deep-frying
Fresh Tomato Salsa (recipe follows)

1. In a medium heavy saucepan, melt the butter over moderate heat. Add the scallion and red pepper, and cook, stirring, until the vegetables are softened, about 2 minutes. Sprinkle on ⅓ cup of the flour and cook, stirring, for 1 minute. Whisk in the milk, broth, salt, and pepper. Bring to a boil, reduce the heat to low, and simmer, whisking often, until thickened, about 2 minutes.

2. In a small bowl, beat the egg yolks. Gradually beat half of the sauce into the egg yolks; stir the mixture back into the remaining sauce in the saucepan. Cook, stirring constantly, until slightly thickened, about 1 minute; do not boil. Stir in the turkey and corn. Transfer to a 9-by-13-inch baking dish lined with plastic wrap, cover, and freeze until firm, about 1 hour.

3. Place the remaining ⅓ cup flour on a plate. In a small bowl, beat the whole eggs. Place the bread crumbs on another plate. Unmold the chilled turkey mixture, peel off the plastic wrap, and cut into 12 rectangles. Dredge each piece in the flour, shaking off any excess. Dip in the beaten eggs and roll in the bread crumbs. Place the croquettes on a wire cake rack and let stand for 30 minutes to set the coating.

4. In a large heavy saucepan, heat 3 inches of vegetable oil over moderately high heat to 360 degrees. Preheat the oven to 200 degrees. Without crowding, deep-fry the croquettes in batches, turning once, until golden brown, about 5 minutes. Adjust the heat to maintain a steady temperature. With a slotted spoon, transfer to a paper towel–lined baking sheet to drain briefly, then keep warm in the oven while preparing the remaining croquettes. Serve hot with tomato salsa on the side.

Fresh Tomato Salsa

Fresh salsa, which is really a tangy uncooked relish, is popular in kitchens all over America. Its exuberant taste adds interest to a variety of dishes without adding a lot of calories. Best of all, it is simple to prepare. Here is an authentic recipe that is not only indispensable with Mexican food and crunchy tortilla chips, but also goes well with Turkey and Corn Croquettes (above), Turkey and Corn Spoon Bread (page 45), and broiled or grilled turkey cutlets.

Makes about 1 cup

6 ripe plum tomatoes (about 1 pound), seeded and chopped
2 tablespoons minced onion
2 tablespoons chopped fresh cilantro (optional)

1 garlic clove, minced
1 jalapeño pepper, seeded and minced
1 tablespoon lime juice
½ teaspoon salt

In a medium bowl, combine all of the ingredients. Cover and refrigerate for 1 hour before serving. (The salsa can be prepared up to 1 day before serving, covered, and refrigerated.)

New Wave Turkey à la King

Shiitake mushrooms, freshly roasted sweet red pepper strips, and a dash of port wine upgrade the familiar Turkey à la King into a luncheon dish for the nineties. Large slices of toasted French bread make a crunchy contrast for the sauced turkey, creating an open-faced sandwich effect.

Makes 4 servings

1 medium red bell pepper
6 ounces mushrooms, preferably shiitake
2 tablespoons unsalted butter
2 tablespoons all-purpose flour
1 cup Homemade Turkey Stock (see page 246) or canned chicken broth
¾ cup half-and-half or light cream
2 cups cooked turkey, cut into 1-inch cubes (about 12 ounces)

1 tablespoon port wine, preferably imported white
½ teaspoon salt
¼ teaspoon freshly ground white pepper
1 large egg yolk
4 thick (½-inch) slices of French or Italian bread, from a large round loaf, or 8 slices from a baguette, grilled or toasted

1. Roast the pepper directly over a gas flame or under a broiler as close to the heat as possible, turning often, until charred and blackened all over, 7 to 10 minutes. Seal in a bag and let steam for 10 minutes. Peel the pepper, discarding the stem, seeds, and ribs. Cut the pepper into ½-by-2-inch strips.

2. If using shiitake mushrooms, remove and discard the tough stems; ordinary white mushrooms do not have to be stemmed. In a medium skillet, heat the butter. Add the mushrooms and cook over moderate heat, stirring often, until the mushrooms have given up their liquid, it evaporates, and they are beginning to brown, 5 to 7 minutes. Sprinkle on the flour and cook, stirring, for 1 minute. Whisk in the turkey stock and half-and-half. Bring to a boil, reduce the heat to low, and simmer for 1 minute, until thickened. Add the cubed turkey, red pepper strips, port, salt, and pepper. Cook until the turkey is heated through, about 2 minutes.

3. In a small bowl, gradually beat about ¼ cup of the sauce into the egg yolk. Stir the egg-yolk mixture back into the skillet and cook, stirring, just until sauce is slightly thickened, about 30 seconds. Serve immediately, spooned over the toasted bread slices.

VARIATION: To make my Great-Aunt Soulima's Traditional Turkey à la King, substitute regular mushrooms for the shiitake mushrooms. Substitute 1 canned pimiento, sliced, for the roasted red pepper. Substitute dry sherry for the white port. Serve the creamed turkey in baked frozen puff-pastry patty shells.

Hash Pancakes O'Brien

Crispy on the outside, creamy within, these savory pancakes are always winners, especially at breakfast with poached eggs.

Makes 8 pancakes

1 cup finely chopped cooked turkey (about 5 ounces)
1 large baking potato (about 8 ounces), peeled and grated
1¼ cups turkey gravy, leftover or canned
¼ cup all-purpose flour

2 tablespoons minced onion
1 small bell pepper, preferably red, finely chopped
1 large egg, lightly beaten
½ teaspoon salt
¼ teaspoon freshly ground pepper
3 tablespoons vegetable oil

1. Preheat the oven to 200 degrees. In a medium bowl, combine all of the ingredients except the oil.

2. In a large skillet, heat the vegetable oil over moderate heat until hot but not smoking. In batches, using ¼ cup for each pancake, spoon the mixture into the skillet and spread out to 4-inch-wide pancakes. Cook, turning once, until golden brown on both sides, about 6 minutes. Transfer the cooked pancakes to a paper towel–lined baking sheet and keep warm in the oven while preparing the remaining pancakes. Serve immediately.

Tearoom Turkey Turnovers

There is a fast-vanishing breed of restaurant known as a "tearoom," where familiar yet comforting meals are served by kindly waitresses in a cozy setting. More often than not, a savory pastry turnover is on the bill of fare. Here's my home-cooked version.

Makes 8 turnovers

1 medium carrot, cut into ½-inch dice
3 tablespoons unsalted butter
3 tablespoons all-purpose flour
1 cup Homemade Turkey Stock
  (see page 246) or canned chicken
  broth
1 tablespoon dry sherry (optional)
½ teaspoon salt

¼ teaspoon pepper
1½ cups finely chopped cooked turkey
  (about ½ pound)
½ cup frozen peas, defrosted
2 sheets frozen puff pastry, defrosted
  (one 17¼-ounce package)
1 large egg yolk, beaten with 1
  tablespoon milk

1. Preheat the oven to 375 degrees. In a medium saucepan of boiling salted water, cook the carrots until crisp-tender, about 3 minutes. Drain and rinse under cold running water.

2. In a heavy medium saucepan, melt the butter over moderately low heat. Whisk in the flour and cook, stirring, for 2 minutes. (Do not let the mixture brown.) Whisk in the stock, sherry (if desired), salt, and pepper. Bring to a boil, reduce the heat to low, and simmer, whisking often, until thickened, about 2 minutes. Stir in the turkey, peas, and carrots; let cool, stirring often, for 10 minutes.

3. On a lightly floured surface, roll out 1 pastry sheet to an 11-inch square. Using a sharp knife, cut the sheet into quarters, giving you four 5½-inch squares. Using a pastry brush, brush away any excess flour on both sides of the squares. Lightly brush the 4 edges of each square with a little of the egg-yolk mixture. Place about ¼ cup of the turkey mixture in the center of each square. Fold the squares in half to form triangles. Press the sides of the triangles shut with the tines of a fork to seal. Place the triangles on an ungreased baking sheet. Repeat the procedure with the remaining ingredients.

4. Lightly brush the tops of the turnovers with some of the egg-yolk mixture and bake until golden brown, 15 to 20 minutes.

Southwestern Stir-fry with Turkey, Peppers, and Corn

Stir-frying is a great, quick way to use up leftovers, so long as you are careful not to overcook the previously roasted meat when you pop it into the wok or skillet. Use this technique with your own inspirations, but always add the meat toward the end.

Makes 4 servings

1 teaspoon cornstarch
½ cup canned chicken broth
2 tablespoons olive oil
1 cup fresh or defrosted frozen corn kernels
1 medium zucchini, thinly sliced
1 medium red or green bell pepper, cut into ½-by-2-inch strips
1 small red onion, thinly sliced

1 fresh jalapeño pepper, minced, or 2 tablespoons chopped canned green chilies
2 garlic cloves, minced
1 tablespoon lime juice
1 tablespoon chili powder
½ teaspoon salt
1 pound cooked turkey, cut into ½-by-2-inch strips

1. In a small bowl, dissolve the cornstarch in the broth; set aside. In a wok or a large skillet, heat the oil over moderately high heat until hot but not smoking. Add the corn, zucchini, red or green pepper, onion, jalapeño pepper, and garlic. Cook, stirring often, until the vegetables are crisp tender, about 2 minutes.

2. Add the lime juice, chili powder, and salt; cook for 30 seconds. Add the turkey meat and cook, stirring often, for 1 minute.

3. Add the cornstarch mixture and cook, stirring, until the sauce thickens and clears, about 1 minute. Serve immediately.

Turkey, Bacon, and Tomato Club Sandwiches with Blue Cheese Mayonnaise

One of Hollywood's top-billed culinary achievements is the cobb salad, named after an owner of the famous Brown Derby Restaurant, and co-starring cooked poultry, crisp bacon, crumbled blue cheese, and romaine lettuce. I've turned this one into my own extravaganza of a sandwich. Like a true native son of the Golden State, I like this on sourdough bread, but large, thin slices of any French or Italian bread, or even toasted white, will do.

Makes 4 servings

1 cup mayonnaise
½ cup crumbled blue cheese, preferably Roquefort
12 thin slices French or Italian bread, from a large, round loaf, grilled or toasted, if desired

1 pound cooked turkey breast, sliced
1 large ripe avocado, thinly sliced
16 slices bacon, crisply cooked
2 medium ripe tomatoes, sliced
4 large romaine lettuce leaves, torn in half crosswise

In a small bowl, mix the mayonnaise and blue cheese until well blended. Spread one-third of the mayonnaise over 4 of the bread slices. Divide the turkey evenly among the slices. Place the avocado slices over the turkey. Spread 4 of the bread slices with another one-third of the mayonnaise and place, dry-side down, on the avocado. Top with the bacon slices, tomato, and lettuce, dividing evenly. Spread the last 4 slices of bread with the remaining blue cheese mayonnaise and place, mayonnaise-side down, on the lettuce. Skewer the sandwiches at both ends with wooden toothpicks to hold the filling in place. Using a serrated knife, cut each sandwich in half, and serve at once.

Toasted Turkey, Cheddar, and Apple Sandwiches

One Thanksgiving, I whipped these up the day after the big feast while we were lazing around, and they have become a tradition ever since. They are a grown-up version of that childhood favorite, grilled cheese sandwiches. Make these with leftover slices of Spice-Rubbed Smoked Turkey (see page 222), and you'll create a toasty lunch treat as good as anything on a menu of an American bistro.

Makes 4 servings

4 tablespoons unsalted butter, melted
8 slices whole wheat bread
3 tablespoons prepared mustard, preferably honey mustard
1 pound cooked turkey breast, either smoked or roasted, sliced

1 large green apple, such as Granny Smith, quartered, cored, and thinly sliced
2 cups grated sharp Cheddar cheese (about ½ pound)

1. Preheat the oven to 400 degrees. Butter one side of 4 slices of the bread and place, buttered sides down, on a baking sheet. Spread the mustard over the sliced bread. Divide the turkey breast evenly over the mustard and arrange the apple slices on top. Sprinkle the cheese evenly over the apples. Butter the remaining 4 slices of bread and place them, buttered sides up, on the cheese, pressing lightly to compact the sandwiches.

2. Bake for 10 minutes, turning once with a metal spatula, until the sandwiches are golden brown and the cheese is melted. With a sharp knife, cut the sandwiches in half diagonally and serve immediately.

Pasta Bow Ties with Smoked Turkey, Sun-Dried Tomatoes, and Basil

It's safe to say that *everyone* loves pasta. The interplaying flavors and textures of smoky turkey chunks, slightly sweet and chewy sun-dried tomatoes, subtle and creamy ricotta, and fragrant basil are refined and gutsy at the same time. (I think you'll be happiest if you use fresh herbs here, so substitute rosemary, sage, or oregano if you can't find basil.)

Makes 4 to 6 servings

1 pound bow-tie pasta or fettuccine
2 tablespoons olive oil
1 cup coarsely chopped sun-dried tomatoes packed in oil, drained (about 6 ounces)
2 garlic cloves, minced
1 pound smoked turkey, cut into 1-inch cubes

¼ cup coarsely chopped Kalamata olives
1 cup part-skim ricotta cheese
¾ cup freshly grated Parmesan cheese
3 tablespoons coarsely chopped fresh basil
Salt and freshly ground pepper

1. In a large saucepan of boiling salted water, cook the pasta until tender but still firm, 10 to 12 minutes. Scoop and reserve 1 cup of the pasta's cooking water. Drain the pasta and place in a large, warmed serving bowl.

2. Meanwhile, in a medium skillet, heat the olive oil. Add the sun-dried tomatoes and garlic. Cook over low heat, stirring often, until the garlic is fragrant, about 1 minute. Add the smoked turkey and olives and cook, stirring often, until the turkey is heated through, about 5 minutes.

3. Pour the warm turkey mixture over the hot cooked pasta. Add the ricotta and Parmesan cheese, basil, and ½ cup of the pasta cooking water. Toss well, adding enough of the remaining pasta cooking water, if necessary, to create a creamy sauce. Season with salt and pepper to taste and serve immediately.

▶ *Sun-dried tomatoes packed in olive oil are available at gourmet shops and Italian delicatessens. The dehydrated sun-dried tomatoes, not in oil, are found in the produce sections of many supermarkets. To rehydrate the dessicated variety, soak them*

*in hot water for 10 minutes, drain, and pat dry with paper
towels. Spread in a single layer on a baking sheet and bake at
200 degrees for 10 minutes. Let cool, then pack in a small
container and cover with olive oil or a combination of olive and
vegetable oils.*

Monte Cristo Sandwiches

Blum's, San Francisco's supreme lunchroom/soda fountain/confectionery of the not-too-distant past, was where thousands of young Californians learned to eat "fancy food." I was one of those kids, and my standing order was for a Monte Cristo Sandwich—a piping hot fork 'n' knife sandwich of meat-and-cheese-filled French toast. When I was in college, I actually worked at one of the last operating Blum's and was in gustatory heaven—imagine having free Monte Cristo Sandwiches every day!

Makes 2 servings

2 large eggs
½ cup milk, regular or low-fat
¼ teaspoon salt
¼ teaspoon freshly ground pepper
4 slices firm-textured white sandwich
   bread

2 tablespoons Dijon-style mustard
4 thin slices Swiss cheese, cut to fit
   bread slices
4 thick slices cooked turkey breast
2 tablespoons unsalted butter
2 tablespoons vegetable oil

1. In a medium bowl, whisk together the eggs, milk, salt, and pepper. Spread one side of each bread slice with 1½ teaspoons of mustard. To make each sandwich, place 1 slice of cheese, 2 slices of turkey, and another slice of cheese on top of 1 slice of mustard-coated bread; top with another slice of bread, mustard-side down.

2. In a large skillet, melt the butter in the oil over moderate heat. Dip the sandwiches briefly in the egg mixture, turning to moisten both sides. Cook, turning once with a pancake turner, until golden brown, about 6 minutes. Adjust the heat as necessary so the sandwiches do not burn. Serve hot.

Nonni's Turkey Vegetable Soup
with Ricotta Dumplings

There are as many recipes for turkey soup as there are recipes for roast turkey. This one gets an added lift from tiny ricotta-and-basil dumplings bobbing in a steaming broth sparkling with fresh vegetable flavors.

Makes 8 servings

1 turkey carcass, chopped into large pieces
2 medium onions, chopped
2 carrots, cut into ½-inch rounds
2 celery ribs, cut into ½-inch slices
About 12 cups cold water
4 sprigs of parsley
1 teaspoon salt
¼ teaspoon pepper
2 tablespoons olive oil
1 medium zucchini, scrubbed, halved lengthwise, and cut into ½-inch slices

¼ pound green beans, trimmed and cut into 1-inch pieces
1 cup drained canned Italian peeled tomatoes, coarsely chopped
½ teaspoon dried marjoram
1 cup freshly grated Parmesan cheese (4 ounces)
½ cup ricotta cheese
¼ cup all-purpose flour
1 large egg, lightly beaten
2 tablespoons minced fresh basil or parsley
Pinch of freshly grated nutmeg

1. In a stockpot or large flameproof casserole, combine the turkey carcass, half of the onion, half of the carrot, and half of the celery; add water to cover. Bring to a boil over moderately high heat; skim off any foam that rises to the surface. Add the parsley, salt, and pepper, reduce the heat to low, and simmer for 2 hours. Set the broth aside.

2. In another pot, heat the oil. Add the remaining chopped onion and cook over moderate heat, stirring, until softened, 2 to 3 minutes. One at a time, add the remaining carrot and celery and the zucchini, green beans, and tomatoes, cooking each for 1 minute before adding the next ingredient. Strain the broth into the saucepan and add the marjoram. Bring to a boil, reduce the heat, and simmer, partially covered, until the vegetables are tender, about 1 hour.

3. In a medium bowl, stir together the Parmesan, ricotta, flour, egg, basil, and nutmeg just until smooth. With a dessert teaspoon, scrape up a heaping

mound (about 1 tablespoon) of the cheese mixture. Using a second spoon, smooth into a dumpling and drop into the simmering soup. Repeat to form all of the dumplings. Simmer, partially covered, until the dumplings are cooked through, about 6 minutes.

Turkey Tostadas Mañana

On Thanksgiving Friday, after a full day of relentlessly patriotic all-American fare, one is sometimes ready to take a culinary trip south of the border. Tostadas are a great way to go, as they couldn't be simpler.

Makes 6 servings

½ cup vegetable oil
6 corn tortillas
½ cup canned chicken broth
1 small onion, thinly sliced
1 pound cooked turkey meat,
  shredded
1 can (16 ounces) refried beans, heated

1 small head iceberg lettuce, shredded
1½ cups Fresh Tomato Salsa
  (see page 57) or Tomatillo Salsa
  (see page 52) or bottled salsa
1 cup grated sharp Cheddar cheese
  (4 ounces)
½ cup sour cream

1. In a large skillet, heat the oil over moderately high heat until very hot but not smoking. In batches, cook the tortillas, turning once, until crisp, about 45 seconds. With tongs, transfer the tortillas to a paper towel–lined baking sheet and let drain.

2. In a medium saucepan, bring the chicken broth and onion to a simmer. Add the shredded turkey and heat, stirring often, over low heat for 5 minutes. Drain the turkey and onions, discarding the liquid.

3. Spread each tortilla with the warm refried beans. Top each with a mound of shredded lettuce, the warm shredded turkey and onions, salsa, and cheese. Top each tostada with a dollop of sour cream and serve.

Old-Fashioned Turkey Vegetable Soup

Turkey and vegetable soup is a time-honored way to use up Thanksgiving leftovers. Use this recipe, fragrant with aromatic herbs and vegetables, as a jumping-off point for your own inspirations, adding whatever vegetables and whole grains you wish.

Makes 6 to 8 servings

1 roast turkey carcass, plus up to 4
    cups leftover turkey meat, cut into
    1-inch cubes
2 tablespoons vegetable oil
About 12 cups cold water
6 large carrots, cut into ½-inch rounds
4 large celery ribs, cut into ½-inch
    slices
2 large onions, chopped
6 sprigs of parsley

1 teaspoon dried thyme
2 imported bay leaves
2 teaspoons salt
½ teaspoon freshly ground
    pepper
4 tablespoons unsalted butter
3 large red potatoes (about 1 pound),
    cut into 1-inch chunks
¼ cup chopped fresh parsley
1 teaspoon dried marjoram

1. Using a heavy cleaver or knife, chop the carcass into large pieces. In a stockpot or a large flameproof casserole, heat the oil. Add the carcass pieces and cook over moderately high heat, turning often, until the pieces are browned, about 10 minutes. Add enough cold water to cover by 2 inches, about 12 cups. Add 2 carrots, 2 celery ribs, and 1 onion. Bring to a simmer; skim off any foam that rises to the top. Add the parsley sprigs, thyme, bay leaves, salt, and pepper. Reduce the heat to low and simmer for at least 2 and up to 4 hours. Strain the turkey broth into a large bowl, press hard on the solids, then discard them. Set the broth aside. Clean the saucepan if you will be using the same one to make the soup.

2. In a large saucepan or flameproof casserole, melt the butter. Add the remaining 4 carrots, 2 celery ribs, and onion. Cook, covered, over moderate heat, stirring occasionally, until the vegetables are softened, about 10 minutes. Add the potatoes, reserved turkey broth, chopped parsley, and marjoram and bring to a boil. Reduce the heat to low and simmer, partially covered, 30 to 40 minutes.

3. Add the cubed turkey and heat through, about 5 minutes.

CREAM OF TURKEY SOUP: Add 1 cup of heavy (whipping) cream to the soup along with the cooked turkey in step 3. Do not boil.

TURKEY NOODLE SOUP: Add 4 ounces of uncooked egg noodles to the soup 15 minutes before the end of the cooking time.

VEGETABLE VARIATIONS: Other vegetables can be added to the soup. Trimmed green beans, broccoli florets, 1/2-inch-thick parsnip rounds, and turnip or rutabaga cut into 1-inch cubes can be added to the vegetables in step 2. Up to 2 cups chopped canned tomatoes also can be added along with the strained turkey broth. Shelled peas and corn kernels should be added along with the turkey meat and cooked for 5 minutes.

PASTA, RICE, AND GRAIN VARIATIONS: Add these ingredients after the soup has simmered for at least 30 minutes. Delete the potatoes, if desired. Tiny pasta shapes, such as *acini de pepe* or orzo, will cook in 5 to 8 minutes. Long-grain rice will cook in about 20 minutes. Brown or wild rice will take up to 1 hour to become tender. Grains, such as barley and wheat kernels, vary greatly in cooking times, depending on how dry the grains are when purchased. Simmer the grains separately in water until tender, drain, and add to the soup with the turkey in step 3.

CHAPTER THREE

White Meat Only

A happy outcome of the new turkey explosion is that you can purchase separately your favorite part of the bird and prepare it to perfection. On a whole turkey, the choice white meat is often difficult to cook precisely. By buying a breast and roasting it alone, you can cook it to perfection and have tender, juicy white meat year-round.

Since turkey breasts are sold half and whole, boned and bone in, skin on and skinned, or tenderloins only, you can choose the size and style that's just right for your needs. With all the possible variations on this theme, you can try such toothsome temptations as Bacon-Wrapped Turkey Roast with Shallot Sauce, Turkey Potpie with Flaky Chive Crust, and even Turkey Breast Pot Roast, laden with vegetables and simmered with white wine and broth.

Nothing makes better salads than braised turkey, and in this chapter you'll find out how to make Basic Braised Turkey Breast, which yields especially moist, succulent meat, perfect for recipes like Orange-Pecan Turkey Salad with Minted Yogurt Dressing or Mediterranean Turkey Salad with Potatoes and Olives. There's also nothing wrong with using this meat for many of the leftover recipes in Chapter 2 as well.

There are a variety of turkey breast products on the poultry shelves. Here's a brief run-through:

Whole turkey breasts, which run about 4½ to 8 pounds, can be purchased fresh or frozen. If frozen, defrost according to the guidelines on page xii. They are sold with the skin and bones attached. If desired, remove the back section so the breast will not roll around on the serving platter. Using a cleaver or heavy knife, chop through where the thin ribs join the meatier area of the breast. Cook the backbone along with the breast to add flavor to the pan drippings or braising liquid, or use it to make stock. Whole breasts are a great way to serve a group, allowing about ¾ pound of a bone-in turkey breast per guest. Boned and stuffed, as in the recipe for Rolled Turkey Roast with French Summer Garden Stuffing, they are an elegant entrée and can substitute for more expensive veal roasts in many recipes.

Half turkey breasts, sold fresh with the bone in and skin on, run 2 to 3½ pounds. They are perfect for smaller groups and make just enough meat and broth for many of the salad and casserole dishes in this book.

Boneless turkey breast roasts are boned breasts, sold fresh, either with skin removed or skin attached. (The skinless variety is a very low-fat product.) They run 1½ to 2½ pounds, depending on the purveyor. Because they are so low in fat, boneless turkey roasts must be handled with care to avoid overcooking and drying out. Butterflied and rolled, they can be stuffed with a variety of ingredients, making colorful roulades.

When roasting a whole or half turkey breast, preheat the oven to 325 degrees. Allow about 20 minutes per pound, and baste often until a meat thermometer inserted in the thick part of the breast without touching a bone reaches 165 to 170 degrees. (I normally roast turkey to the lower temperature needed because the temperature will rise another 5 degrees or so from the residual heat stored in the meat.) When braising, after browning, simmer for 20 to 30 minutes per pound, being sure to turn the meat once or twice for even heating. Use a thermometer to check for doneness.

Boneless roasts are more delicate and should be treated differently. Roast them at 350 degrees for 20 to 25 minutes per pound or braise them for about 20 minutes per pound. With either method, be sure to baste often.

Turkey tenderloins are created from the fillet of the turkey breast and come 2 or 3 to a 1-pound package. As their name suggests, tenderloins are extremely tender, and some processors butterfly them lengthwise, so they can be opened and pounded to an even thickness. Since tenderloins are large, they need to be sautéed about 7 minutes per side. I like to roast them, unopened, as in Deviled Crispy Tenderloins. They can also be cut into pieces for use in stir-fries.

Turkey Breast Pot Roast

A whole turkey breast is browned with bacon, then slowly simmered with loads of fragrant vegetables to make a succulent supper dish par excellence. With the turkey, vegetables, and potatoes in one dish, all you need is a salad—say, curly endive with a Roquefort dressing—to make a meal.

Makes 4 to 6 servings

½ pound thickly sliced bacon, cut crosswise into ½-inch strips
2 tablespoons unsalted butter
1 whole turkey breast (5 pounds), bone in, skin on
12 small white boiling onions (about 1 pound), peeled
6 medium carrots, cut into 2½-inch lengths
4 celery ribs with leaves, cut into 2½-by-½-inch sticks

Salt and freshly ground pepper
1 cup Homemade Turkey Stock (page 246), or ½ cup canned chicken broth mixed with ½ cup water
½ cup dry white wine
1 teaspoon dried thyme
1 bay leaf
8 medium red potatoes (about 1½ pounds), scrubbed
¼ cup finely chopped fresh parsley

1. In a medium saucepan of simmering water, cook the bacon strips for 3 minutes; drain. Rinse the bacon under cold running water, drain again, and pat dry with paper towels.

2. In a heavy oval casserole, melt the butter over moderate heat. Add the bacon and cook, stirring often, until bacon is browned, about 5 minutes. With a slotted spoon, transfer the bacon to a plate, leaving the drippings in the casserole. Add the turkey breast and cook over moderate heat, turning often with two spoons, until browned all over, 10 to 15 minutes. Remove the turkey breast to the plate with the bacon and reserve.

3. Add the onions, carrots, and celery to the casserole and cook over moderate heat, stirring occasionally, until the onions are lightly browned, about 8 minutes. With a slotted spoon, transfer the browned vegetables to a separate plate.

4. Return the turkey breast and bacon to the casserole and season with salt and pepper to taste. Add the stock, wine, thyme, and bay leaf and bring to

a boil. Reduce the heat to low and simmer, covered tightly, for 30 minutes. Add the potatoes and reserved vegetables. Simmer, still covered tightly, about 1 hour, until a meat thermometer inserted in the thick part of the breast, but not touching a bone, registers 165 to 170 degrees. Transfer the turkey breast and the vegetables to a large platter; tent with aluminum foil to keep warm.

5. With a large spoon, skim the fat from the top of the liquid in the pan. Boil over high heat until reduced by one-fourth, about 2 minutes. Season with salt and pepper to taste and pour into a warmed sauceboat. Sprinkle the turkey breast and vegetables with the chopped parsley. Carve the turkey breast and serve with the vegetables and sauce.

REDUCED-FAT AND -CALORIE VARIATION: Omit the bacon from the recipe. Substitute margarine or vegetable oil for the butter.

> ▶ *To peel small boiling onions easily, plunge them into boiling water for 1 minute. Drain, rinse under cold water, and drain again. Pare the loosened peels off with a small, sharp knife. Make small Xs in the root ends of each onion to prevent the onions from bursting.*

Soy-and-Ginger-Braised Turkey Breast

Hanging in the windows of most Chinese food shops are glistening "red-cooked" birds, prepared by gentle simmering in a gingery soy-sauce braising liquid. Here's a home version using turkey that is both easy and incredibly savory. Chunks of leftover Soy-and-Ginger-Braised Turkey Breast make excellent salads, such as Turkey, Pasta, and Vegetable Salad with Spicy Peanut Dressing (see page 100).

Makes 4 to 6 servings

2 cups low-sodium soy sauce
2 cups water
½ cup dry sherry or Chinese rice wine
1 tablespoon coarsely chopped fresh
    ginger
1 whole star anise (see Note), or
    ¼ teaspoon anise seed
1 medium scallion, coarsely chopped

1 whole turkey breast (4½ pounds),
    bone in, skin on
3 tablespoons packed light brown
    sugar
2 teaspoons Oriental sesame oil (see
    Note), or vegetable oil
Lettuce leaves for garnish
    (optional)

1. In a large saucepan, bring the soy sauce, water, sherry, ginger, star anise, and scallion to a simmer over moderate heat. Rinse the turkey breast and dry well with paper towels. Add the turkey breast, skin-side up, to the saucepan. With a bulb baster or large spoon, continuously baste the turkey with the braising liquid until it returns to a simmer, about 1 minute. Cover tightly and simmer over low heat for 20 minutes, basting twice. Turn the turkey breast over carefully with two wooden spoons and stir in the brown sugar. Cover and simmer for 20 minutes longer, basting the turkey twice.

2. Remove the pan from the heat and let the turkey stand in the liquid, tightly covered, for 1 hour, basting every 15 minutes. Turn the turkey breast over carefully with two wooden spoons and let stand, covered, 1 hour longer, again basting every 15 minutes.

3. Remove the turkey breast from the braising liquid and place on a work surface. Brush the skin of the turkey breast with the sesame oil. For the best-looking presentation, chop the turkey breast into pieces Chinese-style: With a heavy cleaver, chop the rib and backbone section away from the meaty portion of the breast. Chop the breast in half vertically down the

breastbone. Chop each breast portion crosswise into 3 or 4 pieces. Chop each piece in half vertically. (Or carve the turkey breast in a conventional manner.)

4. To serve, line a serving platter with the lettuce leaves, if desired, and arrange the turkey pieces on top. Serve at room temperature with some of the braising liquid as a dipping sauce.

> *Note: Star anise and sesame oil are available at Asian markets and many supermarkets, or by mail order from Dean and Deluca, 800-221-7714; 212-431-1691.*

Tandoori Turkey Breast

Marinating turkey breast in spiced yogurt creates an incredibly tender roast with rich aromatic flavor. I recommend serving this with steamed basmati rice tossed with unsweetened coconut flakes and almonds as a foil for the tangy marinade.

Makes 4 to 6 servings

1 whole turkey breast (4½ pounds), bone in, skin on
¼ cup fresh lemon juice
2 teaspoons salt
1 medium onion, quartered
3 garlic cloves, crushed
2 tablespoons coarsely chopped fresh ginger

2 cups plain low-fat yogurt
1 tablespoon ground coriander
1 tablespoon ground cumin
2 teaspoons paprika
½ teaspoon turmeric
½ teaspoon ground cardamom
½ teaspoon ground cinnamon
¼ teaspoon cayenne pepper

1. Using a small, sharp knife, pierce the turkey breast all over at 2-inch intervals, about ½ inch deep. In a large bowl, mix the lemon juice and salt. Place the turkey in the bowl, rub it all over with the lemon mixture, and let stand, turning once or twice, for 30 to 60 minutes at room temperature.

2. Meanwhile, coarsely chop the onion, garlic, and ginger in a food processor. Add the yogurt, coriander, cumin, paprika, turmeric, cardamom, cinnamon, and cayenne, and process until smooth. Pour the yogurt mixture over the turkey, cover tightly, and refrigerate, turning once or twice, for at least 8 hours and up to 24 hours (the longer the better).

3. Preheat the oven to 400 degrees. Place the turkey with marinade in a nonaluminum roasting pan just large enough to hold it comfortably. Bake for 15 minutes. Reduce the heat to 350 degrees, and bake for about 1 hour 15 minutes, until a meat thermometer inserted in the thick part of the breast, but not touching a bone, registers 165 to 170 degrees. Let the turkey breast stand for 10 to 15 minutes, loosely covered with aluminum foil, before carving.

4. To grill the turkey breast, place a heatproof pan, such as a disposable aluminum foil pan, centered on the bottom of a covered charcoal grill. Fill

the pan halfway with water. Build hot charcoal fires (preferably of hardwood charcoal) on both sides of the pan. (You should be able to hold your hand over the fire for only 1 to 2 seconds.) Place the turkey breast over the water-filled pan. Open all of the vents in the grill and cook, covered, until a meat thermometer inserted in the thick part of the breast, but not touching a bone, registers 165 to 170 degrees, about 2 hours. Maintain an even temperature by adding additional hot coals, if necessary.

▶ *How did turkey get its name? When Christopher Columbus first saw a turkey, he thought it was a kind of peacock. Since he mistakenly assumed he was near India, he called it by the Indian word for peacock,* tuka. *(Actually, the turkey is a kind of pheasant.) Other sources say that* turkey *evolved from the Hebrew* tukki, *when the Jews became familiar with the bird during their stay in Spain.*

Turkey Dinner for Two

Not every holiday meal is a huge event with countless hungry relatives. Sometimes it can be an intimate, even romantic, affair for just the two of you. Although this dish is small in scale, it offers many of Thanksgiving's traditional flavors in one dish: turkey, herb stuffing, gravy, carrots, baby onions, and even leftovers!

Makes 2 generous servings, including leftovers

4 tablespoons plus 2 teaspoons
  unsalted butter, softened
1 small onion, finely chopped
1 small celery rib, finely chopped
6 slices of stale white bread, cut
  into ½-inch cubes (about 3 cups)
1¼ cups Homemade Turkey Stock
  (page 246) or canned chicken
  broth
¼ cup chopped fresh parsley
½ teaspoon dried thyme
¼ teaspoon dried sage

¼ teaspoon dried marjoram
¾ teaspoon salt
½ teaspoon freshly ground pepper
1 small whole turkey breast
  (3 pounds), bone in, skin on
4 large carrots, cut into 2-by-
  ½-inch sticks
12 small white boiling onions,
  peeled
2 teaspoons all-purpose flour
1 tablespoon brandy or port wine
  (optional)

1. In a large skillet, melt 2 tablespoons of the butter. Add the onion and celery and cook over moderate heat, stirring often, until softened, about 3 minutes. Off heat, add the bread cubes, ¼ cup of stock, 2 tablespoons of the parsley, the thyme, sage, and marjoram, and ¼ teaspoon each of the salt and pepper. Mix well to combine.

2. Carefully slip your fingers underneath the skin of the turkey breast and separate it from the meat without tearing the skin. (This is easy to do if you make a small incision in the membrane that binds the skin to the meat at the narrow end of the breast and slip your fingers in at that point.) Spread the stuffing evenly underneath the turkey's skin. Rub 2 tablespoons of butter over the skin. Season the top of the breast with the remaining ½ teaspoon salt and ¼ teaspoon pepper. Place in a medium, shallow flameproof baking dish and pour ¼ cup of the stock over it.

3. Preheat the oven to 350 degrees. Roast the turkey breast for 30 minutes, basting occasionally with the pan juices. Arrange the carrot sticks and baby

onions around the turkey, season with additional salt and pepper, and continue roasting, basting occasionally, until a meat thermometer inserted in the thick part of the breast, but not touching the bone, registers 165 to 170 degrees, about 1 hour. Remove the turkey and vegetables to a warmed serving platter. Cover with aluminum foil and let stand 10 minutes before carving.

4. Meanwhile, pour off and discard any fat in the pan, leaving behind the browned bits. Set the roasting pan on top of the stove, add the remaining 2 teaspoons butter, and melt over moderately low heat. Whisk in the flour and cook, whisking constantly and scraping up the browned bits on the bottom of the pan, for 1 minute. Whisk in the remaining ¾ cup of stock and the brandy. Bring to a boil, reduce the heat to low, and simmer, whisking often, for 2 minutes. Pour the gravy into a warmed sauceboat.

5. Sprinkle the turkey breast and vegetables with the remaining 2 tablespoons parsley, carve the turkey breast, and serve immediately with the vegetables and gravy.

Turkey Breast Roast with Peachy Plantation Glaze and Bourbon Gravy

Serve the roast with Rick's Melt-in-Your-Mouth Corn Bread (page 252) for a real taste of the Old South.

Makes 3 to 4 servings

2 teaspoons cornstarch
2 tablespoons bourbon
¼ cup peach preserves
2 tablespoons unsalted butter, softened
1 turkey breast half (2½ pounds), bone in, skin on

¼ teaspoon salt
⅛ teaspoon freshly ground pepper
1 cup water
¾ cup Homemade Turkey Stock (page 246) or canned chicken broth
¼ cup heavy (whipping) cream

1. Preheat the oven to 350 degrees. In a small bowl, dissolve 1 teaspoon of the cornstarch in 1 tablespoon of the bourbon. In a small saucepan, stir together the preserves, 1 tablespoon of the butter, and the bourbon-cornstarch mixture over low heat until melted and thickened, about 1 minute. Set the peach glaze aside.

2. Rub the remaining 1 tablespoon of butter over the turkey breast. Season with the salt and pepper. Place in a medium flameproof roasting pan just large enough to hold the breast. Pour the water into the pan. Bake, brushing often with the pan drippings, for 30 minutes. Continue to bake, basting often with the peach glaze, until a meat thermometer inserted in the thickest part of the breast, but not touching a bone, reads 165 to 170 degrees, 40 to 50 minutes longer. Add a little water to the pan, as necessary, to prevent the drippings from burning.

3. Transfer the turkey to a serving platter and cover loosely with aluminum foil to keep warm. Dissolve the remaining 1 teaspoon cornstarch in the remaining 1 tablespoon bourbon. Set the roasting pan on top of the stove over moderately low heat. Add the stock, heavy cream, and the bourbon mixture to the pan. Bring to a boil, scraping up the browned bits on the bottom of the pan with a wooden spoon. Reduce the heat to a simmer and cook, stirring constantly, for 1 minute. Season with additional salt and pepper to taste. Pour the sauce into a warmed sauceboat and serve with the turkey roast.

Deviled Crispy Tenderloins

Here's a way to achieve a crisp, "deep-fried" crust without loads of oil. Juicy tenderloins—the filet mignons of the turkey breast—are slathered with devilishly spiced yogurt, rolled in bread crumbs, and oven-baked with a little hot oil to give a crunchy result without a high calorie count.

Makes 4 servings

½ cup plain low-fat yogurt
1 tablespoon Dijon mustard
¼ teaspoon hot pepper
   sauce, or more
   to taste
¼ teaspoon salt

2 turkey tenderloins (about 10 ounces
   each), not spread open, tendons
   removed
¼ cup vegetable oil
1 cup fresh bread crumbs
½ teaspoon paprika

1. In a medium bowl, combine the yogurt, mustard, hot sauce, and salt. Add the turkey tenderloins and toss to coat. Let stand 30 minutes at room temperature.

2. Preheat the oven to 425 degrees. Pour the oil into a medium baking dish, set in the oven, and heat until the oil is hot, about 10 minutes. Meanwhile, on a plate, combine the bread crumbs and paprika. Roll the tenderloins in the bread-crumb mixture.

3. When the oil is hot, place the coated turkey tenderloins in the baking dish. Bake, turning once after 15 minutes, until the tenderloins are golden brown and show no trace of pink when pierced with the tip of a knife, about 30 minutes total.

MICROWAVE INSTRUCTIONS: Heat oil in a microwave-safe dish at High (100 percent) for 2 minutes. Add coated tenderloins and cook at High for 10 to 12 minutes, turning once halfway through cooking time. Cover with aluminum foil and let stand for 5 minutes.

Beulah's Turkey Fricassee with Scallion Dumplings

For the ultimate "fricassee experience," you have to go to a clean, comfortable boardinghouse, preferably owned by two friendly sisters in a small Southern town, which sounds exactly like the one my friend Beulah Brown Hesen used to run with her late sister Glendora in Keyser, West Virginia, more than 40 years ago. Although the Sisters Brown used to boil up whole toms for their fricassee to feed hoards of hungry boarders, I have adapted their recipe for a more manageable half breast.

Makes 4 to 6 servings

2 tablespoons unsalted butter
1 turkey breast half (2½ pounds), bone in, skin on
1 large onion, chopped
4 medium carrots, cut into 1-inch lengths
½ pound medium mushrooms, quartered
1¼ cups all-purpose flour
2 cups Homemade Turkey Stock (page 246) or canned chicken broth
1 cup dry white wine or ¾ cup dry vermouth or apple cider

2 teaspoons lemon juice
1½ teaspoons salt
1 teaspoon dried tarragon
½ teaspoon dried thyme
¼ teaspoon white pepper
1 bay leaf
2 teaspoons baking powder
1 large egg, lightly beaten
⅓ cup milk
1 medium scallion, minced
3 large egg yolks
½ cup heavy (whipping) cream

1. In a large saucepan or flameproof casserole, melt the butter over moderate heat. Add the turkey breast and cook, turning once, until lightly browned, about 8 minutes. Add the onion, carrots, and mushrooms. Cover and cook until the vegetables are softened, about 5 minutes.

2. Transfer the turkey breast to a plate. Sprinkle ¼ cup of flour over the vegetables, and cook, stirring, for 1 minute. Stir in the stock, wine, lemon juice, 1 teaspoon of the salt, tarragon, thyme, pepper, and bay leaf. Bring to a boil and reduce the heat to low. Return the turkey breast to the pan, cover, and simmer, turning once, until a thermometer inserted in the thickest part of the breast, but not touching a bone, reads 165 to 170 degrees, 40 to 50 minutes. Transfer the turkey to a cutting board and cool slightly.

3. While the turkey is cooling, make the dumplings. In a medium bowl, stir together the remaining 1 cup flour and ½ teaspoon salt and the baking powder. Stir in the egg, milk, and scallion just until smooth. Drop the dough by heaping teaspoons into the simmering cooking liquid, cover, and cook until the dumplings are firm, about 15 minutes. Using a slotted spoon, transfer the dumplings to a serving dish, cover, and keep warm.

4. While the dumplings are simmering, remove and discard the skin and bones from the turkey breast. Carve the turkey breast meat into 1-inch cubes. In a small bowl, whisk together the egg yolks and cream.

5. After removing the dumplings, add the turkey meat to the fricassee and cook for 1 minute. Gradually stir about ½ cup of the fricassee sauce into the egg mixture, then stir this mixture back into the pan, stirring constantly until the sauce is slightly thickened, about 1 minute; do not boil. Transfer the fricassee to a warmed casserole and serve immediately with the dumplings.

Turkey Breast Roulade with Winter Pesto

Summertime pesto made with fresh basil and pine nuts is glorious, but you can do just fine in winter with a parsley, dried rosemary, and walnut mixture. Here I slather it on a boneless turkey breast roast, which is then braised with broth and wine. The sliced roast could be served with sautéed ribbons of carrots and zucchini to add a touch of color, and steamed rice to soak up the savory juices.

Makes 4 servings

4 garlic cloves, crushed
4 cups chopped flat-leaf Italian parsley
   (about 4 bunches)
1 tablespoon dried rosemary
¾ cup walnut pieces, toasted
   (see page 229)
¾ cup freshly grated Parmesan cheese
1 teaspoon salt
1 cup olive oil

1 boneless turkey breast roast
   (1½ pounds)
⅛ teaspoon freshly ground pepper
2 tablespoons vegetable oil
2 cups Homemade Turkey Stock
   (see page 246), or 1 cup canned
   chicken broth mixed with 1 cup
   water
½ cup dry white wine or dry vermouth

1. In a food processor with the machine on, drop the garlic cloves through the feed tube. Add the parsley, rosemary, walnuts, Parmesan, and ¾ teaspoon of the salt. Process until the mixture forms a paste. With the machine on, gradually add the olive oil, blending until smooth. Transfer the pesto to a bowl and reserve.

2. Place the turkey breast roast, skin-side down, on a work surface. Using a sharp knife, cut a deep incision into the thickest part of the breast on one side of the roast, being careful not to cut completely through. Open this flap like a book to one side, to butterfly the meat. Make another cut on the other side, being careful not to cut completely through, and fold out in the other direction. Pound gently to flatten evenly.

3. Spread ½ cup of the pesto over the surface of the turkey, leaving a 1-inch border around the sides. Starting at a short edge, roll up the breast. Using kitchen string, tie the roast crosswise and lengthwise. Season with the remaining salt and the pepper.

4. In a medium flameproof casserole, heat the vegetable oil. Add the turkey roulade and cook over moderate heat, turning often, until browned all over, about 8 minutes. Add the broth and wine and bring to a simmer. Reduce the heat to low, cover, and simmer, turning once, until a meat thermometer inserted in the center of the breast registers 165 to 170 degrees, 30 to 35 minutes. Transfer the roulade to a serving platter and cover with aluminum foil to keep warm.

5. Boil the cooking liquid in the casserole over high heat until reduced to 1½ cups, 5 to 10 minutes. Remove the kitchen string and carve crosswise into 1-inch-thick slices. Serve with the cooking juices.

▶ *Any leftover pesto is fabulous, of course, on pasta. For every pound of hot, drained cooked pasta, toss with 1 cup of pesto and about ½ cup of reserved hot pasta cooking water. (Add ½ cup low-fat ricotta cheese for extra richness.) Refrigerate the parsley pesto in a tightly covered container with 2 tablespoons of olive oil floating on top.*

Turkey Roast Paprikash

Paprikash is a satisfying Hungarian stew whose hallmark is a paprika-flavored tomato sauce, tinted pink with a swirl of sour cream. Do try to search out real Hungarian sweet paprika for this dish—it is distinctly tastier. Here is an elegant version that uses boneless turkey breast. Serve with egg noodles.

Makes 3 to 4 servings

1 boneless turkey breast roast
  (2 pounds)
¼ teaspoon salt
⅛ teaspoon freshly ground pepper
1 tablespoon unsalted butter
1 tablespoon vegetable oil
1 medium onion, chopped

1 tablespoon paprika, preferably
  Hungarian sweet
1 tablespoon all-purpose flour
1 cup tomato puree
½ cup Homemade Turkey Stock (page
  246) or canned chicken broth
½ cup sour cream

1. Roll the turkey breast lengthwise into a cylinder and tie in several places with kitchen string. Season the breast with salt and pepper.

2. In a large flameproof casserole, melt the butter in the oil over moderate heat. Add the turkey breast and cook, turning often, until browned all over, about 8 minutes. Transfer the turkey to a plate.

3. Add the onion and cook, stirring often, until softened, about 3 minutes. Add the paprika and flour and cook, stirring, for 1 minute. Stir in the tomato puree and broth; return the breast to the casserole and bring to a simmer.

4. Cover and bake until a meat thermometer inserted in the breast reads 170 degrees, 40 to 50 minutes. Transfer to a plate, cover loosely with foil, and let stand for 5 to 10 minutes before slicing.

5. Just before serving, place the casserole over low heat, add the sour cream, and stir just to warm the sauce through, about 1 minute; do not boil. Remove the strings from the turkey and carve crosswise into 1-inch slices. Arrange the slices overlapping on a platter and pour the sauce over the turkey.

Bacon-Wrapped Turkey Roast with Shallot Sauce

A meaty turkey breast, wrapped with smoky bacon strips that baste the bird as they brown, is presented with new potatoes in their jackets that are roasted right alongside.

Makes 4 to 6 servings

1 whole turkey breast (5 pounds), bone in, skin on
¾ teaspoon salt
½ teaspoon freshly ground pepper
8 strips bacon
½ cup water
12 small red potatoes (about 2 pounds), well scrubbed and halved

¾ teaspoon dried thyme
¼ cup chopped fresh parsley
3 medium shallots or scallions (white part only), minced
2 tablespoons all-purpose flour
2 cups Homemade Turkey Stock (page 246), or 1 cup canned chicken broth mixed with 1 cup water

1. Preheat the oven to 350 degrees. Season the turkey with ¼ teaspoon each salt and pepper. Arrange the bacon lengthwise over the breast. Place on a rack in a roasting pan. Pour the water into the bottom of the pan.

2. Bake for 30 minutes, basting frequently. Arrange the potatoes around the turkey, sprinkle with the remaining ½ teaspoon salt, ¼ teaspoon pepper, and the thyme, and toss the potatoes to coat with the drippings and seasonings. Continue baking, basting and turning the potatoes often, until a meat thermometer inserted in the thickest part of the breast reads 170 degrees and the potatoes are tender, an additional 1¼ to 1½ hours. (Total cooking time is 1¾ to 2 hours.) Transfer the roast and the potatoes to a serving dish, cover loosely with aluminum foil, and keep warm.

3. Pour off all but 2 tablespoons of the pan drippings. Set the roasting pan on top of the stove over moderately low heat. Add the shallot and stir until softened, about 1 minute. Sprinkle in the flour and cook, whisking constantly, for 1 minute. Whisk in the turkey stock and bring to a simmer; cook until slightly thickened, about 5 minutes. Pour the sauce into a sauceboat and serve with the turkey breast and potatoes.

Turkey Potpie with Flaky Chive Crust

This is a surefire recipe for an old favorite, chock-full of baby onions, carrots, and peas in a silky sauce, and topped with a melt-in-your-mouth pastry crust. If you're in a hurry, you could use a prepared pie crust.

Makes 4 to 6 servings

Flaky Chive Pastry
  (recipe follows)
6 tablespoons unsalted butter
1 turkey breast half (2½ pounds),
  bone in, skin on
½ teaspoon salt
¼ teaspoon freshly ground pepper
12 small white boiling onions,
  peeled
2 medium carrots, cut into ¼-inch-
  thick rounds

2 cups Homemade Turkey Stock (page
  246), or 1 cup canned chicken broth
  mixed with 1 cup water
½ cup dry vermouth, dry white wine,
  or additional stock
2 tablespoons chopped fresh parsley
½ teaspoon dried thyme
½ cup peas, fresh or defrosted
¼ cup all-purpose flour
1 large egg
1 tablespoon milk

1. Make the Flaky Chive Pastry. Let stand at room temperature until malleable before rolling out.

2. In a large saucepan or flameproof casserole, melt 2 tablespoons of butter over moderate heat. Add the turkey breast, season with the salt and pepper, and cook, turning once, until lightly browned, about 8 minutes. Add the onions and carrots, cover, and cook until the vegetables are slightly softened, about 5 minutes. Add the stock, vermouth, parsley, and thyme. Bring to a boil, reduce the heat to low, cover, and simmer, turning the breast after 25 minutes, until a thermometer inserted in the thickest part of the meat reads 170 degrees, 40 to 50 minutes in all. During the last 10 minutes of the cooking time, add the peas.

3. Transfer the turkey breast to a cutting board. Using a slotted spoon, transfer the vegetables to a bowl. Remove and discard the skin and bones from the turkey, and carve the meat into 1-inch cubes. Strain the cooking liquid and add enough water, if necessary, to measure 2 cups.

4. In a heavy medium saucepan, melt 4 tablespoons butter over moderately

low heat. Whisk in the flour and cook, stirring, for about 2 minutes, without letting the mixture brown. Whisk in the 2 cups of cooking liquid and bring to a boil. Reduce the heat and simmer, whisking often, until thickened, about 3 minutes. Add the turkey and vegetables. Transfer the pie filling to a round 2-quart baking dish, such as a soufflé dish, and let cool completely, stirring occasionally. (The filling can be prepared up to 1 day ahead, cooled, covered, and refrigerated.)

5. Preheat the oven to 375 degrees. On a lightly floured work surface, roll out the pastry into an 11- to 12-inch circle about ⅛ inch thick. (If the dough cracks while rolling, it is too cold; let it stand at room temperature for 5 minutes and proceed.) Cut out a circle of dough 1 inch larger than the top of the baking dish. (If desired, use the pastry scraps to cut out decorations, such as leaves or circles, with a sharp knife or cookie cutter.) In a small bowl, beat together the egg and milk to make a glaze. Brush the edge of the baking dish with some of the egg glaze. Place the pastry round on top of the dish, and press the pastry onto the edge to adhere. Fold up the overhanging pastry and pinch the dough to form a thick edge around the top of the dish; crimp decoratively. Brush the dough lightly with some of the egg glaze. If using pastry decorations, place them on top of the crust and brush again lightly with the glaze. Using a sharp knife, cut a small X in the center of the dough to allow the steam to escape.

6. Bake the potpie until the top of the dough is golden brown, 35 to 40 minutes. Serve immediately.

Flaky Chive Pastry

Makes enough for one 9-inch single crust

1½ cups all-purpose flour
1 teaspoon salt
⅓ cup vegetable shortening,
   chilled

3 tablespoons unsalted butter, chilled,
   cut into ½-inch cubes
2 tablespoons minced fresh chives, or
   1½ teaspoons dried
About ¼ cup ice water

1. In a medium bowl, stir together the flour and salt. Using a pastry blender or two knives, cut the shortening and butter into the flour until the mixture resembles small peas. Stir in the chives.

2. Tossing the mixture with a fork, gradually sprinkle in the ice water, mixing just until the dough is moist enough to hold together when pinched between the thumb and forefinger. (You may need to add more ice water.) Gather the dough into a thick, flat disc, wrap in wax paper, and chill for at least 1 hour, or overnight.

Basic Braised Turkey Breast

A basic braised breast like this makes the most succulent, flavor-packed turkey salads ever, and creates cooked turkey for any of the recipes in Chapter 2 when leftovers from a roasted bird are not on hand. It also yields the added bonus of a stock from the leftover cooking liquid, which can be frozen for future use.

Makes about 4 cups cubed cooked turkey, or 4 servings

1 tablespoon vegetable oil	About 6 cups water
1 turkey breast half (2½ pounds), bone in, skin on (see Note)	3 sprigs of parsley
	½ teaspoon dried thyme
1 medium onion, chopped	1 bay leaf
1 medium carrot, chopped	½ teaspoon salt
1 medium celery rib, chopped	¼ teaspoon peppercorns

1. In a large saucepan, heat the oil. Add the breast, skin-side down, and cook over moderate heat, turning often, until lightly browned all over, about 8 minutes. Add the onion, carrot, and celery. Cover and cook until the vegetables are slightly softened, about 3 minutes.

2. Turn the breast skin-side down. Add enough water to cover the breast at least halfway. Increase the heat to high and bring to a boil, skimming off the foam. Reduce the heat to low and add the parsley, thyme, bay leaf, salt, and peppercorns. Cover and simmer for 25 minutes. Turn the breast over and continue to cook until a meat thermometer inserted in the thickest part of the breast reads 165 to 170 degrees, 20 to 25 minutes. Off heat, let the turkey breast cool, uncovered, in the liquid, if time allows.

3. Remove the turkey breast from the cooking liquid; reserve the liquid for stock, if desired. Remove the skin and bones. Wrap the meat and refrigerate for up to 3 days before using. Cut the turkey as required by your needs shortly before serving or using as an ingredient.

Note: A half breast is the easiest cut to handle for braising. However, for a large yield of 8 cups of meat, use a whole breast, split in half lengthwise down the back and breastbone. Double all the above ingredients and follow the same procedure. A 5-pound whole breast, unsplit, needs 75 to 90 minutes of covered simmering. (Turn the whole breast often to be sure the meaty portions cook evenly, unless you have a huge pot, big enough to cover the breast completely with water.) For reduced-fat diets, a 1½-pound skinless, boneless breast roast, tied into a cylinder with kitchen string, will take 35 to 40 minutes, with a yield of about 2½ cups cubed meat. (Beware of overcooking the boneless roast.)

Classic Turkey Salad

Classic turkey salad on whole wheat toast flecked with celery seed and accented with a dash of lemon will please everyone in the family. For fancier affairs, you might take advantage of the variations—Turkey Salad Véronique or Turkey Tarragon and Walnut Salad. They're blue-blooded salads to serve on your finest china with the most delicate Bibb lettuce.

Makes 4 to 6 servings

1 cup mayonnaise
1½ teaspoons lemon
   juice
1¼ teaspoons celery seed
¾ teaspoon salt
½ teaspoon white pepper

4 cups (about 1⅓ pounds) cubed
   cooked turkey, preferably braised
   (see page 93)
1 large scallion, minced
1 celery rib, finely chopped
3 tablespoons minced fresh parsley

In a medium bowl, whisk together the mayonnaise, lemon juice, celery seed, salt, and white pepper. Add the turkey, scallion, celery, and parsley. Mix to combine.

TURKEY SALAD VÉRONIQUE: Omit the scallion. Add 1 cup halved seedless grapes, ½ cup toasted sliced almonds, and an additional ¼ cup mayonnaise. This is excellent served in ripe seeded papaya halves.

TURKEY TARRAGON AND WALNUT SALAD: Substitute 1 tablespoon chopped fresh tarragon or 1 teaspoon dried tarragon for the celery seed. Add ½ cup toasted walnut halves.

TURKEY SALAD WALDORF. Omit the scallion. Add 1 tart apple, cored and diced, and ½ cup toasted walnut halves.

REDUCED-FAT VARIATION. Substitute ½ cup nonfat plain yogurt and ½ cup reduced-calorie mayonnaise for the regular mayonnaise. Fold—do not whisk—the yogurt and mayonnaise together; whisking will thin out the yogurt.

Turkey and Grapefruit Salad with Poppy Seed Dressing

Grapefruit and turkey make a pretty pair when joined with a fruity poppy seed dressing. It is delicious year-round, but I am especially fond of it in wintertime, when grapefruit's citrusy tang is invigorating.

Makes 4 to 6 servings

2 pink grapefruit
2 white grapefruit
2 tablespoons lemon juice or white wine vinegar
2 tablespoons minced onion
2 teaspoons sugar
½ teaspoon salt

¾ cup vegetable oil
2 tablespoons poppy seeds
4 cups (about 1⅓ pounds) cubed cooked turkey, preferably braised (see page 93)
Thinly sliced red onion and red-leaf lettuce, for garnishes

1. Finely grate the zest from one grapefruit and reserve. (There should be about 1 tablespoon.) Using a serrated knife, cut the ends off all four grapefruit and cut off the peel, removing all of the bitter white pith. Holding the grapefruit over a medium bowl to catch the juice, cut down along both sides of each membrane to remove the grapefruit sections. Strain and reserve ¼ cup of the juice. Place the peeled grapefruit sections in a medium bowl.

2. In a blender or food processor, combine the reserved grapefruit juice, the lemon juice, minced onion, sugar, and salt. Blend briefly. With the machine on, gradually add the vegetable oil. Add the poppy seeds and pulse once or twice, just to mix.

3. Add the cubed turkey to the grapefruit sections; add about ½ cup of the poppy seed dressing and toss gently to coat. Serve the turkey and grapefruit salad, garnished with red onion rings, on a bed of red lettuce leaves. Pass the remaining dressing on the side.

Cold Turkey Breast with Italian Tuna Sauce

Thin slices of poached turkey breast are cloaked with the same tart tuna sauce that makes the Italian veal antipasto dish *vitello tonnato* so popular. Since loin of veal is one of the most expensive items you will ever find in the butcher case, I am happy to report that using a skinless, boneless turkey breast roast will give incredible results for a fraction of the cost. Either as an appetizer or as a cold entrée, it is *bellissimo*.

Makes 4 to 6 servings

1 boneless turkey roast (1½ pounds), skin removed
6 cups water
½ cup dry white wine
1 small onion, chopped
1 small carrot, chopped
1 small celery rib, chopped
½ teaspoon salt
¼ teaspoon peppercorns

1 can (6½ ounces) tuna, preferably imported Italian packed in olive oil
2 tablespoons fresh lemon juice
4 canned anchovy fillets, rinsed
¾ cup olive oil
1 tablespoon capers, rinsed, chopped if large
1 medium lemon, thinly sliced

1. Roll the turkey into a cylinder and tie in several places with kitchen string. In a medium saucepan, combine the water, wine, onion, carrot, celery, salt, and peppercorns. Bring to a simmer over low heat. Cook, partially covered, for 15 minutes. Add the turkey breast and simmer, covered, until a meat thermometer inserted in the breast reads 165 degrees, 35 to 40 minutes. Let cool completely in the cooking liquid. (The temperature will rise to 170 degrees upon standing.)

2. Transfer the cooled turkey breast to a work surface; discard the cooking liquid or save for stock. Remove and discard the kitchen string and carve the breast into slices about ¼ inch thick. Arrange the slices, overlapping, on a serving platter.

3. In a blender or food processor, combine the tuna, lemon juice, and anchovies. With the machine on, very gradually add the olive oil, blending until smooth. Using a rubber spatula, spread the tuna sauce over the turkey slices, masking them completely. Cover the platter tightly in plastic wrap and refrigerate for at least 4 hours or, preferably, overnight.

4. Remove the platter from the refrigerator about 1 hour before serving. Just before serving, sprinkle the capers over the sauce and garnish the platter with the lemon slices.

Guacamole Turkey Salad

If possible, serve this multilayered salad in a large glass bowl, to showcase its colors. Romaine lettuce, grated Cheddar cheese, cubed turkey, avocado slices, and spicy tomato salsa are accented by a lime vinaigrette. Since the ingredients are chopped, this salad is easy to eat with just a fork, so it makes a fine buffet dish. Tortilla chips are a great accompaniment.

Makes 8 to 10 servings

⅓ cup fresh lime juice
½ teaspoon salt
¼ teaspoon freshly ground pepper
1 cup olive oil
1 medium head romaine lettuce, torn into 2-inch pieces
4 cups (about 1⅓ pounds) cubed cooked turkey, preferably braised (see page 93)

1 cup tomato salsa, bottled or fresh (see page 57), drained of excess liquid
3 ripe avocados, preferably Hass, pitted, skinned, and cut into 1-inch cubes
1 cup grated sharp Cheddar cheese (about 4 ounces)

1. In a medium bowl, whisk the lime juice, salt, and pepper. Gradually whisk in the oil.

2. Place the chopped lettuce in a large bowl, preferably glass. Add ½ cup of the dressing and toss. Add the turkey cubes and drizzle with ¼ cup of the remaining dressing. Cover the turkey with the salsa. Top the salsa with the avocado cubes; drizzle the remaining dressing over the avocados. Sprinkle the Cheddar over the top. Dig down into the bowl to get a little of each ingredient.

Turkey Breast Antipasti Roulade

Prosciutto, provolone cheese, roasted red pepper, and black olives make a beautiful spiral pattern in a rolled, boneless turkey breast roast. Served hot, with a simple white wine sauce, it is nice with orzo, a rice-shaped pasta, tossed with butter and Parmesan cheese.

Makes 4 to 6 servings

1 boneless turkey breast roast (about 2½ pounds), skin on
4 slices prosciutto
4 slices provolone cheese
1 small canned roasted red pepper, rinsed and cut into ¼-inch-wide strips

8 oil-cured black olives, pitted and coarsely chopped
2 tablespoons unsalted butter
1 tablespoon vegetable oil
1 cup dry white wine
⅓ cup water

1. Preheat the oven to 350 degrees. Place the turkey breast, skin-side down, on a work surface. Using a sharp knife, cut a deep incision into the thickest part of the meat on one side of the roast, being careful not to cut completely through. Open this flap like a book to one side to butterfly the roast. Make another cut on the other side, being careful not to cut completely through, and fold out in the other direction. Pound gently to flatten evenly.

2. Arrange the prosciutto slices, overlapping slightly, over the surface of the meat. Top the prosciutto with overlapping slices of provolone. Arrange the roast pepper strips in a 1-inch-wide row, 1 inch from the right-hand edge of the roulade. Arrange the chopped olives in a row down the center of the red peppers. Starting at the right edge, roll up the breast. Using kitchen string, tie the roast crosswise and lengthwise.

3. In a medium flameproof casserole, heat the butter and oil. Add the turkey breast and cook over moderate heat, turning often, until browned all over, about 8 minutes. Add ½ cup of the white wine and bring to a simmer. Place the casserole in the oven and bake, uncovered, basting often with the remaining ½ cup white wine, for 50 to 60 minutes, until a meat thermometer inserted in the center of the breast reads 170 degrees. Transfer the turkey to a serving platter, cover with aluminum foil, and let stand for 10 minutes before carving. Remove the string and carve the meat into 1-inch-thick slices.

Arrange the slices, slightly overlapping, on the platter and cover with foil to keep warm.

4. Tip the casserole so all of the juices gather in one corner and skim off the fat. Place the casserole on top of the stove over moderately high heat. Add the water and boil, stirring up any browned bits from the bottom of the pan with a wooden spoon, until the liquid has thickened and reduced to about ⅓ cup. Drizzle the sauce over the roulade and serve.

▶ *California has the highest annual turkey consumption, with about 23 pounds per person. (It's obvious to me that Californians have taken to turkey's low-fat profile and use it year-round on the grill.)*

Turkey, Pasta, and Vegetable Salad in Spicy Peanut Dressing

This exotic-sounding dish with Oriental flair is a frequent visitor to my buffet table. Unsalted peanut butter is important here because of the saltiness of the soy sauce.

Makes 6 to 8 servings

½ pound corkscrew or shell pasta
¼ cup plus 1 tablespoon Oriental sesame oil (see Note)
1 bunch of broccoli
2 tablespoons minced fresh ginger
3 garlic cloves
⅓ cup low-sodium soy sauce
½ cup unsalted peanut butter, well stirred
¼ cup vegetable oil

¼ cup reserved cooking liquid from Basic Braised Turkey Breast (see page 93) or canned chicken broth
2 teaspoons packed light brown sugar
¼ teaspoon crushed hot pepper flakes
4 cups (about 1⅓ pounds) cubed cooked turkey, preferably braised (see page 93)
1 large red bell pepper, cut into strips
1 tablespoon sesame seeds, for garnish

1. In a large pot of boiling salted water, cook the pasta over high heat until just tender, about 10 minutes. Drain, rinse with cold running water, and drain well. In a large bowl, toss the pasta with 1 tablespoon of the sesame oil. Set aside.

2. Separate the stems from the broccoli tops. Peel the stems and cut crosswise into ½-inch-thick slices. Cut the broccoli tops into 1-inch florets. In another pot of boiling salted water, cook the broccoli stems over high heat for 1 minute. Add the florets and cook until both are crisp-tender, about 2 minutes. Drain and rinse under cold running water; drain well.

3. In a blender or a food processor, blend the ginger, garlic, soy sauce, and peanut butter. Add the remaining sesame oil, the vegetable oil, the reserved cooking liquid, brown sugar, and hot pepper flakes. Process until smooth.

4. Add the turkey, broccoli, and sweet red pepper to the pasta. Add the peanut dressing and toss well to coat. Sprinkle with sesame seeds.

Note: Oriental sesame oil, as opposed to cold-pressed, is available at Asian markets and in many supermarkets, or by mail order from Dean and Deluca, 800-221-7714; 212-431-1691.

Turkey Salad with Asparagus, Mushrooms, and Walnuts

Turkey and asparagus are a great match. This salad can be served for a lunch or dinner entrée, or even in small portions as a first course.

Makes 4 to 6 servings

1 pound asparagus, trimmed, peeled, and cut into 1-inch pieces
¼ cup sherry vinegar or red wine vinegar
¼ teaspoon salt
¼ teaspoon freshly ground pepper
1 cup walnut or olive oil

Arugula, endive, or curly lettuce leaves, for garnish
1½ pounds sliced cooked turkey breast
½ pound medium mushrooms, thinly sliced
½ cup walnut halves, toasted (see page 229)

1. Bring a large saucepan of lightly salted water to a boil over high heat. Add the asparagus and cook until just crisp-tender, about 2 minutes. Drain, rinse well under cold running water, and drain again. Immediately pat the asparagus dry with paper towels.

2. In a medium bowl, whisk together the vinegar, salt, and pepper until the salt is dissolved. Gradually whisk in the oil.

3. Line a large serving platter with the arugula, endive, or lettuce leaves. Arrange overlapping slices of the turkey on top and garnish with the asparagus. Sprinkle the mushrooms and walnuts over the turkey. Toss the salad with ½ cup of the dressing and pass the remaining dressing on the side.

▶ *Add vinaigrettes to salads containing asparagus, broccoli, or green beans at the last minute to keep the vegetables bright green.*

Mediterranean Turkey Salad
with Potatoes and Olives

What's summer without potato salad? I used to serve plain potato salad as a side dish, but when I finally noticed that it was always the first dish to disappear at a picnic, I decided to make it a main dish with the addition of turkey chunks and vegetables.

Makes 6 to 8 servings

¼ pound green beans, trimmed, cut into 2-inch lengths
3 tablespoons white wine vinegar
3 anchovy fillets, mashed to a paste
¼ teaspoon salt
¼ teaspoon freshly ground pepper
¾ cup olive oil
1 pound small waxy boiling potatoes, scrubbed
¼ cup dry white wine or dry vermouth

4 cups (about 1⅓ pounds) cubed cooked turkey, preferably braised (see page 93)
2 medium red bell peppers, seeds and ribs removed, cut into ½-by-2-inch strips
2 scallions, chopped
½ cup oil-cured black olives, pitted and coarsely chopped
¼ cup finely chopped fresh basil or parsley

1. Bring a large saucepan of lightly salted water to a boil over high heat. Add the green beans and cook until just crisp-tender, 2 to 3 minutes. Drain, rinse well under cold running water, drain again, and reserve.

2. In a small bowl, whisk together the vinegar, anchovies, salt, and pepper. Gradually whisk in the oil.

3. Cook the potatoes in a large saucepan of lightly salted boiling water until just tender, 15 to 20 minutes. Drain, rinse well under cold running water, and drain again. As soon as the potatoes are cool enough to handle, cut into 1-inch pieces.

4. In a large bowl, toss the warm potatoes with the wine. Add the turkey, red pepper, scallion, olives, and basil. Pour on the dressing and toss carefully to combine. (The salad can be made up to 1 day ahead. Adjust seasonings, including oil and vinegar, before serving.) Just before serving, add the reserved green beans and toss.

▶ *Boiling potatoes with firm, waxy flesh (such as Red Bliss or Yukon Gold) make better potato salad than mealy baking potatoes (such as Idaho or Russet), because they won't break up easily while tossing.*

Curried Turkey Salad Madras

Curried turkey salad has been around for years, but it has rarely been this good! First, I use half low-fat yogurt and half mayonnaise in the dressing—not only does the yogurt save a few calories, it enhances the flavor immensely. Next, raisins and cashews add their irresistible appeal. A dash of chutney balances the spiciness of the curry, which has been toasted to enliven the flavor. Curried turkey salad hits the spot in a pita pocket. But my favorite poolside lunch is curried turkey salad heaped on a lettuce-lined platter, surrounded by luscious tropical fruits—bananas, strawberries, papaya, kiwi, and mango.

Makes 4 to 6 servings

2½ tablespoons curry powder, preferably Madras brand
¾ cup plain low-fat yogurt
¾ cup mayonnaise
2 tablespoons mango chutney, chopped
¼ teaspoon salt

4 cups (about 1⅓ pounds) cubed cooked turkey meat, preferably braised (see page 93)
½ cup raisins
½ cup coarsely chopped roasted cashews, rinsed briefly to remove salt

1. Heat a medium dry skillet over moderate heat. Add the curry powder and cook, stirring constantly, until very fragrant, 45 to 60 seconds. Do not let the curry scorch. Pour immediately into a medium bowl.

2. Add the yogurt, mayonnaise, chutney, and salt. Stir until well blended. Add the turkey meat, raisins, and cashews. Mix to combine.

REDUCED-FAT VARIATION: Substitute reduced-calorie mayonnaise for regular mayonnaise.

Orange-Pecan Turkey Salad
with Minted Yogurt Dressing

Looking for a low-fat salad with no compromise on flavor? Here it is—thin slices of poached turkey, alternating with orange rounds, served with a slimming reduced-calorie yogurt-mayonnaise dressing. I designed this recipe originally for my friends at Perdue Farms, whom I thank for allowing me to use it here.

Makes 4 to 6 servings

4 medium navel oranges
½ cup plain low-fat yogurt
½ cup reduced-calorie mayonnaise
1 tablespoon finely chopped fresh
   mint, or 1 teaspoon dried
½ teaspoon salt
¼ teaspoon freshly ground white
   pepper

1 boneless turkey breast roast
   (1½ pounds)
3 tablespoons vegetable oil
1¾ cups canned chicken broth
2 medium scallions, finely chopped
2 bunches of watercress
2 tablespoons chopped pecans
Fresh mint sprigs, for garnish

1. Grate the zest of 1 orange into a medium bowl. Squeeze the juice from 2 oranges into a small bowl. Add 3 tablespoons of the orange juice to the zest; reserve the remaining juice.

2. Add the yogurt, mayonnaise, mint, ¼ teaspoon of the salt, and ⅛ teaspoon of the pepper to the zest in the medium bowl. Fold gently to combine. (Do not whisk, or the yogurt will thin out.) Cover tightly and refrigerate until ready to use. (The dressing can be made up to 1 day ahead, covered, and refrigerated.)

3. Roll the roast into a cylinder, tying in three or four places with kitchen twine. Season with the remaining ¼ teaspoon salt and ⅛ teaspoon pepper. In a large saucepan, heat the oil. Add the roast and cook over moderate heat, turning often, until browned all over, about 8 minutes. Pour off the oil. Add the chicken broth, ¼ cup of the reserved orange juice, and half of the chopped scallions. Bring to a simmer, reduce the heat to low, cover tightly, and simmer, turning the roast once, until a meat thermometer inserted in the center of the roast reads 155 degrees, 35 to 40 minutes. Remove from the heat. (The temperature of the roast will increase to 160 upon

standing.) Allow the turkey to cool completely in the cooking liquid. Transfer the turkey to a cutting board; discard the cooking broth or reserve for stock. Remove the string and cut the turkey into ½-inch slices. (The turkey can be prepared up to 1 day ahead, covered, and refrigerated.)

4. Using a serrated knife, cut the ends off the remaining 2 oranges, peel them, and remove all the bitter white pith. Cut the oranges crosswise into ½-inch-thick slices. Arrange the watercress on a serving platter. Arrange alternating slices of the turkey and oranges in a circle on the greens. Drizzle one-third of the dressing over the turkey and oranges. Sprinkle the pecans and remaining scallions over the salad. Garnish with sprigs of fresh mint and pass the remaining dressing on the side.

▶ *Historians are not positive that turkey was served at the first Pilgrim Thanksgiving. The only record we have of the meal mentions "fowling," which could mean ducks, geese, and/or turkeys.*

Rolled Turkey Roast with Summer Garden Stuffing

A whole turkey breast, boned and stuffed with whatever makes you happy, is a luxurious way to feed a crowd. My inspiration for this recipe, with a fresh-tasting filling of zucchini, mushrooms, and sweet red pepper, comes from Simone "Simca" Beck, the divine French cooking authority. Served warm with its sublime brown sauce, it is a spectacular dinner party entrée. I serve it most often as the main event on a cold buffet with a dab of Green Herb Sauce (recipe follows).

Makes 8 to 10 servings

1 whole turkey breast (about 6 pounds), bone in, skin on
2 packages (3 ounces each) cream cheese, softened
¾ cup fresh bread crumbs
1 large egg
2 medium zucchini, grated
1½ teaspoons salt
1 stick plus 1 tablespoon unsalted butter
3 medium scallions, finely chopped
1 medium red bell pepper, seeds and ribs removed, cut into ¼-inch dice
10 ounces fresh mushrooms, sliced

3 tablespoons finely chopped fresh parsley
1¼ teaspoons dried tarragon
¼ teaspoon freshly ground pepper
½ cup freshly grated Parmesan cheese
2 tablespoons Dijon mustard
¼ cup vegetable oil
2 medium onions, chopped
2 medium carrots, chopped
3 cups water
1 cup dry white wine
½ teaspoon dried thyme
4 sprigs of fresh parsley
¼ teaspoon peppercorns

1. To bone the turkey breast, use a thin-bladed, sharp knife. Make an incision down the backbone. Using short strokes, with the point of the knife pointing in toward the bone, start cutting at the point where one-half of the turkey breast meets the backbone, peeling the meat and skin back as you go and leaving as little meat on the bone as possible. Stop when you meet the breastbone. Repeat the procedure with the other side. Carefully cut the meat away from the breastbone, taking care not to cut through the skin.

2. Place the boned turkey breast, skin-side down, on a work surface. Cut away and discard the white tendons that run vertically along each side of the breast. Make a deep incision in the thickest part of one side of the breast at about a 45-degree angle, being careful not to cut completely through. Open this flap like a book, butterflying and increasing the surface of the meat.

Butterfly the other side of the breast. Repeat this procedure on the opened portion of the meat to open up the breast further. Using a cleaver or a heavy knife, chop the bones into large pieces, and set aside. (The breast can be boned up to 2 days ahead, wrapped well, and refrigerated.)

3. In a medium bowl, work the cream cheese with the back of a wooden spoon until smooth. Add the bread crumbs and the egg, work together until well combined, and reserve.

4. In a colander, sprinkle the zucchini with 1 teaspoon of salt and let stand for 15 minutes. Rinse the zucchini well under cold running water. By hand-fuls, squeeze out the excess moisture; reserve the zucchini.

5. In a large skillet, heat 3 tablespoons of the butter. Add the scallions and red pepper and cook over moderate heat, stirring, until the scallions are wilted, about 1 minute. Add the mushrooms, parsley, tarragon, and pepper, increase the heat to moderately high, and cook until the mushrooms have given up their liquid, it evaporates, and they become lightly browned, 6 to 8 minutes. Add the reserved zucchini and cook, stirring constantly, until the zucchini is somewhat drier, 1 to 2 minutes. Add the vegetable mixture to the cream cheese mixture and beat well to combine. Stir in the Parmesan.

6. Spread the turkey breast evenly with the mustard, then the zucchini filling, leaving a 1-inch border around all four sides. Starting at a short end, roll the breast into a cylinder. Using kitchen twine, tie the roll crosswise in four or five pieces. Rinse a large double-thickness piece of cheesecloth under cold running water and squeeze out. Wrap the turkey completely in cheese-cloth. Tie the cheesecloth at both ends to enclose the breast, and crosswise in another four or five places to form a compact sausage shape.

7. In a large oval flameproof casserole, heat the oil over moderately high heat until very hot but not smoking. Add the turkey breast and cook, turning occasionally, until browned all over, about 10 minutes. Transfer the turkey breast to a plate. Add the chopped bones to the casserole and cook, turning occasionally, until browned, 10 to 15 minutes. Transfer the bones to a plate. Add the chopped onions and carrots and cook, turning occasionally, until lightly browned, about 10 minutes. Return the breast and bones to the casserole. Add the water and wine, and bring to a simmer, skimming off any foam that rises to the surface. Add the thyme, parsley, and peppercorns, reduce the heat to low, cover tightly, and simmer, turning the breast halfway through cooking, until a meat thermometer inserted in the center of the roll reads 160 to 165 degrees, 75 to 90 minutes. Transfer the breast to a work surface and wrap loosely in aluminum foil to keep warm.

(continued)

8. Strain the cooking liquid into a large saucepan and let stand for 5 minutes; skim off any of the clear fat that rises to the surface. Bring the liquid to a boil over high heat and cook until reduced to 1½ cups, about 20 minutes. Remove from the heat and whisk in the remaining 6 tablespoons of butter, 1 tablespoon at a time. Pour the sauce into a warmed sauceboat.

9. Remove the foil, strings, and cheesecloth from the roll. Using a serrated knife, cut the roast crosswise into ¾-inch-thick slices and arrange overlapping on a large platter. Serve immediately with the sauce.

VARIATION: To serve the rolled roast cold, cook the breast to 160 degrees and let the roll cool completely in the cooking liquid. Follow the instructions for Galantine of Turkey, page 204, steps 8 and 9, to make a glaze for the roll. Serve with Green Herb Sauce (recipe follows).

Green Herb Sauce

Makes about 1 cup

½ cup packed fresh parsley
2 tablespoons coarsely chopped fresh
    basil, or 1 teaspoon dried
¼ cup blanched slivered
    almonds

1½ teaspoons Dijon mustard
1½ teaspoons lemon juice
1 small garlic clove, crushed
¼ teaspoon salt
½ cup olive oil

In a food processor, process the parsley, basil, almonds, mustard, lemon juice, garlic, and salt until the herbs and almonds are finely chopped. With the machine on, slowly add the oil, stopping and scraping down the sides of the bowl as necessary; process until smooth. Transfer the sauce to a small bowl. (The sauce can be made up to 2 days ahead, covered, and refrigerated. Let return to room temperature and stir well before serving.)

Four Seasons Corn and Turkey Chowder

Of course this soup can be made from leftovers from a whole roast turkey. But with half breasts so easily available, you don't have to wait to savor this soothing soup.

Makes 6 to 8 servings

3 tablespoons unsalted butter
1 turkey breast half (2 pounds), bone in, skin on
1 large baking potato, peeled and cut into 2-inch chunks
1 medium onion, chopped
1 medium carrot, chopped
1 celery rib, chopped
4 cups corn kernels, fresh or defrosted

6 cups Homemade Turkey Stock (see page 246), or 3 cups canned chicken broth mixed with 3 cups water
½ teaspoon dried marjoram
¼ teaspoon dried rosemary
½ teaspoon salt
¼ teaspoon freshly ground pepper
1 cup heavy (whipping) cream

1. In a large saucepan, melt the butter over moderate heat. Add the breast and cook, turning once, until lightly browned, about 5 minutes. Add the potato, onion, carrot, celery, and 2 cups of the corn. Cover and cook until the onion is softened, 3 to 4 minutes. Add the stock and bring to a simmer. Skim off any foam that rises to the surface. Add the marjoram, rosemary, salt, and pepper. Reduce the heat to low and simmer, covered, turning once, until a meat thermometer inserted in the thickest part of the breast reads 170 degrees, 40 to 50 minutes. Remove the breast from the liquid and let cool.

2. While the breast is cooling, use a slotted spoon to transfer about half of the soup vegetables to a food processor or blender. Add about 1 cup of the soup liquid and puree.

3. Remove the meat from the breast and discard the skin and bones. Cut the turkey into 1-inch cubes. Add the vegetable puree, cubed turkey, remaining 2 cups corn kernels, and heavy cream to the saucepan. Bring to a simmer over low heat, stirring constantly. Serve the soup hot or at cool room temperature.

▶ *One medium ear of corn will yield about ½ cup of kernels. I always buy one or two extras to make sure I have enough.*

CHAPTER FOUR

Some Like It Dark

I have always enjoyed the rich flavor and succulent texture of dark-meat turkey. In fact, every Thanksgiving of my childhood and a couple of my adulthood, I remember some heated arguments with my two brothers over how the lone pair of drumsticks would be divided. (Three does not go into two, especially in a family with a trio of hungry boys.) Nowadays, I always buy a separate package of drumsticks and roast them in the pan with the whole turkey, so everyone is satisfied.

Dark meat, as flavor-packed as it is, is not as chameleonlike as other turkey parts. For example, it does not sauté particularly well. In fact, to be at its best, it calls for long, slow cooking. Moist-heat cooking methods also complement dark meat, making it ideal for stews, soups, and pasta sauces. Dark meat in any kind of poultry is always tougher than white meat and needs long, tenderizing cooking, as the legs and wings are well exercised during the bird's life.

Dark turkey meat is slightly higher in calories and fat than white meat, coming in at about 150 calories per 3-ounce portion. (On an average, whole roasted turkey comes in at about 130 calories.) However, as with all poultry, if you remove the skin, where most of the fat resides, you will reduce your calorie and fat intake considerably. Under any circumstances, the saturated fat content of turkey is far below that of other meats.

Substitute 1½-inch cubes of skinless turkey thigh for beef, lamb, or pork in your favorite stews. Be sure to adjust the cooking times accordingly, since the turkey thighs will be done in about 45 minutes. In cases where long simmering is important to the flavor of the finished stews, brown the turkey cubes first, remove them from the pan, and set them aside in the refrigerator. Then proceed with the recipe; return the browned cubes to the sauce about 45 minutes before the end of the cooking period.

Dark-meat parts available in supermarkets include:

Turkey drumsticks, in sizes from 12 ounces to 1½ pounds each. When roasting, bake at 325 degrees, covered with aluminum foil, for 1½ to 2 hours. Remove the foil during the last 30 minutes to allow for browning. Braised drumsticks, after browning in a little oil or butter, need at least 1½ hours to cook until tender. Drumsticks can be grilled, too; see Chapter 8, "Turkey on the Grill, for complete instructions.

Turkey thighs run from ½ to 1½ pounds each. (It is difficult to give exact weights on any turkey products, because you never know if a processor will use small hens or large toms for the parts.) Roast turkey thighs at 325 degrees, loosely covered with aluminum foil, for about 1½ hours, depending on size, removing the foil during the last 30 minutes to brown. Braise turkey thighs for at least 1¼ hours.

Boneless turkey drumsticks and thighs are sold with and without the skin. Cut them into 1- to 2-inch cubes for stews, casseroles, and even kebabs. They take well to marinades. Kebabs can be cooked under the broiler or on the grill.

Turkey wings can weigh anywhere from ¾ to 1¼ pounds. The meaty first joints are often separated and sold as *turkey drumettes*, the first "all-white drumstick." *Turkey wing portions* are the wings separated into the drumettes and the flat, but equally meaty, second joint portion. The wing tips are very bony and are often put to best use in the stockpot. But if you like gnawing on things, they are flavorful. Turkey wings make great hors d'oeuvres; just be sure to have plenty of bowls on hand to collect bones. Turkey wings need about 1½ hours of roasting at 325 degrees, covered with aluminum foil at first, or 1½ hours of simmering. Turkey wings, because of the high proportion of skin and bone, add extra flavor to stews and stocks.

Turkey tails and necks, incredibly inexpensive, are also available. I use the tails for stock, but my grandfather would have roasted them and savored a whole plateful. Necks also go into a stockpot, and for about a dollar's worth of meat, you can have a quart of fantastic homemade turkey stock.

Turkey Drumsticks Osso Buco–Style

As soon as your guests walk in the door, they'll remark on the wonderful aroma floating from the kitchen. And why not, with white wine, turkey, tomatoes, garlic, onions, carrots, celery, and herbs simmering to make one of the most luscious sauces in the Italian recipe repertoire?

Makes 6 servings

6 turkey drumsticks (about 12 ounces each)
½ cup all-purpose flour
¼ cup olive oil
1 large onion, chopped
1 large carrot, chopped
1 large celery rib, chopped
1 large garlic clove, minced
¾ cup dry white wine
1½ cups Homemade Turkey Stock (see page 246) or canned chicken broth

1 can (14 ounces) Italian peeled tomatoes, with their juice, coarsely chopped
½ teaspoon dried basil
¼ teaspoon dried rosemary
½ teaspoon salt
¼ teaspoon freshly ground pepper
¼ cup chopped fresh parsley
Grated zest from 1 lemon

1. Roll the drumsticks in the flour to coat lightly, shaking off any excess. In a large flameproof casserole, heat the oil. Add the drumsticks in batches without crowding and cook over moderately high heat, turning often, until browned all over, about 8 minutes. Transfer the browned drumsticks to a plate. (If the flour in the casserole burns, wipe it out with paper towels and add 2 tablespoons additional olive oil before cooking the next batch.)

2. Reduce the heat to moderate. Add the onion, carrot, celery, and garlic to the casserole. Cook, stirring often, until the vegetables are softened, about 5 minutes. Add the white wine and cook until the wine is reduced by half, about 2 minutes. Add the stock, tomatoes with their juice, basil, rosemary, salt, and pepper and bring to a boil. Reduce the heat to low, cover, and simmer until the drumsticks are tender, about 1¼ hours.

3. With tongs, transfer the drumsticks to a serving platter and keep warm. Increase the heat to high and boil until the sauce has evaporated by half, about 5 minutes. Pour the sauce over the drumsticks. In a small bowl, mix together the parsley and lemon zest; sprinkle over the drumsticks.

Braised Turkey Drumsticks with Olives over Pasta

Tasty turkey drumsticks are braised in a medley of Mediterranean ingredients, combining to create a piquant sauce that is perfect ladled over chunky pasta shapes. Remember, olives and bacon are naturally salty, so do not add salt (or top pasta with Parmesan cheese) until after finishing the sauce, and only if you are positive it's necessary.

Makes 4 to 6 servings

¾ pound large green olives, drained, pitted, and coarsely chopped
⅓ cup diced bacon
4 turkey drumsticks (12 to 14 ounces each)
1 large onion, coarsely chopped
2 medium celery ribs, coarsely chopped
1 large carrot, coarsely chopped
1 can (35 ounces) Italian peeled tomatoes, drained, seeded, and coarsely chopped

1 cup Homemade Turkey Stock (see page 246), or ½ cup canned chicken broth mixed with ½ cup water
¾ cup dry white wine
2 tablespoons tomato paste
1½ teaspoons chopped fresh rosemary, or ¾ teaspoon dried
½ teaspoon crushed hot pepper flakes
1 pound pasta, such as penne, cooked and drained
Grated Parmesan cheese (optional)

1. In a medium saucepan, cover the olives with cold water, bring to a boil over high heat, and cook for 1 minute. Drain, rinse, drain again, and set aside.

2. In a large flameproof casserole, cook the bacon over moderately high heat until crisp, about 3 minutes. Remove the bacon with a slotted spoon and set aside, leaving the drippings in the casserole. In batches, if necessary, add the turkey drumsticks to the casserole, and cook, turning often, until browned, about 10 minutes. Remove the drumsticks and set aside.

3. Add the onion, celery, and carrot to the casserole. Reduce the heat to moderate and cook, stirring often, until softened, about 5 minutes. Add the tomatoes, stock, white wine, tomato paste, rosemary, hot pepper flakes, ⅓ cup of the olives, and the reserved bacon. Bring to a simmer. Return the drumsticks to the casserole. Cover tightly, reduce the heat to low, and simmer, turning the drumsticks occasionally, for 1½ hours. Uncover, raise the heat to moderately high, and cook for 15 minutes.

4. Remove the drumsticks and set aside, covered loosely with aluminum foil to keep warm. Pour the remaining contents of the casserole into a food processor or blender and puree until smooth. Return the sauce to the casserole, add the remaining olives, and bring to a simmer.

5. Place the hot pasta in a warm serving dish. Pour the sauce over the pasta, arrange the drumsticks on top, and serve sprinkled with the Parmesan, if desired.

MICROWAVE INSTRUCTIONS: In a conventional broiler, broil the turkey drumsticks about 4 inches from the heat source, turning, until the skin is brown, about 10 minutes. In a 4-cup glass measuring cup, cover the olives with water and cook on High (100 percent) for 3 minutes. Drain, rinse, and set aside. Place the bacon in a microwave-safe casserole, and cover loosely with paper towels. Cook on High for 3 minutes. Discard the paper towels. Remove the bacon with a slotted spoon and set aside. Add the onion, celery, and carrot, cover with a casserole lid or plastic wrap, and cook on High for 2 minutes, until softened. Add the tomatoes, stock, wine, tomato paste, rosemary, hot pepper flakes, ⅛ cup olives, reserved bacon, and turkey drumsticks, and cook, covered on High for 25 minutes. Let stand, covered, for 10 minutes. Remove and reserve the drumsticks. Puree the sauce, return to the casserole, add the remaining olives, and cook on High for 1 minute.

REDUCED-FAT VARIATION: Replace the ⅛ cup diced bacon with 1 tablespoon olive oil. In regular recipe, heat the oil in casserole until very hot, and brown the turkey drumsticks in the hot oil, rather than the rendered bacon fat. In microwave version, heat the oil on High for 1 minute, add the vegetables, and proceed.

> ▶ *For best flavor, pit large green olives from the delicatessen, and avoid the canned varieties. To pit olives easily, smash them one at a time under the wide, flat part of a large knife, with the tip of the knife levered on the work surface.*

Spinach-and-Feta-Stuffed Drumsticks

Plump drumsticks are made even plumper, stuffed under the skin with a spinach-and-feta filling, and then braised in a cinnamon-and-oregano-spiced tomato sauce. The stuffing procedure may seem odd at first, but it's just like rolling a sock down and up over your ankle. The drumsticks are especially good when served with boiled orzo, a rice-shaped pasta.

Makes 2 to 3 servings

1 tablespoon olive oil
1 small onion, finely chopped
1 garlic clove, minced
1 package (10 ounces) frozen chopped
   spinach, defrosted, squeezed to
   remove excess moisture
½ cup fresh bread crumbs
⅓ cup crumbled feta cheese

¼ teaspoon salt
¼ teaspoon freshly ground pepper
3 turkey drumsticks (about 12 ounces
   each)
1 cup tomato puree
1 tablespoon honey
¼ teaspoon dried oregano
⅛ teaspoon ground cinnamon

1. In a medium skillet, heat the oil. Add the onion and garlic and cook over moderate heat, stirring often, until the onion turns golden, about 4 minutes. Add the spinach and cook, stirring constantly to evaporate excess moisture, about 1 minute. Stir in the bread crumbs, feta, salt, and pepper.

2. Preheat the oven to 350 degrees. Push the skin of each drumstick down to the leg bone. Divide the stuffing among the drumsticks, patting the stuffing around the meat, and bring the skin back up to enclose the stuffing. Place the drumsticks in a lightly oiled baking dish.

3. In a small bowl, combine the tomato puree, honey, oregano, and cinnamon. Pour the sauce over the drumsticks and cover them tightly with aluminum foil. Bake for 1¼ hours. Remove the foil and continue baking until the drumsticks are tender, 15 to 25 minutes.

Oven-BBQ'd Turkey Thighs

These tender thighs, baked in their own spicy-sweet tomato sauce, can be made oven ready in minutes. The recipe multiplies easily, which is good news, because kids love this dish.

Makes 2 to 3 servings

¾ cup chili sauce
1 tablespoon brown sugar
1 tablespoon Worcestershire sauce
2 teaspoons prepared mustard

2 turkey thighs
    (about 12 ounces each)
1 teaspoon chili powder
¼ teaspoon garlic salt

1. Preheat the oven to 350 degrees. In a small nonreactive baking dish, combine the chili sauce, brown sugar, Worcestershire, and mustard. Place the thighs, skin side down, in the dish; turn to coat. Season the skin with the chili powder and garlic salt. Cover the dish tightly with aluminum foil.

2. Bake for 45 minutes. Remove the foil and continue baking, basting occasionally with the sauce, until the thighs are tender, 15 to 25 minutes.

MICROWAVE INSTRUCTIONS: Place all ingredients in a microwave-safe baking dish. Tent with wax paper. Cook on High (100 percent) for 5 minutes. Cook on Medium (50 percent) for 20 minutes. Let stand, covered with aluminum foil, for 10 minutes.

> ▶ *The Pilgrims were well acquainted with the turkey, since it had been introduced to Europe in about 1511, and to England circa 1524.*

Mexican Turkey and Hominy Soup

As a student, I lived with a Mexican family while attending the University of Guadalajara. I confess that I spent more time at the elbow of the family cook than I did studying Spanish literature, but her recipes have served me well over the years. She made *pozole* with a pig's head. I like this equally tasty, lighter version, made rich with turkey drumsticks and colorful with two kinds of hominy. Hot buttered flour tortillas are a must as accompaniment.

Makes 6 to 8 servings

2 tablespoons olive oil
3 turkey drumsticks
   (about 12 ounces each)
1 medium onion, coarsely chopped
2 garlic cloves, minced
1 jalapeño pepper, minced, or 2
   tablespoons canned chopped green
   chilies
6 cups Homemade Turkey Stock (see
   page 246), or 3 cups canned chicken
   broth mixed with 3 cups water

1½ teaspoons dried oregano
1½ teaspoons dried marjoram
1 can (16 ounces) white hominy,
   drained and rinsed
1 can (16 ounces) golden hominy,
   drained and rinsed
Salt and freshly ground pepper
Grated radishes, cubed avocado,
   sliced lime, and grated
   Monterey jack cheese,
   for garnishes

1. In a large saucepan or flameproof casserole, heat the olive oil. Add the drumsticks and cook over moderately high heat, turning occasionally, until browned all over, about 10 minutes. Add the onion, garlic, and jalapeño; cook over moderate heat, stirring often, until the vegetables are lightly browned, about 5 minutes.

2. Add the stock and bring to a simmer, skimming off any foam that rises to the surface. Add the oregano and marjoram and simmer over low heat until the drumsticks are tender, about 1½ hours.

3. Remove the drumsticks and let cool slightly. Remove the meat from the bones and cut into 1-inch chunks, discarding skin, tendons, and bones. Place the turkey chunks in the soup with the white and golden hominy and simmer for 10 minutes. Season to taste with salt and pepper.

4. Place the radishes, avocado cubes, lime, and grated cheese in separate bowls. Serve the hot soup with the garnishes, allowing each diner to add garnishes to taste.

Low-Fat Turkey Chorizo

Bruce Aidells, one of the best sausage makers around, helped me with this recipe for a lean-and-mean Mexican turkey sausage. A superlative and easy eye-opener when formed into patties and served with eggs for breakfast, it also makes excellent Mexican enchiladas, burritos, and tacos.

Makes 1¼ pounds, or 6 patties

2 turkey thighs (about 12 ounces each), bones removed, skin removed and reserved
2 tablespoons lime juice
2 tablespoons minced onion
1 small fresh jalapeño pepper, seeded and minced

2 teaspoons chili powder
2 teaspoons paprika, preferably Hungarian sweet
½ teaspoon salt
¼ teaspoon freshly ground black pepper
⅛ teaspoon cayenne pepper
1 tablespoon olive oil

1. Cut the boned turkey thighs into 2-inch pieces. Freeze the meat and skin for 30 minutes, until very firm but not frozen. In a food processor, process the skin alone until very finely ground. Add the turkey meat and pulse until coarsely ground.

2. Transfer the ground turkey to a bowl. Stir in the lime juice, onion, jalapeño pepper, chili powder, paprika, salt, black pepper, and cayenne. Cover and refrigerate for at least 4 hours or overnight. Shape the mixture into 6 patties about 4 inches in diameter.

3. In a large skillet, heat the olive oil. Cook the patties over moderate heat, turning once, until browned on both sides, about 8 minutes total. Transfer to paper towels to drain briefly before serving.

Turkey Minestrone

Minestrone is a personal matter to Italian chefs, and many a heated discussion has occurred over exactly what belongs in this soup. Therefore, if you would like to include such additions as cubed potatoes, rice, small pasta shapes, zucchini, yellow squash, pesto, or peas—be my guest. My recipe is a streamlined version, but nonetheless tasty, thanks to the addition of meaty turkey drumsticks.

Makes 8 servings

1 tablespoon olive oil
1 tablespoon unsalted butter
3 turkey drumsticks
  (about 12 ounces each)
1 large onion, chopped
2 large carrots, chopped
2 celery ribs, chopped
¼ pound green beans, trimmed, cut
  into 1-inch pieces
1 can (14 ounces) Italian peeled
  tomatoes, with their juice

8 cups water
½ teaspoon dried basil
1 teaspoon salt
¼ teaspoon freshly ground black
  pepper
1 can (16 ounces) white
  cannellini beans, drained and
  rinsed
½ cup freshly grated Parmesan
  cheese

1. In a large flameproof casserole or large saucepan, heat the oil and butter. Add the drumsticks and cook over moderately high heat, turning often, until lightly browned all over, about 10 minutes. Transfer the drumsticks to a plate.

2. Add the onion, carrots, and celery to the casserole. Cook, stirring often, until the vegetables are softened, about 5 minutes. Return the drumsticks to the casserole. Add the green beans, tomatoes, and water. Bring to a boil, skimming off any foam that rises to the surface. Add the basil, salt, and pepper. Reduce the heat to low and simmer until the drumsticks are tender, about 1 hour 20 minutes.

3. Remove the drumsticks and let cool for 30 minutes, while continuing to simmer the soup. Remove the meat from the bones and cut into 1-inch chunks, discarding skin, tendons, and bones.

4. Place the turkey chunks and the drained white beans in soup and heat through. Stir in the Parmesan.

REDUCED-FAT VARIATION: Delete oil, butter, and cheese. Broil drumsticks, turning often, until browned all over, about 10 minutes. Place drumsticks in casserole. Add all vegetables and water at the same time, and simmer until done. Let soup stand 10 minutes, or cool and refrigerate until fat solidifies on surface. Skim off and discard all fat.

Buffalo Turkey Wings with Blue Cheese Dip

Spicy deep-fried chicken wings are a staple munchie in Buffalo, New York. I think I have improved on the original. First of all, these crunchy wings are baked, not fried. Second, you get enough meat on the hefty wings to turn this finger-licking dish into a fun-filled entrée, instead of just another appetizer.

Makes 3 to 4 servings

4 turkey wings (about 1 pound each), or 4 pounds pre-cut turkey wing drumettes or wing portions
6 tablespoons unsalted butter, melted
2 tablespoons lemon juice
½ teaspoon salt
½ teaspoon cayenne pepper, or more to taste

1 cup mayonnaise
½ cup sour cream
½ cup crumbled blue cheese
1 scallion, minced
¼ teaspoon freshly ground black pepper

1. Preheat the oven to 375 degrees. Using a large sharp knife or cleaver, chop the wings at the joints to make 3 sections each.

2. In a baking dish just large enough to hold the wing sections, combine the melted butter, 1 tablespoon of the lemon juice, the salt, and the cayenne. Add the wing sections and turn to coat with the butter. Bake, turning once, until golden brown and tender, 1 to 1¼ hours.

3. While the turkey wings are roasting, make the blue cheese dip. In a medium bowl, combine the mayonnaise, sour cream, blue cheese, remaining 1 tablespoon lemon juice, scallion, and pepper. Mix to blend well. Cover and refrigerate. Serve the wings hot or warm with the cold dip.

Chunky Turkey Chili

Now, I know some folks like their chili made from ground meat, but I am from the camp that prefers their "bowl of red" with big, juicy chunks of meat poking through a tomatoey sauce. Freshly baked corn bread and a romaine salad with oranges and red onions are perfect sidekicks.

Makes 4 servings

2 tablespoons olive oil or vegetable oil
2 turkey thighs (12 to 14 ounces each), skin and bones removed, cut into 1½-inch chunks
1 medium onion, chopped
1 medium green bell pepper, chopped
1 jalapeño pepper, seeded and minced, or 2 tablespoons canned chopped green chilies
2 garlic cloves, chopped
¼ cup chili powder
1 can (8 ounces) tomato sauce

1 can (14 ounces) peeled Italian tomatoes, drained and coarsely chopped
½ cup beer, preferably dark imported
½ cup Homemade Turkey Stock (see page 246) or canned chicken broth
1 can (16 ounces) dark kidney beans, drained
2 tablespoons yellow cornmeal
Salt and freshly ground pepper
Sour cream or plain yogurt, for garnish

1. In a large saucepan or flameproof casserole, heat the oil. Add the turkey chunks and cook over moderately high heat, stirring often, until they are lightly browned, about 5 minutes. With a slotted spoon, transfer the turkey chunks to a plate and reserve, leaving the oil in the saucepan.

2. Add the onion, bell pepper, jalapeño, and garlic to the oil in the saucepan and cook over moderate heat, stirring often, until the vegetables are softened, about 5 minutes. Add the chili powder and cook, stirring, for 1 minute. Add the reserved turkey, tomato sauce, tomatoes, beer, and stock. Simmer until the turkey chunks are tender, about 45 minutes. Stir in the kidney beans and cook until the beans are heated through, about 5 minutes.

3. Whisk the cornmeal into ¼ cup water until smooth. Stir the cornmeal mixture into the chili and simmer for 5 minutes, until thickened. Season with salt and pepper to taste. Serve in soup bowls, topped with a dollop of sour cream.

▶ *Keep turkey chili in mind when you have to feed a crowd. It multiplies readily, keeps refrigerated (and improves in flavor) for up to 3 days, and freezes well.*

Turkey Wing and Winter Vegetable Stew

I look forward to winter's bounty as much as to summer's garden offerings. Root vegetables of all kinds—turnips, celeriac, parsnips, rutabagas, carrots—find their way into my cold-weather menus in stews, purees, and gratins. Here, turkey wings are braised in an old-fashioned ragoût that is highlighted by a collection of these vegetables. Spoon the light sauce over boiled rice to enjoy every last drop.

Makes 3 to 4 servings

4 turkey wings (about 10 ounces each), or 3½ pounds pre-cut turkey wing drumettes or wing portions
3 tablespoons unsalted butter
3 medium carrots, cut into 1-inch chunks
2 medium parsnips, cut into 1-inch chunks
1 medium celeriac (celery root), peeled and cut into 1-inch cubes

1 medium onion, chopped
1 cup Homemade Turkey Stock (see page 246) or canned chicken broth
½ teaspoon salt
½ teaspoon dried marjoram
¼ teaspoon freshly ground pepper
2 tablespoons minced fresh parsley, for garnish

1. Using a large sharp knife or cleaver, chop the whole wings at the joints to make 3 sections each. In a large saucepan, heat the butter. Add the wings and cook over moderately high heat, turning once, until lightly browned, about 7 minutes.

2. Add the carrots, parsnips, celeriac, and onion. Cover and cook until the onion is softened, about 5 minutes.

3. Add the stock, salt, marjoram, and pepper. Bring to a boil, reduce the heat to low, cover, and simmer until the wings are very tender, 1¼ to 1½ hours. Sprinkle with parsley and serve.

Turkey Thighs in Herbed Tomato Sauce with Polenta

Italians can take a simple culinary element, such as polenta, and embellish it to new heights. Turkey thighs in an herb-laced tomato sauce are served next to a golden mound of cheesy, piping-hot polenta. The dish is also great with pasta or rice.

Makes 4 servings

1 ounce dried imported mushrooms,
  either porcini (see Note) or Polish
½ cup boiling water
2 tablespoons olive oil
2 turkey thighs (about 1 pound each)
1 medium onion, chopped
1 garlic clove, minced
1 can (35 ounces) Italian peeled
  tomatoes, coarsely chopped,
  juices reserved

½ cup dry red wine
¾ teaspoon dried basil
½ teaspoon dried oregano
1¾ teaspoons salt
¼ teaspoon freshly ground pepper
3 cups cold water
1 cup yellow cornmeal, preferably
  stone-ground
½ cup freshly grated Parmesan cheese
3 tablespoons unsalted butter

1. In a small bowl, cover the porcini with the boiling water. Let stand until softened, 20 to 30 minutes. Lift out the porcini; reserve the liquid. Rinse the porcini well to remove any hidden grit and chop coarsely. Strain the liquid through a paper coffee filter or a double layer of cheesecloth and reserve.

2. In a large saucepan, heat the oil. Add the turkey thighs and cook over moderately high heat, turning once, until browned, about 10 minutes. Transfer the turkey thighs to a plate and reserve. Add the onion and garlic and cook, stirring often, until the onion is softened, about 3 minutes. Add the tomatoes and their juices, chopped mushrooms and their liquid, red wine, basil, oregano, ¾ teaspoon of the salt, and pepper and bring to a simmer. Return the thighs to the saucepan, reduce the heat to low, cover, and simmer, stirring occasionally, until the thighs are tender, 1¼ to 1½ hours. Transfer the thighs to a cutting board and carve into 1-inch pieces, discarding the bones. Return the turkey pieces to the sauce and keep warm.

3. Meanwhile, make the polenta. In a medium heavy-bottomed saucepan, bring the water and the remaining 1 teaspoon salt to a boil over high heat. Very gradually whisk in the cornmeal, so the water doesn't lose its boil. Reduce the heat to low and cook, stirring frequently, until the whisk can

stand in the polenta, 15 to 20 minutes. Off heat, stir in the Parmesan and butter until combined. Serve the polenta immediately, topped with the turkey and tomato sauce.

Note: Porcini mushrooms are available by mail order from Dean and Deluca, 800-221-7714; 212-431-1691.

Sauerkraut-Smothered Smoked Turkey Drumsticks

Buried deep in a simmering pot of sauerkraut, apples, and onions, these savory drumsticks slowly turn tender and succulent. Serve with steamed new potatoes and sharp mustard.

Makes 4 servings

2 tablespoons vegetable oil
1 medium onion, thinly sliced
1 medium green apple, such as Granny
  Smith, cored and thinly sliced
2 small carrots, cut into
  ½-inch dice
1 garlic clove, minced
2 pounds sauerkraut, well rinsed,
  squeezed to remove excess moisture

¾ cup dry white wine
¾ cup canned chicken broth
2 tablespoons gin
½ teaspoon salt
¼ teaspoon freshly ground pepper
4 smoked turkey drumsticks (about 12
  ounces each)

In a large saucepan, heat the oil. Add the onion, apple, carrots, and garlic. Cook, stirring, until the onion is softened, about 3 minutes. Add the sauerkraut, wine, broth, gin, salt, and pepper. Bring to a simmer. Bury the drumsticks deep in the sauerkraut, cover, and simmer until the drumsticks are tender, 1¼ to 1½ hours.

▶ *Many recipes call for just a tablespoon or so of liquor. If you don't feel like buying a whole bottle, purchase a miniature, which holds about 3 tablespoons.*

Turkey and Smoked Turkey Sausage Gumbo

An authentic gumbo is the quintessential autumn meal-in-a-pot. When I served this version to N'Awlins-born jazz-musician friends, they refused to believe that the whole tureen of it wasn't flown in from the Big Easy. Then I told them that I used turkey kielbasa instead of the traditional spicy pork *andouille* sausage, and they wrote me off as a lyin' Yankee. Serve with warm, crusty garlic bread and a simple salad dressed with a Creole mustard vinaigrette.

Makes 6 to 8 servings

½ cup vegetable oil
¾ pound smoked turkey, beef, or pork kielbasa or *andouille*, cut into ½-inch-thick slices
½ cup all-purpose flour
2 celery ribs with leaves, chopped
1 medium onion, chopped
2 medium green bell peppers, chopped
¾ pound okra, cut into ½-inch slices
3 garlic cloves, chopped
1 can (35 ounces) Italian peeled tomatoes, drained and coarsely chopped

¼ cup coarsely chopped flat-leaf parsley
2 turkey drumsticks (about 1 pound each)
6 cups Homemade Turkey Stock (see page 246), or 3 cups canned chicken broth mixed with 3 cups water
1 teaspoon dried thyme
½ teaspoon cayenne pepper
¼ teaspoon black pepper
2 bay leaves
Salt and hot pepper sauce
4 cups hot, freshly cooked long-grain rice

1. In a large nonreactive saucepan or flameproof casserole, heat the oil. Add the kielbasa slices and cook over moderately high heat, stirring often, until they are lightly browned on both sides, about 4 minutes. With a slotted spoon, transfer the kielbasa to a plate and reserve, leaving the oil in the pan.

2. Raise the heat to high and heat oil until smoking. Gradually whisk in the flour and reduce the heat to moderate. Cook, whisking constantly, until the flour mixture is nut brown, 3 to 4 minutes. Add the celery, onion, and green peppers and cook, stirring often, until the vegetables are softened, about 5 minutes. Add the okra and garlic and cook for 2 minutes. Add the tomatoes and parsley and bring to a simmer. Add the drumsticks, reserved kielbasa, stock, thyme, cayenne, black pepper, and bay leaves. Simmer, partially covered, until the drumsticks are tender, about 1½ hours.

3. Remove the drumsticks and let cool slightly. Remove the meat from the bones and cut into 1-inch chunks, discarding skin, tendons, and bones. Place turkey chunks in gumbo and heat through. Season to taste with salt and hot sauce.

4. To serve, place a large spoonful of cooked rice in each soup bowl and ladle the gumbo over the rice.

▶ *Gumbo gets its name from the African word for okra, which plays a big part in this dish. Okra lends both flavor and thickening to the soup. Gumbo without okra must be thickened in another fashion, usually with filé (powdered sassafras leaves). Don't be tempted to cook the rice in the soup—it soaks up too much liquid.*

CHAPTER FIVE

Turkey Cutlets:
The New Scallopini

Turkey breast cutlets, which are just making a splash in American markets, have been a staple of Italian cuisine for years. An enterprising Italian chef noted the similarities between thin-sliced boneless turkey breast and the more expensive veal scallopini, and capitalized on the match. Turkey cutlets are the foundation for one of the most popular dishes in Italian cooking, Turkey Cutlets with Prosciutto and Parmesan (see page 142), served in its native Bologna with a shower of shaved white truffles.

While the mild flavor of turkey cutlets is similar to the neutral taste of veal, you shouldn't treat them interchangeably. For example, if turkey cutlets are seared over high heat, they easily toughen and dry out. Always cook turkey cutlets over *moderate* heat.

Turkey cutlets, skinless and relatively fat free, are adaptable to a number of treatments and cuisines. Cut into strips, they can be stir-fried in Chinese dishes, such as Cantonese Turkey and Vegetable Stir-fry with Ginger Sauce, or scattered over the top of a pizza crust along with sweet peppers and corn for an up-to-the-minute Heartland Pizza. They can be pounded into scallopine and sautéed quickly for delectable French-style Turkey Cutlets in a Creamy Cider Sauce or Turkey and Mushroom Stroganoff, a Russian classic. Or they can be cut extra-thick into meaty turkey steaks.

Some recipes call for pounding the cutlets to ¼-inch thickness. Tear off two 16-inch lengths of wax paper and place the sheets on a work surface. Moisten your hand with cold water and flick the water from your fingertips over the wax paper sheets. Arrange the cutlets on one sheet, and cover with the second sheet, moistened-side down. Gently pound the cutlets to ¼-inch thickness, using a flat meat pounder, a rolling pin, or even the bottom of a heavy saucepan. (An empty wine bottle will work in a pinch, too.)

Turkey breast cutlets are found in packages that run from 1 pound to 1⅓ pounds. Each processor slices his cutlets a little thinner or thicker than the next, so the cutlets range in weight from 3 to 5 ounces each. I assume an average weight of about 4 ounces per cutlet. If you find that your cutlets are of dramatically different weight, adjust the cooking times accordingly. I gauge about ⅓ pound per person, especially when a sauce is involved. If your recipe is fairly plain, you may want to plan on as much as ½ pound of cutlets per guest. Whole cutlets cook very quickly: they only need about 2 minutes per side over moderate heat to cook through. They are the perfect entrée when you need something classy but quick.

Turkey steaks are cut a little over ⅝-inch thick and weigh about 8 ounces each. They are a good substitute for red meat steaks, but be sure to cook them until well done. This is one steak you don't eat rare. If you sauté them over moderate heat for 6 to 8 minutes, turning once or twice, you should have a minimum of shrinkage and moisture loss.

Lemon-Tarragon Turkey Cutlets

There is nothing simpler, tastier, or more elegant than these quickly sautéed turkey scallops finished off with a tangy sauce. While my favorite herb to use here is tarragon, fresh dill is also a fine match with the lemon and white wine flavors. Be sure to serve the cutlets with steamed rice and a bright green vegetable such as broccoli or asparagus.

Makes 2 to 3 servings

4 turkey breast cutlets
  (about 4 ounces each)
⅓ cup all-purpose flour
¼ teaspoon salt
⅛ teaspoon freshly ground pepper
2 tablespoons unsalted butter

2 tablespoons olive oil
½ cup dry white wine
2 tablespoons fresh lemon juice
½ teaspoon dried tarragon
1 small lemon, thinly sliced, for
  garnish

1. Pound the turkey cutlets between 2 sheets of moistened wax paper until flattened evenly to ¼-inch thickness. On a plate, mix together the flour, salt, and pepper. Dredge the cutlets in the seasoned flour, shaking off any excess.

2. In a large skillet, heat 1 tablespoon of the butter in 1 tablespoon of the oil over moderate heat. Add as many cutlets as will fit in a single layer and cook until lightly browned, turning once, about 2 minutes per side. Transfer the browned cutlets to a plate and set aside. Repeat with the remaining butter, oil, and turkey.

3. Increase the heat to high, add the wine, lemon juice, and tarragon to the skillet, and bring to a boil. Cook for 1 minute to reduce slightly. Return the cutlets to the pan, reduce heat to moderately low, and cook, turning once, until the sauce is thickened and the cutlets are heated through, about 1 minute. Season the sauce with additional salt and pepper to taste, and serve.

Cantonese Turkey and Vegetable Stir-fry with Ginger Sauce

What is unusual about this great-looking Chinese dish is that there isn't a smidgen of soy sauce, giving it a clean and vibrant taste that allows the turkey and vegetables to shine through. While I normally serve this with rice, it is also delicious served with thin egg noodles.

Makes 4 servings

1 large egg white
2 tablespoons dry sherry
1 tablespoon plus 1 teaspoon cornstarch
1 pound turkey breast cutlets, cut into ½-by-2-inch strips
2 tablespoons canned chicken broth or water
¼ cup vegetable oil

1 tablespoon minced fresh ginger
1 garlic clove, minced
1 cup broccoli florets
1 medium carrot, cut crosswise on the diagonal into ¼-inch slices
1 medium zucchini, scrubbed, cut crosswise on the diagonal into ¼-inch slices

1. In a medium bowl, beat the egg white until foamy. Beat in 1 tablespoon of the sherry. Add 1 tablespoon cornstarch and stir until dissolved. Add the turkey strips and toss to coat. Let marinate, if time allows, covered and refrigerated, for at least 30 minutes, or up to 4 hours.

2. In a small bowl, combine the remaining 1 tablespoon sherry and the chicken broth or water. Add the remaining 1 teaspoon cornstarch and stir until dissolved.

3. Heat a wok or large skillet over moderately high heat until very hot. Add 2 tablespoons of the oil and heat until hot but not smoking. Add the ginger and garlic and stir until fragrant but not browned, about 30 seconds. Add the broccoli and carrots; stir-fry for 1 minute. Add the zucchini and stir-fry until the vegetables are crisp-tender, about 1 minute. Transfer the vegetables to a plate.

4. Add the remaining 2 tablespoons oil to the wok and swirl to coat the inside of the pan; heat until hot but not smoking. Reduce the heat to moderate and add the marinated turkey strips. Cook, stirring often, until cooked

through, 2 to 3 minutes. Add the reserved vegetables and the sherry-broth mixture. Bring to a boil, stirring constantly, until the turkey and vegetables are glossy with the ginger sauce, about 30 seconds. Serve immediately.

▶ *Timing is everything in Chinese cooking. While the turkey is marinating, prepare the vegetables. (When pressed for time, I often buy pre-cut raw vegetables at the salad bar.) Have the chopped ginger and garlic and the cornstarch-sherry-broth mixture at your side before starting to stir-fry.*

Turkey Cutlets in a Creamy Cider Sauce

I can hardly wait until autumn, when apples are at their peak, to pre-pare this French specialty. Search out tart roadside cooking apples and the best unfiltered cider to make them truly special. The creamy cider sauce is heavenly, so serve plenty of steamed wild rice alongside to soak up every last bit.

Makes 2 to 3 servings

4 turkey breast cutlets
   (about 4 ounces each)
⅓ cup all-purpose flour
½ teaspoon salt
⅛ teaspoon white pepper
2 to 3 tablespoons unsalted
   butter
2 to 3 tablespoons vegetable
   oil

2 tart green cooking apples, such as
   Pippin or Granny Smith, peeled,
   cored, and thinly sliced
1 tablespoon fresh lemon juice
2 tablespoons finely chopped shallot
¼ cup applejack, Calvados, or brandy
⅓ cup apple cider, preferably fresh
   and unfiltered
1 cup heavy (whipping) cream

1. Preheat the oven to 200 degrees. Pound the cutlets between 2 sheets of moistened wax paper until evenly flattened to ¼-inch thickness. Cut each cutlet in half crosswise. On a plate, combine the flour, salt, and pepper. Dredge the cutlets in the seasoned flour, shaking off any excess.

2. In a large skillet, melt 2 tablespoons butter in 2 tablespoons oil. In batches, cook the cutlets in a single layer over moderate heat, turning once, until lightly browned on both sides, about 2 minutes per side. Transfer the cooked cutlets to a heatproof platter, cover with aluminum foil, and keep warm in the oven.

3. Add additional butter and oil to the skillet, if necessary. Toss the apples with the lemon juice to coat. Add to the skillet along with the shallots and cook over moderately high heat, stirring occasionally, until the apples are crisp-tender, about 2 minutes. Add the applejack and cider. Cook over high heat until liquid is reduced to about 2 tablespoons, about 2 minutes. Add the cream and cook until slightly thickened, about 2 minutes. Season the sauce with additional salt and white pepper to taste, pour over the warm cutlets, and serve.

Szechuan Turkey with Red and Green Peppers

All Chinese takeout should taste as good as this! It has a tantalizing, authentic favor, yet uses supermarket ingredients.

Makes 4 servings

1 large egg white
1 tablespoon dry sherry
1 tablespoon cornstarch
1 pound turkey breast cutlets, cut into
 ½-by-2-inch strips
2 tablespoons soy sauce
1 tablespoon plus 1 teaspoon rice
 vinegar or distilled white vinegar
2½ teaspoons sugar

¼ cup vegetable oil
2 teaspoons minced fresh ginger
2 garlic cloves, minced
¼ teaspoon crushed hot pepper flakes
1 small green bell pepper, cut into
 ½-by-2-inch strips
1 small red bell pepper, cut into
 ½-by-2-inch strips
2 large scallions, coarsely chopped

1. In a medium bowl, beat the egg white until foamy. Beat in the sherry. Add the cornstarch and stir until dissolved. Add the turkey strips and toss to coat. Let the strips marinate, if time allows, covered and refrigerated, for at least 30 minutes or up to 4 hours.

2. In a small bowl, combine the soy sauce and vinegar. Add the sugar and stir until dissolved. Reserve.

3. Heat a wok or large skillet over moderately high heat until very hot. Add 1 tablespoon oil and heat until hot but not smoking. Add the ginger, garlic, and pepper flakes. Stir-fry until fragrant but not browned, about 30 seconds. Add the sweet peppers and scallions and stir-fry until crisp-tender, about 1 minute. Transfer the vegetables to a plate.

4. Add the remaining 3 tablespoons of oil to the wok and swirl to coat the inside of the pan; heat until hot but not smoking. Reduce heat to moderate and add the marinated turkey strips. Cook, stirring often, until cooked through, 2 to 3 minutes. Add the cooked vegetables and the soy sauce mixture. Bring to a boil, stirring constantly, until the turkey and vegetables are glossy with the sauce, about 30 seconds. Serve immediately.

Spaghetti with Provençale Turkey Stir-fry

This is a real lifesaver when you need something fast, colorful, and flavorful for a group. The concept of a Chinese stir-fry can be happily applied to other cuisines, as this crowd pleaser demonstrates.

Makes 4 to 6 servings

¼ cup olive oil
1 pound turkey breast cutlets, cut into ½-by-2inch strips
1 medium onion, sliced
2 garlic cloves, minced
2 medium zucchini, scrubbed and cut into ½-inch rounds
1 pound fresh plum tomatoes, peeled and cut crosswise into ¼-inch slices

¼ cup pitted black olives
2 tablespoons chopped fresh basil, or 1 teaspoon dried
¾ teaspoon salt
¼ teaspoon pepper
1 pound spaghetti
½ cup freshly grated Parmesan cheese

1. In a large skillet, heat 3 tablespoons of olive oil. Add half the cutlet strips and cook over moderate heat, stirring occasionally, until lightly browned all over, 2 to 3 minutes. With a slotted spoon, transfer the cooked turkey strips to a plate and cover with foil; repeat with the remaining turkey strips. Remove them to the plate.

2. Add the remaining 1 tablespoon olive oil to the skillet. Increase heat to moderately high and add the onion and garlic. Cook, stirring often, until beginning to brown, about 2 minutes. Add the zucchini and cook, stirring often, for 1 minute. Add the reserved turkey strips, tomatoes, olives, basil, salt, and pepper. Cook, stirring often, until the tomatoes are heated through, about 2 minutes.

3. Meanwhile, in a large saucepan of boiling salted water, cook the spaghetti until just tender, 8 to 10 minutes. Drain well. Transfer the spaghetti to a warmed serving dish.

4. Arrange the cooked spaghetti on a warmed platter. Pour the turkey stir-fry over the spaghetti and sprinkle the Parmesan over the top. Serve immediately, with additional Parmesan on the side, if desired.

REDUCED-FAT VARIATION: Use a nonstick skillet. Reduce the amount of olive oil for stir-frying cutlet strips to 1 tablespoon. Replace remaining 3 tablespoons olive oil with 3 tablespoons low-sodium chicken broth. Stir-fry vegetables with broth, adding more if necessary to keep vegetables from sticking. Reduce Parmesan to ¼ cup.

▶ *Israel has the world's highest annual turkey consumption. Red meat is very expensive in Israel, and turkey's high meat-to-bone ratio brings it in at 28 pounds per capita.*

Sausage-Stuffed Turkey Rollatini

Delectable turkey cutlets rolled with a moist Italian sausage filling are always popular. I make them well ahead; then all they need is a quick trip to the skillet.

Makes 6 servings

12 turkey breast cutlets
  (3 to 4 ounces each)
½ cup fresh bread crumbs
¼ cup milk
2 tablespoons unsalted butter
½ pound Italian-style pork sausage,
  casing removed
2 tablespoons freshly grated Parmesan
  cheese

1 large egg, lightly beaten
¼ cup chopped fresh parsley
¼ teaspoon dried marjoram
¼ teaspoon salt
¼ teaspoon freshly ground
  pepper
1 tablespoon vegetable oil
1 cup dry white wine

1. Pound the turkey cutlets between 2 sheets of moistened wax paper until evenly flattened to ¼-inch thickness. In a medium bowl, soak the bread crumbs in the milk for 5 minutes. Squeeze the milk from the crumbs and return the moistened crumbs to the bowl.

2. In a medium skillet, melt 1 tablespoon of the butter over moderate heat. Add the sausage and cook, stirring and breaking up the meat with a wooden spoon, until it loses its pink color, about 5 minutes. Add to the moistened crumbs with cheese, egg, 2 tablespoons of parsley, and the marjoram; mix well. Place about 1 tablespoon of the sausage filling in the center of each turkey cutlet. Fold in the sides, then roll up to form cylinders. Secure each roll lengthwise with a wooden toothpick. (The rollatini can be made up to 4 hours ahead, covered, and refrigerated.) Season the cutlets with the salt and pepper.

3. In a large skillet, melt the remaining 1 tablespoon of butter in the oil. Add the rollatini in batches, if necessary, and cook over moderately high heat, turning often, until browned all over, about 5 minutes. Add the wine, reduce the heat to moderately low, cover, and simmer until cooked through, 8 to 10 minutes. With tongs or a slotted spoon, transfer the rollatini to a plate and cover loosely with aluminum foil to keep warm.

4. Bring the wine to a boil over high heat and cook until reduced by half, about 2 minutes. Pour the sauce over the rollatini, garnish with the remaining 2 tablespoons parsley, and serve.

Turkey Saltimbocca

There is something particularly charming about the look of this dish, with a fresh sage leaf and a slice of prosciutto skewered onto a turkey cutlet with a toothpick. *Saltimbocca* is Italian for "jump-in-mouth," and that's exactly what this dish will do! It is a many-faceted dish—simple enough for an informal supper, yet elegant enough for an upscale dinner.

Makes 4 servings

¼ teaspoon dried sage
⅛ teaspoon freshly ground
  pepper
4 turkey breast cutlets
  (about 4 ounces each)

4 slices prosciutto or ham, trimmed to
  fit cutlets
4 fresh sage leaves, if available
2 tablespoons unsalted butter
2 tablespoons olive oil

1. Preheat the oven to 225 degrees. Sprinkle the dried sage and pepper over the cutlets. Place a prosciutto slice on each cutlet. Please a sage leaf in the center. Using wooden toothpicks, attach the prosciutto and sage leaf together to the cutlet.

2. In a large skillet, melt the butter in the oil. Add as many cutlets as will fit in one layer, prosciutto-side down, and cook over moderate heat for 2 minutes. Turn and cook until the underside is lightly browned. Transfer the cutlets to a baking sheet and keep warm in the oven. Repeat the procedure with the remaining cutlets. Transfer the cutlets to a warmed serving platter and serve.

Breaded Turkey Cutlets with Parmesan Cheese

Like everyone else who'll admit it, I love any dish that has a fried, crunchy, crisp, golden-brown crumb coating. As these cutlets are on the plain side, I like to accompany them with a colorful, strongly seasoned vegetable, such as zucchini slices in an oregano-infused tomato sauce.

Makes 2 servings

4 turkey breast cutlets (about
   4 ounces each)
½ cup all-purpose flour
½ teaspoon salt
⅛ teaspoon freshly ground
   pepper

3 large eggs
¼ cup plus 3 tablespoons vegetable oil
⅛ teaspoon hot pepper sauce
2 cups fresh bread crumbs
½ cup freshly grated Parmesan cheese
Lemon wedges, for garnish

1. Pound the turkey cutlets between 2 sheets of moistened wax paper until flattened evenly to ¼-inch thickness. On a plate, combine the flour, salt, and pepper. In a shallow bowl, whisk together the eggs, 1 tablespoon of the oil, and the hot sauce. On another plate, combine the bread crumbs and Parmesan; toss to mix.

2. Using one hand, dredge one cutlet at a time in the flour mixture, shaking off any excess. Using the same hand, dip the cutlet in the egg mixture, letting excess drip back into the bowl. Using the other hand, coat the cutlet in the crumb mixture, patting gently to help the crumbs adhere. Place on a baking sheet. Refrigerate the coated cutlets for at least 30 minutes and up to 2 hours.

3. Preheat the oven to 200 degrees. In a large skillet, heat 3 tablespoons of the vegetable oil until very hot. Cook as many cutlets as will fit in a single layer over moderate heat, turning once, until both sides are golden brown, 2 to 3 minutes per side. Transfer the fried cutlets to a heatproof serving platter and keep warm in the oven. Add the remaining 3 tablespoons of oil to the skillet and heat. Repeat with the remaining cutlets. Serve them at once, squeezing the lemon wedges over each serving to taste.

▶ *Be sure to chill the breaded cutlets for 30 minutes before frying, and your coating will adhere beautifully and not come off in the hot oil.*

Stuffed Turkey Rolls with Herbed Cheese

I have served these hot out of the oven, the warm cheese oozing out of the cutlets to form its own sauce. Then again, I've served them in overlapping slices on a cold buffet, served with tomato salsa or Italian green sauce. Either way, they're delicious.

Makes 4 servings

4 turkey breast cutlets (about 4 ounces each)	⅛ teaspoon freshly ground pepper
1 package (3 ounces) cream cheese	¼ cup milk
1 garlic clove, crushed through a press	1 large egg, lightly beaten
2 teaspoons minced fresh chives, or ¾ teaspoon dried	¼ teaspoon salt
¼ teaspoon dried tarragon	1 cup fresh bread crumbs
	½ cup freshly grated Parmesan cheese
	3 tablespoons unsalted butter, melted

1. Preheat the oven to 375 degrees. Pound the turkey cutlets between 2 sheets of moistened wax paper until evenly flattened to ¼-inch thickness.

2. In a small bowl, mix together the cream cheese, garlic, chives, tarragon, and pepper. Place one-quarter of the cheese mixture in the center of each cutlet. Fold in the sides and roll up into a cylinder. Repeat with the remaining herbed cream-cheese mixture and cutlets.

3. In a medium bowl, beat the milk, egg, and salt until well blended. On a plate, combine the bread crumbs and Parmesan. Dip the stuffed turkey rolls in the egg mixture, then dredge in the bread-crumb mixture to coat.

4. Place the butter in a 9-inch-square baking dish and bake until the butter is melted and hot, about 5 minutes. Place the rolls in the dish and bake, turning once, until browned outside with no sign of pink inside when pierced with a knife, about 20 to 25 minutes.

Turkey Cutlets with Prosciutto and Parmesan

Turkey is very popular in Italy, especially as scallopini. Here I've paired turkey with two of Italy's signature ingredients: prosciutto and Parmesan. If your market doesn't carry prosciutto, substitute Black Forest or Smithfield ham.

Makes 2 to 3 servings

4 turkey breast cutlets
  (about 4 ounces each)
½ cup all-purpose flour
¼ teaspoon salt
¼ teaspoon freshly ground
  pepper
2 tablespoons unsalted butter

2 tablespoons olive oil
4 slices prosciutto or ham, trimmed to
  fit cutlets
½ cup freshly grated Parmigiano
  Reggiano cheese (see Note), or 4
  thin slices mozzarella
½ cup dry white wine

1. Preheat the oven to 400 degrees. Pound the turkey cutlets between 2 sheets of moistened wax paper until evenly flattened to ¼-inch thickness. On a plate, mix together the flour, salt, and pepper. Dredge the scallopini in the seasoned flour and shake off any excess.

2. In a large skillet, melt the butter in the oil over moderate heat. Add as many scallopini as will fit in a single layer, and cook, turning once, until lightly browned, about 2 minutes per side. Transfer the browned scallopini to a baking sheet. Repeat with the the remaining scallopini, adding additional oil to the skillet, if necessary. Transfer the second batch to the baking sheet; set the skillet aside.

3. Place a slice of prosciutto on top of each scallopini; sprinkle each with 2 tablespoons Parmesan. Bake just until the cheese is almost melted, about 4 minutes.

4. Meanwhile, heat the skillet over high heat. Add the wine and cook, scraping up the browned bits from the bottom of the pan with a wooden spoon, until reduced to ¼ cup, about 3 minutes. Transfer the scallopini to a warmed serving platter and drizzle the sauce over the top.

Note: While less-expensive grating cheeses, such as Pecorino, Romano, or domestic or Argentinian Parmesan, can sometimes be substituted for imported Parmigiano Reggiano, they are much too salty to be served with the prosciutto here. If you cannot find the real thing, substitute thin slices of mozzarella.

Sweet-and-Sour Baked Turkey Cutlets

Baked in their own tangy marinade, these turkey cutlets are steeped with flavor. Sprinkle them with something green and fresh—I use scallion, but chives, parsley, or basil are also nice.

Makes 4 servings

¼ cup lemon juice
¼ cup olive oil
1 tablespoon honey
1 teaspoon dried basil
½ teaspoon salt

⅛ teaspoon freshly ground pepper
4 turkey cutlets
   (about 4 ounces each)
1 small scallion, finely chopped, for
   garnish

1. In a nonreactive 11-by-7-inch baking dish, mix the lemon juice, olive oil, honey, basil, salt, and pepper. Add the turkey cutlets, slightly overlapping. Cover and refrigerate for 1 hour.

2. Preheat the oven to 350 degrees. Bake the turkey cutlets uncovered, turning once, until firm, with no sign of pink when pierced with a knife, 20 to 25 minutes. Transfer the cutlets to a warm serving platter, cover with aluminum foil, and keep warm.

3. Pour the pan juices into a small saucepan and boil over high heat until reduced to about 3 tablespoons. Pour over the cutlets, sprinkle with the scallion, and serve.

Pasta with Turkey and Artichokes in Garlic Cream

In northern California, where I was raised, artichokes were as common as corn in Iowa. So when I make fettuccine in a silken turkey-and-artichoke sauce, it reminds me of the casseroles my Mom would cook up. If you don't feel like paring down fresh artichokes—it can be a chore—feel free to substitute a 12-ounce package of defrosted artichoke hearts.

Makes 4 to 6 servings

1 large lemon
6 medium artichokes, or 1 package (12 ounces) frozen artichoke hearts, thawed and quartered
4 tablespoons unsalted butter
1 small onion, finely chopped
2 garlic cloves, finely chopped
½ cup dry white wine
1 tablespoon chopped fresh rosemary, or 1 teaspoon dried

½ teaspoon salt
⅛ teaspoon freshly ground pepper
1 pound turkey breast cutlets, cut into ½-by-1½-inch strips
1½ cups heavy (whipping) cream
1 pound fettuccine
¾ cup freshly grated Parmesan cheese
2 medium scallions, thinly sliced

1. Halve the lemon and squeeze the juice into a large bowl of water; place the lemon halves in the bowl. While paring the artichokes, dip them often in the lemon water to avoid discoloration. Working with one artichoke at a time, cut off the stem. Bend back and pull off almost all of the tough, dark green leaves from around the base. Cut the top third off and split them in half lengthwise. Cut out the fuzzy chokes in the centers, rinsing the artichoke halves in the lemon water. Cut each artichoke lengthwise into thin slices. Place the slices in the lemon water. (The defrosted artichoke hearts need no preparation.)

2. In a large skillet, melt 2 tablespoons of the butter. Add the onion and garlic and cook over moderate heat, stirring often, until the onions are softened, about 2 minutes. Drain the artichoke slices. Add the artichokes, wine, and rosemary to the skillet. Simmer over moderate heat, covered, until the artichokes are tender, about 12 minutes. Transfer the artichoke slices to a bowl and season with the salt and the pepper. (The artichokes can be prepared up to 2 hours in advance and set aside at room temperature.)

3. In the same skillet, melt the remaining 2 tablespoons butter. Cook half of the turkey strips over moderate heat, turning often, until lightly browned on all sides, 2 to 3 minutes. With tongs, transfer the cooked turkey strips to a plate, cover with foil, and brown the remaining turkey strips.

4. Add the heavy cream, reserved turkey strips, and artichoke slices to the skillet and cook over high heat until the cream has reduced by one-third, about 2 minutes. Remove from the heat and cover to keep warm.

5. Meanwhile, in a large pot of boiling salted water, cook the fettuccine until tender but still firm, 1 to 2 minutes for fresh, 10 to 12 minutes for dried. Drain well.

6. In a large warmed serving bowl, toss the turkey-artichoke sauce and Parmesan with the cooked pasta. Season with additional salt and pepper to taste. Sprinkle with the scallions and serve immediately, with additional Parmesan on the side, if desired.

Turkey and Mushroom Stroganoff

Proof positive of how turkey cutlets can be easily transformed into fresh interpretations of familiar classics. As an extra bonus, this recipe is very quick to prepare. You'll want something to sop up the mushroom and sour cream sauce, so toss freshly cooked egg noddles with butter and poppy seeds to go alongside. Steamed baby carrots with fresh dill will add color and authentic Russian flavor to the plate.

Makes 2 to 3 servings

4 to 5 tablespoons unsalted butter
1 medium onion, thinly sliced
½ pound medium mushrooms, sliced
1 garlic clove, minced
½ cup all-purpose flour
1 teaspoon paprika, preferably
  imported Hungarian sweet
½ teaspoon salt
⅛ teaspoon freshly ground pepper

1 pound turkey breast cutlets, cut into
  ½-by-1½-inch strips
¼ cup dry white wine or dry vermouth
1 cup Homemade Turkey Stock
  (page 246) or canned chicken
  broth
¾ cup sour cream
2 teaspoons Dijon mustard
Chopped fresh parsley, for garnish

1. In a large skillet, melt 2 tablespoons of the butter. Add the onion and cook over moderate heat, stirring often, until the onion is softened, about 4 minutes. Add the sliced mushrooms and garlic and cook, stirring often, until the mushrooms are lightly browned, about 5 minutes. Transfer the mushroom mixture to a plate and reserve. (Can be prepared up to 3 hours in advance.)

2. On a plate, combine the flour, paprika, salt, and pepper; toss to mix. Dredge half the turkey strips in the seasoned flour, shaking off any excess. In a large skillet, melt the remaining 2 tablespoons butter. Add the turkey strips and cook over moderate heat, turning occasionally, until lightly browned all over, 2 to 3 minutes. With tongs, transfer the turkey strips to a plate and cover with foil to keep warm. Dredge the remaining turkey strips and brown them as above, adding additional butter, if necessary.

3. Increase the heat to high, add the wine to the skillet, and bring to a boil, scraping up any browned bits with a wooden spoon. Cook until the wine is reduced to 2 tablespoons, about 1 minute. Add the stock, and reserved

mushrooms and turkey strips, and bring the sauce to a simmer, stirring often. Cook until the sauce is thickened, about 1 minute. Reduce the heat to low and stir in the sour cream and mustard. Cook just until sauce is heated through; do not boil sauce after sour cream has been added. Season sauce with additional salt and pepper to taste, and serve immediately, sprinkled with chopped parsley, if desired.

▶ *"Truth is, my fine fellow of the distensible weskit, your annual gratitude is a sorry pretense, a veritable sham, a cloak, dear man, to cover your unhandsome gluttony; and when by chance you actually do take to your knees on one day of the year it is for physical relief and readier digestion of your bird. Nevertheless, there is truly a subtle but significant relation between the stuffing of the flesh and the gratitude of the spirit . . ."*

—Ambrose Bierce, "Thanksgiving Day"

Turkey Scallopini Marsala with Mushrooms

Now I can enjoy one of my favorite dishes often, made with reasonably priced turkey cutlets instead of veal. If I'm feeling flush, I will use stemmed, sliced shiitake mushrooms instead of regular mushrooms, for a real treat.

Makes 6 servings

6 turkey breast cutlets
  (about 4 ounces each)
1 stick plus 1 tablespoon unsalted
  butter
10 ounces medium mushrooms, thinly
  sliced

2 medium scallions, chopped
½ cup all-purpose flour
½ teaspoon salt
¼ teaspoon freshly ground pepper
2 to 3 tablespoons vegetable oil
¾ cup dry Marsala

1. Preheat the oven to 225 degrees. Gently pound the turkey cutlets between 2 sheets of moistened wax paper until evenly flattened to ¼-inch thickness.

2. In a large skillet, melt 2 tablespoons of the butter over moderately high heat. Add the mushrooms and scallions, and cook until the mushrooms give up their liquid, it evaporates, and they become lightly browned, 6 to 8 minutes. Transfer the mushrooms to a plate and reserve.

3. On a plate, mix together the flour, salt, and pepper. Dredge the cutlets in the seasoned flour, shaking off any excess. In a large skillet, melt 4 tablespoons butter in 2 tablespoons oil. Add as many cutlets as will fit in a single layer and cook over moderate heat, turning once, until lightly browned, about 2 minutes per side. Transfer the browned cutlets to a baking sheet, and keep warm in the oven. Repeat with the remaining cutlets, adding additional oil to the skillet, if necessary.

4. Discard the oil in the skillet and wipe out with paper towels. Heat the skillet over high heat. Add the Marsala and boil, scraping up any browned bits from the bottom of the pan with a wooden spoon, until reduced to ½ cup. Return the mushrooms to the skillet and cook until the mushrooms are heated through, about 1 minute. Off heat, stir in the remaining 3 tablespoons butter. Transfer the cutlets to a warmed serving platter, pour the mushroom sauce over all, and serve.

Turkey Cutlets en Papillote with Zucchini, Red Peppers, and Scallions

Turkey cutlets and slivers of zucchini, red pepper, and scallion stew together in individual packages, their flavors mingling with a dash of dry vermouth and butter. In fact, there's so little butter in each portion that this is one of my favorite low-cal dishes, and one that I can serve with pride to the pickiest guest when I'm counting calories and they're not.

Makes 4 servings

½ teaspoon dried chervil,
or ¼ teaspoon dried
tarragon
¼ teaspoon salt
⅛ teaspoon freshly ground pepper
4 turkey cutlets
(about 4 ounces each)

1 medium zucchini, scrubbed, cut into
¼-by-2-inch strips
1 small red bell pepper, seeded and
cut into ¼-by-2-inch strips
2 medium scallions, finely chopped
4 teaspoons unsalted butter
½ cup dry vermouth

1. Preheat the oven to 375 degrees. In a small bowl, combine the chervil, salt, and pepper. Sprinkle evenly over the turkey cutlets. Place each cutlet on the bottom half of four 12-inch squares of aluminum foil. Combine the zucchini, sweet red pepper, and scallions, and place one-quarter of the mixed vegetables on top of each cutlet. Place 1 teaspoon butter and 2 tablespoons vermouth on each cutlet. Fold over the foil to enclose the cutlets and vegetables. Crimp the 3 open sides closed on each packet. (The packages can be prepared and refrigerated up to 4 hours ahead of time.)

2. Bake for 20 to 25 minutes. To test, open up 1 package and pierce the cutlet with a knife to check that there is no sign of pink. If necessary, reclose the package tightly and continue baking until done. Serve immediately, and let each guest open his or her own package.

Heartland Pizza

Yes, turkey *pizza*. Thin strips of turkey cutlets cook up to juicy perfection as a topping for a toothsome cornmeal pizza-dough base. A whole harvest of vegetables join the turkey to create a pizza that may not be 100 percent Italian but is so totally mouthwatering, you'll never miss the pepperoni. One note—the directions may seem lengthy, but the procedure is very straightforward, and most of all, fun!

Makes two 12-inch pizzas, 4 to 6 servings

Food Processor Pizza Dough
(recipe follows)
2 cups grated extra sharp Cheddar
cheese (about ½ pound)
7 medium plum tomatoes (about 1
pound), cut crosswise into ½-inch-
thick slices
1 pound turkey breast cutlets, cut
crosswise into ½-inch strips
⅔ cup corn kernels, fresh or frozen,
defrosted

1 medium red onion, thinly sliced
1 medium red bell pepper,
cut lengthwise into ½-inch
strips
3 garlic cloves, finely chopped
¼ cup freshly grated Parmesan
cheese
2 tablespoons olive oil
2 tablespoons chopped fresh sage, or
1½ teaspoons crumbled dried
Crushed hot pepper flakes

1. Prepare Food Processor Pizza Dough. Position two racks in the top and bottom thirds of the oven. Place two rimless baking sheets, at least 12 inches wide, in the oven and preheat oven to 500 degrees.

2. Punch down the pizza dough. Divide the dough in half. On a lightly floured surface, roll out half of the dough into a 12-inch circle. Roll the dough up onto the rolling pin and unroll onto a double thickness of aluminum foil 14 inches square. Fold over 1 inch of the pizza dough's edge, then flute with your thumb and forefinger to form a decorative rim.

3. Sprinkle ½ cup of Cheddar over the dough. Arrange half of the tomatoes in concentric circles over the cheese. Arrange half of the turkey strips in a spoke pattern on the tomatoes. Scatter half of the corn, sliced red onion, red pepper strips, and chopped garlic on top. Sprinkle another ½ cup of Cheddar and 2 tablespoons of Parmesan over the vegetables. Drizzle with about 1 tablespoon olive oil. Repeat with the remaining dough and ingredients to make a second pizza.

4. Carefully slide one of the pizzas on its foil onto one of the hot cookie sheets. Repeat procedure with second pizza. Bake pizzas until crusts are golden brown and turkey slices are cooked through, 15 to 18 minutes. Remove pizzas from oven and sprinkle on sage. Season pizzas to taste with hot pepper flakes. Cut each pizza into wedges and serve while hot.

Food Processor Pizza Dough

Makes enough dough for two 11-inch pizzas

1 teaspoon sugar
¾ cup plus 2 tablespoons warm
   (100 to 110 degrees) water
1 package (¼ ounce) active
   dry yeast

2½ cups unbleached all-purpose flour
½ cup yellow cornmeal, preferably
   stone-ground
1 teaspoon salt
2½ tablespoons olive oil

1. In a small cup, dissolve the sugar in the warm water. Add the yeast and let stand until foamy, about 10 minutes.

2. In a food processor, pulse the flour, cornmeal, and salt to combine. With the machine on, add the yeast mixture and 2 tablespoons olive oil through the feed tube in a steady stream. Process until the dough forms a ball on top of the blade. (If the dough is too wet or too dry, the dough will not form a ball. Feel the dough, and if it is sticky and wet, add additional flour, 2 tablespoons at a time, processing after each addition, until the dough forms a ball. If the dough is crumbly and dry, follow the same procedure, adding additional water 1 tablespoon at a time.) Process the ball of dough for 45 seconds to knead. (To make the dough by hand, in a large bowl, combine the flour, cornmeal, and salt. Make a well in the center and add the yeast mixture and olive oil. Using a wooden spoon, blend the flour into the well to make a stiff dough. Turn the dough out onto a lightly floured surface and knead until smooth and elastic, 10 to 15 minutes.)

3. Grease a medium bowl with the remaining ½ tablespoon oil. Gather up the dough and form into a neat ball; place in the bowl and turn to coat with the oil. Cover with a kitchen towel and set aside in a warm, draft-free place until the dough is doubled in bulk, about 1 hour.

Turkey Cutlets with Asparagus and Fontina Cheese

When cooking against the clock, thin-sliced turkey breast can be your best friend. Crisp-tender asparagus tops cutlets, which are then cloaked with melted Fontina cheese and finished off with a Marsala sauce.

Makes 4 servings

16 asparagus spears, trimmed
4 turkey breast cutlets
  (about 4 ounces each)
½ cup all-purpose flour
½ teaspoon salt
⅛ teaspoon freshly ground pepper
5 tablespoons unsalted butter, chilled

2 to 3 tablespoons olive or
  vegetable oil
¼ pound thinly sliced Italian or
  Swedish Fontina
1 cup dry Marsala
Minced fresh chives or chopped fresh
  parsley, for garnish

1. Bring a large pot of salted water to a boil over high heat. Cook the asparagus for 1 to 2 minutes, depending on the thickness of the spears, until just crisp-tender. Drain, rinse under cold water, and set aside. Cut each asparagus spear in half crosswise.

2. Cut each turkey cutlet in half crosswise, keeping them as uniform as possible. On a plate, mix together the flour, salt, and pepper. Dredge the turkey pieces in the seasoned flour mixture, shaking off any excess.

3. Preheat the oven to 200 degrees. In a large skillet, melt 2 tablespoons of the butter in 1 tablespoon of the oil over moderate heat. Add as many cutlets as will fit in a single layer and cook until the undersides are lightly browned, about 2 minutes. Turn and place 4 asparagus pieces on each turkey piece. Divide half of the cheese slices among the turkey pieces, covering the asparagus on each piece with a few slices of cheese. Cover and cook until turkey is cooked through and the cheese is melted, about 2 minutes. Transfer the turkey pieces to a baking sheet and keep warm in the oven while repeating with remaining cutlets, asparagus, and cheese. Add additional oil to the skillet, if necessary.

4. Add the Marsala to the skillet and boil over high heat for about 1 minute, until reduced to ⅔ cup. Off heat, whisk in the remaining 3 tablespoons butter, 1 tablespoon at a time, until smooth. Drizzle the sauce over the cutlets and garnish with the chives.

Chicken-Fried Turkey Steaks
with Ranch-House Milk Gravy

Turkey steaks, slabs of breast meat over ½ inch thick, are hefty portions that take well to hearty preparations. These crispy steaks are dipped in a spicy coating, then served with a milk gravy that would make any cowhand ask for seconds.

Makes 4 servings

3 large eggs
1 cup all-purpose flour
1½ teaspoons poultry
   seasoning
¾ teaspoon salt

½ teaspoon freshly ground pepper
4 turkey breast steaks
   (about 8 ounces each)
¼ cup vegetable oil
1½ cups milk

1. Preheat the oven to 200 degrees. In a medium bowl, beat the eggs well. On a medium plate, combine the flour, poultry seasoning, ½ teaspoon of the salt, and ¼ teaspoon of the pepper. Dip the turkey steaks in the beaten eggs, then dredge in the seasoned flour, shaking off any excess. Reserve the remaining seasoned flour.

2. In a large skillet, heat the oil. Add the steaks and cook over moderate heat, turning once, until golden brown outside with no sign of pink when pierced with a knife, 6 to 8 minutes. Transfer the browned steaks to a baking sheet, cover loosely with foil, and keep warm in the oven.

3. Pour off all but 2 tablespoons of the oil and return the skillet to moderately low heat. Sprinkle on 2 tablespoons of the reserved seasoned flour and cook, whisking constantly, for 1 minute. Whisk in the milk and bring to a boil. Reduce the heat to a simmer and cook, whisking often, until thickened, about 2 minutes. Whisk in the remaining ¼ teaspoon each salt and pepper, and serve the milk gravy over the steaks.

Creole Turkey Steaks

For my version of *grillades*, a popular New Orleans brunch dish, turkey steaks are simmered in a chunky tomato sauce, flavored with celery, peppers, onions, garlic, and a jumble of spices and herbs. Serve over creamy-textured grits or rice for breakfast (if you don't plan on eating anything else all day), or for lunch or dinner.

Makes 6 servings

3 tablespoons unsalted butter
1 medium onion, chopped
1 medium celery rib, chopped
1 medium green bell pepper,
  chopped
2 garlic cloves, minced
1 can (28 ounces) crushed tomatoes
1 cup canned chicken broth
½ teaspoon dried thyme
½ teaspoon dried basil

1 bay leaf
1 cup all-purpose flour
½ teaspoon garlic salt
½ teaspoon paprika, preferably
  Hungarian sweet
¼ teaspoon freshly ground black
  pepper
⅛ teaspoon cayenne pepper
6 turkey steaks (about 8 ounces each)
About ¼ cup vegetable oil

1. In a large skillet, melt the butter over moderately high heat. Add the onion, celery, green pepper, and garlic. Cook, stirring often, until the vegetables are softened, about 5 minutes. Add the tomatoes, broth, thyme, basil, and bay leaf. Bring to a boil, reduce the heat to very low, partially cover, and simmer, stirring often, until thickened, 45 minutes to 1 hour. (This creole sauce can be prepared up to 1 day ahead, covered, and refrigerated. Bring to a simmer over low heat before continuing.)

2. On a medium plate, combine the flour, garlic salt, paprika, pepper, and cayenne. Dredge the steaks in the seasoned flour and shake off any excess.

3. In a large skillet, heat the oil over moderate heat. In batches, cook the steaks, turning once, until lightly browned on both sides, about 4 minutes total. (If the steaks are slightly pink in the center, don't worry, since they will be cooked further.) Transfer the steaks to a plate as they are browned.

4. Place the turkey steaks in the hot creole sauce and simmer for 5 minutes, turning once. Serve the turkey steaks with the sauce.

CHAPTER SIX

Great Ground Turkey

I have been lucky enough to travel all over the country "talking turkey," teaching cooking classes on America's favorite bird. Everywhere I go, I hear the same thing: "I made chili out of ground turkey, and it was fabulous!" or "I secretly made burgers out of ground turkey, and my family didn't even know it wasn't beef!" While I am thrilled that these people are incorporating the health benefits of turkey into their diets, I think that their experiments with ground turkey could be even more successful than they seemed to be. Ground turkey is not ground beef, and substitutions should be made with a little care.

Ground turkey is made from white and dark meat combined. The proportion of dark to white meat varies from brand to brand. Because the dark meat is higher in fat, the fat content in ground turkey changes from 7 to 15 percent, depending on the producer. It's interesting that until recently ground turkey was considered a dark-meat product, but as consumers became interested in low-fat, red-meat substitutes, more processors changed their formulas to include the more expensive, but leaner, white meat. Skin on the meat is ground in as well, because the fat found in the skin adds needed moisture.

If you are concerned about saturated fat and cholesterol, read package labels on the ground turkey you buy. One brand, Perdue, lists the average calories in a 3-ounce serving of their ground turkey as a low 114, with 8 grams of fat. Yet another study of the eight leading turkey brands came out with an average of 195 calories and 9 grams of fat. That compares with 266 for beef, with 16 grams of fat, and 200 for extra-lean beef, with 11 grams of fat. While the figures look close when you get down to the extra-lean beef, keep in mind that turkey is exceptionally low in saturated fat, so it's still your best choice if your goal is to reduce cholesterol consumption. If you are on a highly restricted diet, buy skinless white meat and have the butcher grind it or do it yourself in a food processor. Just remember that it will be quite dry unless you add a little olive or canola oil—2 teaspoons for every pound of meat—to make up for the lack of turkey fat.

To compensate for its low fat content, cook all ground turkey over moderate heat to minimize shrinkage and dryness. When forming into patties or loaves, add rolled oats, bread crumbs, or crushed crackers to help retain moisture.

Because ground turkey has a very mild flavor, I like to zip it up in hearty pasta sauces such as Turkey Tomato Sauce Pronto, and ethnic casseroles, such as Turkey Tamale Pie and Turkey-Macaroni Bake, which is my version of Greek pastitsio. When grilling turkey burgers, brush them with sauce or serve them with lots of condiments, as in Backyard Turkey Burgers. Try a few of the following recipes, follow my simple guidelines, and I guarantee, you'll find your family clamoring for more.

Truck Stop Turkey Loaf

Here's a reduced-fat version of a family favorite that would still satisfy the hungriest truck driver. Poultry broth provides moisture, while replacing some of the calories and saturated fats in more traditional recipes. Save any leftovers for fantastic sandwiches!

Makes 4 servings

1 cup fresh bread crumbs
½ cup Homemade Turkey Stock (page 246) or canned chicken broth
1½ pounds ground turkey
1 medium onion, finely chopped
1 large celery rib with leaves, finely chopped

1 small red or green bell pepper, finely chopped
¼ cup finely chopped fresh parsley
1 tablespoon poultry seasoning
2 large egg whites, lightly beaten
1 teaspoon salt
¼ teaspoon freshly ground pepper
⅓ cup ketchup

1. Preheat the oven to 375 degrees. In a large bowl, moisten the bread crumbs with the broth. Add the turkey, onion, celery, bell pepper, parsley, poultry seasoning, egg whites, salt, and pepper. Pack into a lightly buttered 9-by-5-by-3-inch loaf pan.

2. Bake, uncovered, for 45 minutes. Spread the ketchup over the top of the loaf and continue baking until a meat thermometer inserted in the center of the loaf reads 160 to 165 degrees, about 15 minutes more. Let the loaf stand for 5 to 10 minutes before unmolding and slicing.

MICROWAVE INSTRUCTIONS: Bake, uncovered, in a 9-by-5-by-3-inch heatproof glass loaf pan for 12 minutes on High (100 percent) power. Spread loaf with ketchup and cook an additional 2 to 5 minutes, until a meat thermometer reads 150 degrees. Let stand, covered with foil, 10 minutes.

Russian Turkey "Cutlets"

Pojarski, breaded ground chicken or veal patties shaped into oval cutlet shapes and sautéed, have been a signature dish of Russian cuisine ever since a Mr. Pojarski put them on his inn's menu in the 1700s. They are even tastier, and more economical, when made with ground turkey.

Makes 8 cutlets

3 cups fresh bread crumbs
½ cup heavy (whipping) cream
1 pound ground turkey
¾ teaspoon salt
¼ teaspoon freshly ground
   pepper

¼ teaspoon freshly grated nutmeg
1 large egg
1 tablespoon water
3 tablespoons unsalted butter
3 tablespoons vegetable oil
Lemon wedges, for garnish

1. In a medium bowl, combine 1 cup of the bread crumbs and the heavy cream. Add the turkey, salt, pepper, and nutmeg; mix well. Using lightly floured hands, form the mixture into 8 oval cutlets, about ¾ inch thick.

2. In a medium bowl, beat the egg with the water. Place the remaining 2 cups bread crumbs on a plate. Dip the cutlets in the egg mixture, then coat with the bread crumbs. Refrigerate the cutlets for 15 minutes to set the coating.

3. In a large skillet, melt the butter in the oil over moderate heat. Cook the cutlets, turning once, until golden brown on both sides, about 6 minutes. (Adjust the heat as necessary to avoid burning the crust.) Transfer the cutlets to paper towels to drain briefly, then serve immediately, with lemon wedges for squeezing over the top.

> ▶ *A quick sauce for pojarski:* Combine ½ cup sour cream or plain yogurt, 1 minced scallion, 2 tablespoons prepared white horseradish, and 1½ teaspoons lemon juice. Let stand for 30 minutes at room temperature so the flavors can blend.

Dallas Turkey Loaf

Just a tad spicier than your usual meat loaf, this slices like a dream. It's so good cold that I sometimes tote it along on a picnic and serve it like a pâté.

Makes 4 servings

¾ cup chili sauce
¼ cup water
¾ cup rolled oats
1 large egg, lightly beaten
1 tablespoon chili powder
1 tablespoon Worcestershire
   sauce

1 teaspoon salt
1½ pounds ground turkey
1 small sweet red or green bell pepper,
   finely chopped
1 small onion, finely chopped
1 cup fresh or defrosted frozen corn
   kernels

1. Preheat the oven to 350 degrees. In a large bowl, combine ½ cup of the chili sauce with the water. Add the oats, egg, chili powder, Worcestershire, and salt, and mix well. Add the turkey, bell pepper, onion, and corn, and mix well. Spread in a lightly greased 9-by-5-by-3-inch loaf pan.

2. Bake, uncovered, for 45 minutes. Spread the remaining ¼ cup chili sauce over the top of the loaf and bake until a meat thermometer inserted in the center of the loaf registers 165 degrees, about 15 minutes longer. Let the loaf stand for 5 to 10 minutes before slicing.

MICROWAVE INSTRUCTIONS: Cook, uncovered, in a 9-by-5-by-3-inch heatproof glass loaf pan on High (100 percent) for 12 minutes. Spread chili sauce over loaf and cook until a meat thermometer inserted in center reads 150 degrees. Let stand, uncovered, for 10 minutes.

Scandinavian Meatballs in Dilled Yogurt Sauce

Here's a versatile dish you can enjoy over noodles as a dinner entrée or on toothpicks as a hot appetizer at cocktail parties. I always serve these at my holiday buffets, as even dieting guests can indulge in these treats—light turkey meatballs flavored with dill and lemon in a tangy low-fat yogurt sauce.

Makes 4 servings as a main course, 7 servings as an hors d'oeuvre

1¼ pounds ground turkey
½ cup fresh bread crumbs
3 tablespoons finely chopped onion
1 large egg
3 tablespoons finely chopped fresh dill, or 2 teaspoons dried
¾ teaspoon salt
½ teaspoon freshly ground pepper

½ cup all-purpose flour
1 tablespoon unsalted butter
1 tablespoon vegetable oil
1½ cups Homemade Turkey Stock (page 246) or canned chicken broth
2 teaspoons cornstarch dissolved in 1 tablespoon cold water
Grated zest of 1 lemon
½ cup plain low-fat yogurt

1. In a medium bowl, combine the turkey, bread crumbs, onion, egg, 1 tablespoon fresh dill or ½ teaspoon dried dill, ½ teaspoon salt, and ¼ teaspoon pepper. Roll level tablespoons of the mixture between your palms into balls, dredge in the flour to coat, and place on a baking sheet.

2. In a large skillet, melt the butter in the oil over moderately high heat. Add the meatballs and cook, turning often, until they are browned all over, about 8 minutes. Add the stock and bring to a simmer. Reduce the heat to low, cover, and simmer until the meatballs are cooked through, about 5 minutes.

3. Stir in the dissolved cornstarch and lemon zest and cook until the sauce thickens, about 1 minute. Stir in the yogurt, 2 tablespoons fresh dill or 1½ teaspoons dried dill, ¼ teaspoon salt, and ¼ teaspoon pepper. Cook just until the yogurt is heated through; do not let boil after adding the yogurt.

REDUCED-FAT VARIATION: Omit the butter and vegetable oil from the recipe. Bake the meatballs in a preheated 400-degree oven for 15 to 20 minutes, turning occasionally, until browned. Transfer the meatballs to a large skillet and proceed with the recipe. Use nonfat yogurt.

Sloppy Toms

This is what I whip up for youngsters at parties where the grown-ups are enjoying more sophisticated fare. They love them, and so do I.

Makes 4 sandwiches

2 tablespoons vegetable oil or unsalted
  butter
1 small onion, chopped
1 small green bell pepper,
  chopped
1 celery rib, chopped
1 garlic clove, minced

1 pound ground turkey
¾ teaspoon salt
¼ teaspoon freshly ground pepper
¾ cup ketchup, chili sauce, or chunky
  taco sauce
1 teaspoon Worcestershire sauce
4 hamburger buns, toasted

1. In a large skillet, heat the oil. Add the onion, green pepper, celery, and garlic. Cook over moderate heat, stirring often, until the vegetables are softened, about 3 minutes.

2. Add the ground turkey, salt, and pepper. Cook, breaking up the meat with a spoon, until the turkey loses its pink color, about 3 minutes.

3. Add the ketchup, chili sauce, or taco sauce and Worcestershire. Cook, stirring often, until thickened, about 1 minute. Serve on toasted hamburger buns.

REDUCED-FAT VARIATION; Use a nonstick skillet. Reduce oil to 1 tablespoon. Cook vegetables *covered* until softened.

▶ *Only toms "gobble"; hens make a clicking noise.*

Oriental Turkey Meatball Soup

Tiny spoonfuls of an Oriental-flavored turkey mixture are cooked in a simmering broth full of green vegetables to make a quick and satisfying lunch. Of course, you could add other vegetables on hand—carrots, broccoli, red bell peppers, green beans—so long as you slice them thinly enough to cook in 3 minutes.

Makes 8 servings

3 scallions
2 garlic cloves
1¼ pounds ground turkey
½ cup fresh bread crumbs
1 large egg, lightly beaten
2 teaspoons minced plus 3 slices fresh ginger
1 tablespoon plus 1 teaspoon soy sauce
2 teaspoons sesame oil
¼ teaspoon freshly ground pepper

3 quarts Homemade Turkey Stock (see page 246), or 1½ quarts canned chicken broth mixed with 1½ quarts water
2 celery ribs, cut diagonally into ½-inch slices
1 medium zucchini, scrubbed, halved lengthwise, and cut diagonally into ½-inch slices
1 cup fresh or defrosted frozen peas

1. Mince 1 scallion and 1 garlic clove. In a medium bowl, combine the ground turkey, bread crumbs, egg, minced scallion, minced garlic, ginger, soy sauce, sesame oil, and pepper. Cover and refrigerate while making the broth.

2. Crush the remaining garlic clove. In a large saucepan, bring the stock, sliced ginger, and crushed garlic to a boil over moderate heat. Reduce the heat to low and simmer for 15 minutes. Slice the remaining 2 scallions and set aside. Using a slotted spoon, remove the ginger slices and garlic from the stock.

3. Add the celery, sliced scallions, zucchini, and peas. Return to a simmer. Drop heaping teaspoons of the turkey mixture into the soup and simmer for 3 to 5 minutes, or until the meatballs are cooked through and the vegetables are crisp-tender.

Little Tom's Special

Little Joe's is a restaurant in the San Francisco Bay area that has a specialty of an omeletlike mélange of ground beef, eggs, spinach, and cheese. My rendition boasts the more delicate flavor of ground turkey. As an after-theater supper, this dish can't be beat.

Makes 4 servings

3 tablespoons olive oil
1 medium onion, chopped
1 cup sliced fresh mushrooms
1 pound ground turkey
1 package (10 ounces) frozen chopped spinach, defrosted, squeezed to remove excess moisture

3 large eggs, lightly beaten
½ teaspoon salt
¼ teaspoon hot pepper sauce
¼ cup freshly grated Parmesan cheese

1. In a large skillet, heat the oi!. Add the onion and cook over moderate heat, stirring often, until golden, about 4 minutes.

2. Add the mushrooms and cook, stirring often, until lightly browned, about 3 minutes.

3. Add the ground turkey and cook, breaking up the turkey with a spoon, until it loses its pink color, about 3 minutes.

4. Add the spinach and cook for 1 minute. Add the eggs, salt, and hot pepper sauce, and cook, stirring occasionally, until the eggs are set, about 1 minute longer. Sprinkle with the cheese and serve immediately.

REDUCED-FAT VARIATION: Use a nonstick skillet. Reduce oil to 1 tablespoon. Cook onions and mushrooms together, covered, until softened. Reduce cheese to 2 tablespoons.

Turkey Picadíllo in Acorn Squash

Ground meat is often served in this fashion south of the border. I've seen *picadíllo* baked in a whole pumpkin, but I like the individual serving size of acorn squash.

Makes 4 servings

2 acorn squash (1½ pounds each), halved lengthwise and seeds removed
2 tablespoons olive oil
1 small onion, finely chopped
1 small red bell pepper, finely chopped
1 garlic clove, minced
1 pound ground turkey
1 can (14 ounces) Italian peeled tomatoes, drained and coarsely chopped

¼ cup dark raisins
¼ cup green pimiento-stuffed olives, chopped
½ teaspoon salt
¼ teaspoon dried oregano
¼ teaspoon dried thyme
¼ teaspoon freshly ground pepper
¼ cup chopped toasted almonds, for garnish

1. Preheat the oven to 375 degrees. Trim a thin slice off the bottom of each squash half so it stands flat without rolling. Place the squash, seeded sides down, on a baking sheet. Bake until tender, about 1 hour.

2. Meanwhile, make the *picadíllo*. In a large nonreactive skillet, heat the oil. Add the onion, red pepper, and garlic. Cook over moderate heat, stirring often, until the vegetables are softened, about 3 minutes. Add the ground turkey and cook, stirring often and breaking up any lumps with a wooden spoon, until the turkey loses its pink color, about 3 minutes. Add the tomatoes, raisins, olives, salt, oregano, thyme, and pepper. Cook until thickened, about 15 minutes.

3. When the squash are done, transfer them to a serving platter. Spoon the hot *picadíllo* into them, sprinkle the almonds over the *picadíllo*, and serve.

Farmer's Turkey Potpie with Mashed Potato Crust

Here is another informal casserole to warm up a cold winter's night, featuring steaming turkey-and-gravy filling under a golden mashed-potato crust.

Makes 4 to 6 servings

4 tablespoons unsalted butter
1 medium onion, chopped
1 medium green bell pepper, chopped
1 pound ground turkey
2 tablespoons all-purpose flour
⅔ cup canned chicken broth
¼ teaspoon dried marjoram

¼ teaspoon dried savory
1 teaspoon salt
¾ teaspoon freshly ground pepper
2 pounds baking potatoes, peeled and
   cut into 2-inch chunks
⅓ cup milk
½ teaspoon paprika

1. Preheat the oven to 350 degrees. In a large skillet, melt 2 tablespoons of the butter over moderate heat. Add the onion and green pepper and cook, stirring often, until the vegetables are softened, about 3 minutes. Add the ground turkey and cook, stirring and breaking up the meat with a wooden spoon, until it loses its pink color, about 3 minutes. Sprinkle on the flour and cook, stirring constantly, for 1 minute. Stir in the broth, marjoram, savory, ½ teaspoon of the salt, and ½ teaspoon of the pepper. Bring to a boil, reduce the heat to low, and simmer the filling for 5 minutes. Lightly butter a 9-inch-square baking dish; spoon the filling into the dish, spreading evenly.

2. Meanwhile, cook the potatoes in a large pot of lightly salted boiling water until tender, about 20 minutes. Drain and mash with the milk and the remaining 2 tablespoons butter, ½ teaspoon salt, and ¼ teaspoon pepper. Spread the warm mashed potatoes evenly over the filling. Score the top decoratively with the tines of a fork and sprinkle with the paprika.

3. Bake until the potato crust is beginning to brown, 30 to 35 minutes.

Sweet-and-Sour Turkey Cabbage Rolls

You can't live in New York City for very long without somebody's aunt giving you a recipe for stuffed cabbage. The sweet-and-sour piquancy of this sauce, along with the elusive flavor of maple syrup, adds a new dimension to the traditional dish.

Makes 18 rolls

2 small heads cabbage (about 1 pound each), cored (see Note)
2 tablespoons unsalted butter
2 medium onions, chopped
2 pounds ground turkey
2 large eggs, lightly beaten
½ teaspoon salt
½ teaspoon freshly ground pepper

1 can (28 ounces) Italian peeled tomatoes, coarsely chopped, juice reserved
1 medium carrot, sliced
1 medium celery rib, sliced
½ cup maple syrup
2 tablespoons brown sugar
2 tablespoons lemon juice
1 teaspoon dried marjoram

1. Preheat the oven to 400 degrees. Cook the cabbages, one at a time, in a large pot of lightly salted boiling water until the outer layers of leaves peel off easily, about 5 minutes. Peel off the tender cabbage leaves and choose the largest 18. (Set aside the remaining cabbage for another use.) Cut away and discard the thick rib in each leaf.

2. In a medium skillet, heat the butter. Add half of the onion and cook over moderate heat, stirring often, until the onion is softened, about 3 minutes. In a large bowl, combine the ground turkey, cooked onion, eggs, salt, and pepper.

3. Lightly butter a 9-by-13-inch baking dish. Place about 2 tablespoons of the ground turkey mixture in the center of a cabbage leaf, fold in the sides, and roll into a cylinder. Place the roll, seam-side down, in the baking dish and repeat with the remaining leaves and filling.

4. In a medium bowl, stir together the tomatoes with their juice, the remaining chopped onion, the carrot, celery, maple syrup, brown sugar, lemon juice, and marjoram; pour over the cabbage rolls. Cover with aluminum foil and bake for 30 minutes. Reduce the heat to 325 degrees, remove the foil, and bake until the rolls are beginning to brown, 45 minutes to 1 hour longer.

Note: Only the outside leaves of the cabbage are used for this recipe. Small heads yield the most tender results. That's why I use 2 rather than 1 large head. Shred the leftover cabbage and stir-fry it in butter with caraway seeds as a side dish for next evening's supper, or make a batch of coleslaw.

Turkey Burgers au Poivre

How can a dinner dish be upscale and down home at the same time? When it's this turkey burger, which goes to the Ritz with a dash of Cognac in an easy, low-fat sauce made right in the pan.

Makes 4 servings

1 pound ground turkey
2 teaspoons Worcestershire sauce
¼ teaspoon salt
1 teaspoon coarsely cracked pepper
2 teaspoons vegetable oil
2 teaspoons unsalted butter

1 tablespoon chopped shallots or scallions
¼ cup canned chicken broth
¼ cup Cognac or brandy
1 tablespoon chopped fresh chives or parsley, for garnish

1. In a medium bowl, combine the turkey, Worcestershire, and salt; mix to blend well. Shape into 4 patties about 4 inches in diameter. Sprinkle the pepper over both sides of the patties.

2. In a large nonstick skillet, heat the oil. Add the turkey burgers and cook over moderate heat, turning once, until they are browned on both sides and cooked through and the meat springs back when pressed lightly with a finger, 6 to 8 minutes. Transfer the burgers to a plate and cover loosely with aluminum foil to keep warm.

3. Add the butter to the pan and melt. Add the shallots and cook, stirring, until softened, about 1 minute. Add the chicken broth and scrape up the brown bits on the bottom of the pan. Carefully add the Cognac. Averting your face, light the Cognac with a match, let the flames subside, and cook until the liquid is reduced by half. Pour the sauce over the burgers, sprinkle with chives, and serve.

Turkey-Macaroni Bake

I have served pan after pan of this cinnamon-scented casserole over the years. Inspired by Greek *pastitsio,* it is a handsome-looking dish, with layers of macaroni and meat and an inviting golden custard topping.

Makes 6 to 8 servings

1 stick unsalted butter
½ cup all-purpose flour
4 cups milk, scalded
¼ teaspoon grated nutmeg
6 large eggs, at room temperature
2 cups freshly grated Romano or
    Parmesan cheese (about 8 ounces)
2 tablespoons olive oil
1 medium onion, chopped
2 garlic cloves, minced

1½ pounds ground turkey
1 can (6 ounces) tomato paste
½ cup dry red wine
½ cup water
1 teaspoon dried basil
1 teaspoon dried oregano
½ teaspoon ground cinnamon
½ teaspoon salt
¼ teaspoon freshly ground pepper
1 pound elbow macaroni

1. Preheat the oven to 350 degrees. In a medium saucepan, melt the butter over moderately low heat. Whisk in the flour and cook, stirring frequently, for 2 minutes, without letting the mixture brown. Whisk in the milk, bring to a boil, and cook, whisking often, until slightly thickened, about 2 minutes. Beat in the nutmeg. In a large bowl, beat the eggs well. Gradually whisk the sauce into the eggs. Stir 1 cup of the grated cheese into the sauce.

2. In a large skillet, heat the oil. Add the onion and garlic and cook, stirring often, until the onion is softened, about 3 minutes. Add the ground turkey and cook, stirring and breaking up the meat with a wooden spoon, until it loses its pink color, about 3 minutes. Add the tomato paste, wine, water, basil, oregano, cinnamon, salt, and pepper. Bring to a boil, reduce the heat to low, and simmer until thickened, about 15 minutes.

3. Meanwhile, cook the macaroni in a large pot of boiling salted water until just tender, 10 to 12 minutes. Drain into a colander, rinse briefly under cold running water, and drain well.

4. Lightly butter a 9-by-13-inch baking dish. Place half the macaroni in the baking dish; spread half the sauce over the macaroni. Cover with all of the

turkey filling and top with the remaining macaroni. Spoon the remaining sauce over the top and sprinkle with the remaining 1 cup grated cheese. Place the baking dish on a baking sheet to catch any drips.

5. Bake until the sauce is bubbling and the top is golden brown, 50 to 60 minutes. Let the casserole stand for 10 minutes before cutting into squares.

▶ *The first official national Day of Thanksgiving was pro-claimed by the Continental Congress in 1781, to acknowledge the victory at Saratoga over General Burgoyne. It had nothing to do with the Pilgrims. In fact, there was always opposition to establishing the holiday in conjuction with the Pilgrims legend. Detractors felt that there were other things in America to be thankful for than the fate of twenty-one "religious fanatics."*

Turkey Tamale Pie

Tamale pie, that steaming dish of spicy meat with a delicious cornmeal crust, is comfort food ne plus ultra. This topping is much creamier and cheesier than most, perfect with the zesty turkey chili filling beneath.

Makes 4 to 6 servings

2 tablespoons olive oil
1 medium onion, chopped
1 medium green bell pepper, chopped
2 garlic cloves, minced
1 pound ground turkey
2 tablespoons chili powder
1½ teaspoons salt
1 teaspoon dried oregano
½ teaspoon ground cumin
¼ teaspoon cayenne pepper
  (optional)

1 can (28 ounces) Italian peeled
  tomatoes, drained and coarsely
  chopped
1½ cups tomato sauce
1½ cups sliced pitted black olives
1 cup fresh or defrosted frozen corn
  kernels
2 cups water
1 cup yellow cornmeal, preferably
  stone ground
2 cups grated sharp Cheddar cheese

1. In a large skillet, heat the oil. Add the onion, green pepper, and garlic. Cook over moderate heat, stirring often, until the vegetables are softened, about 3 minutes. Add the ground turkey and cook, stirring and breaking up the meat with a wooden spoon, until it loses its pink color, about 3 minutes.

2. Add the chili powder, 1 teaspoon of the salt, the oregano, cumin, and cayenne. Cook, stirring, for 1 minute. Add the tomatoes, tomato sauce, olives, and corn. Bring to a boil, reduce the heat to moderately low, and simmer until the filling is thickened, 15 to 20 minutes. Lightly butter a 9-inch-square baking dish and spoon in the filling, spreading evenly.

3. In a medium saucepan, bring the water and the remaining ½ teaspoon of salt to a boil over high heat. Gradually whisk in the cornmeal, reduce the heat to low, and cook, whisking constantly, for 1 minute. Spread the warm cornmeal topping over the filling. (The tamale pie can be made to this point up to 1 day ahead, covered, and refrigerated.)

4. Preheat the oven to 375 degrees. Bake for 30 minutes, or 40 minutes if pie was refrigerated. Sprinkle the grated cheese over the top and continue baking until the cheese is melted, about 10 minutes.

Turkey Tacos

Turkey tacos are fun to make and to eat. I prepare them often, especially when there are children around. Set out the different components on a platter, so everyone can mix and match to their own taste. This recipe doubles easily.

Makes 6 tacos

1 tablespoon olive or vegetable oil
1 small onion, chopped
1 garlic clove, minced
1 pound ground turkey
2 tablespoons chili powder
½ teaspoon ground cumin
¼ teaspoon salt
¼ teaspoon freshly ground pepper
1 can (8 ounces) tomato sauce

6 taco shells
½ small head lettuce, shredded
2 medium tomatoes, seeded and chopped
1 cup grated Cheddar cheese (about 4 ounces)
Fresh Tomato Salsa (see page 57) or bottled taco sauce
Guacamole (see page 213)

1. In a large skillet, heat the olive oil. Add the onion and garlic and cook over moderately high heat, stirring often, until the onion is softened, about 3 minutes. Add the ground turkey and cook, stirring often and breaking up the meat with a wooden spoon, until it loses its pink color, about 3 minutes. Add the chili powder, cumin, salt, and pepper. Cook, stirring, for 1 minute. Stir in the tomato sauce. Bring to a boil, reduce the heat to low, and simmer until thickened, about 10 minutes.

2. On a large platter, arrange the taco shells, shredded lettuce, tomatoes, and grated cheese. Set out small bowls of the salsa and guacamole and a larger bowl of the warm filling. Allow guests to fill their own taco shells and add garnishes as desired.

Turkey and Tomato Pasta Sauce Presto

This is the gutsy quick red sauce I make when there is only an hour to pull it all together. And when prepared in the microwave, it is *really* "presto."

Makes about 3 cups

2 tablespoons olive oil
1 medium onion, chopped
2 garlic cloves, minced
1 pound ground turkey
1 can (28 ounces) Italian peeled
    tomatoes in puree, coarsely chopped

1 can (6 ounces) tomato paste
½ cup dry red wine
1 teaspoon dried basil
1 teaspoon dried oregano
¼ teaspoon crushed hot pepper
    flakes

1. In a medium saucepan, heat the olive oil. Add the onion and cook over moderate heat, stirring often, until the onion is softened, about 3 minutes. Add the garlic and cook for 1 minute. Add the ground turkey and cook, stirring and breaking up the meat with a wooden spoon, until it loses its pink color, about 3 minutes.

2. Stir in the tomatoes with their puree, the tomato paste, red wine, basil, oregano, and hot pepper flakes. Bring to a boil, reduce the heat to low, and simmer for 45 minutes, until slightly thickened.

VARIATION: To make Turkey Sausage and Tomato Sauce Presto, substitute 1 pound of Italian-style turkey sausage, casings removed, for the ground turkey.

REDUCED-FAT VARIATION: Omit the olive oil. In a large nonstick skillet, cook the turkey, onion, and garlic in ¼ cup of the dry red wine over moderate heat until the turkey loses its pink color. Proceed with the recipe, adding the remaining ¼ cup wine with the tomatoes.

MICROWAVE INSTRUCTIONS: In a 2-quart microwave-safe baking dish, heat the olive oil for 2 minutes on High (100 percent). Add the onion and garlic, cover tightly with microwave-safe plastic wrap, and cook for 2 minutes on High. Add the turkey and cook, uncovered, for 6 minutes on High, stirring twice. Add the remaining ingredients and cook, uncovered, on Medium-High (75 percent) for 15 minutes.

Turkey Pasta Sauce Bolognese

Delicately seasoned, subdued, and refined, this is a long-simmering sauce for your finest pasta dishes. I always have a pint or so of this superlative sauce in my freezer, ready to make a quick supper at a moment's notice.

Makes about 4 cups

3 tablespoons unsalted butter
1 small onion, finely chopped
1 small carrot, finely chopped
1 small celery rib, finely chopped
1 pound ground turkey
¾ cup dry white wine

¾ cup milk
1 can (35 ounces) Italian peeled tomatoes, coarsely chopped, juices reserved
¼ teaspoon salt
¼ teaspoon freshly ground pepper

1. In a large saucepan or flameproof casserole, melt the butter over moderate heat. Add the onion, carrot, and celery and cook, stirring often, until the vegetables are softened, about 5 minutes. Add the ground turkey and cook, stirring and breaking up the meat with a wooden spoon, until the turkey loses its pink color, about 3 minutes.

2. Add the wine and cook until reduced to about ¼ cup, 3 to 5 minutes. Add the milk and cook until the liquid is again reduced to about ¼ cup, 3 to 5 minutes. Add the tomatoes with their juice, the salt, and the pepper. Bring to a boil, reduce the heat to low, and simmer, uncovered, stirring occasionally, until thickened, about 2 hours.

MICROWAVE INSTRUCTIONS: In a 2-quart microwave-safe baking dish, heat the butter for 2 minutes on High (100 percent). Add the onion, carrot, and celery, cover tightly with microwave-safe plastic wrap, and cook on High for 2 minutes. Add the turkey and cook, uncovered, on High, for 6 minutes, stirring twice. Add the wine and cook on High for 2 minutes. Add the milk, tomatoes, salt, and pepper. Cook, uncovered, on Medium-High (75 percent), until reduced to about 4 cups, about 45 minutes.

Backyard Turkey Burgers

The beef burger on a bun is practically an icon in our country's culinary heritage. But with their high fat content, even hamburgers are not immune to the political theory that idols are made to be toppled. Turkey burgers have come to the rescue to give America a healthier, low-fat alternative. Here is my favorite recipe for turkey burgers brushed with a tangy barbecue sauce, as well as ideas for other burgers.

Makes 8 burgers

1 bottle (10 ounces) chili sauce
3 tablespoons cider vinegar
3 tablespoons brown sugar
1 tablespoon Worcestershire
   sauce
½ teaspoon hot pepper sauce
2 pounds ground turkey

1 teaspoon salt
¼ teaspoon freshly ground pepper
8 hamburger buns
Tomato slices, lettuce leaves, and
   onion slices, for garnish

1. In a nonreactive medium saucepan, combine the chili sauce, vinegar, brown sugar, Worcestershire, and hot pepper sauce. Bring to a simmer over moderately low heat, stirring constantly. Cook, stirring often, until slightly thickened, about 5 minutes.

2. In a medium bowl, combine the ground turkey, salt, and pepper. Form into 8 patties 4 inches in diameter. Lightly grease the rack and build a charcoal fire in the grill. Let the fire burn down to moderately hot. (You should be able to hold your hand over the fire for 3 to 4 seconds.) Grill the turkey burgers 6 inches away from the coals, turning once, for 4 minutes. Brush with the sauce and cook for 1 minute. Turn, brush again, and cook until the burgers are browned outside and cooked through and the meat springs back when lightly pressed with a finger, 1 to 2 minutes. (When grilling burgers without sauce, cook for a total of 6 to 8 minutes, turning once.) Serve on hamburger buns with tomato, lettuce, onion, and desired condiments.

BROILER VARIATION: To broil the burgers indoors, cook in a preheated broiler, about 4 inches from the heat source, turning once, until the burgers are cooked through and the meat springs back when pressed lightly with a finger, 6 to 8 minutes.

MEXICAN BURGERS: Add 2 tablespoons chili powder to the ground turkey. Serve on fried tortillas with guacamole, salsa, and sour cream.

GREEK BURGERS: Add 1 teaspoon dried oregano to the ground turkey. After turning the burgers, top with thin slices of feta cheese and grill, covered, or broil to melt the cheese. Serve burgers in mini-pitas with chopped cucumbers, chopped tomatoes, and yogurt.

ITALIAN BURGERS: Add 1 teaspoon dried basil to the ground turkey. After turning the burgers, top with thin slices of mozzarella cheese and grill, covered, or broil to melt the cheese. Serve burgers on toasted Italian bread slices with tomato slices marinated in Italian salad dressing.

▶ *The first professional football game on Thanksgiving was played by the Detroit Lions and the Chicago Bears in 1934.*

Turkey and Ricotta Manicotti

Manicotti, those big tubes of pasta loved by both grown-ups and kids, are stuffed here with a delicate filling of ground turkey and Italian cheeses, then baked with a rosemary-scented tomato sauce. I always use part-skim cheeses when possible, but you can also use whole-milk products.

Makes 6 servings

¼ cup olive oil
1 medium onion, finely chopped
1 garlic clove, minced
2 cans (28 ounces each) Italian peeled tomatoes, coarsely chopped, juices reserved
1 tablespoon chopped fresh rosemary, or 1 teaspoon dried
¼ teaspoon freshly ground pepper
8 ounces manicotti shells

1½ pounds ground turkey
1 cup part-skim ricotta
4 ounces part-skim mozzarella, grated (about 1 cup)
¼ cup freshly grated Parmesan cheese
1 large egg plus 1 egg white, lightly beaten
¼ cup finely chopped fresh parsley
2 teaspoons dried basil

1. In a large nonreactive saucepan or flameproof casserole, heat 2 table-spoons of the olive oil. Add the onion and cook over moderate heat, stirring often, until the onion is softened, about 3 minutes. Add the garlic and cook for 1 minute. Add the tomatoes with their juices, the rosemary, and the pepper. Bring to a boil, reduce the heat to low, and simmer, stirring often, until slightly thickened, about 1 hour. Lightly oil a 9-by-13-inch baking dish. Spread a thin layer of the tomato sauce on the bottom of the dish.

2. In a large saucepan of boiling salted water, cook the manicotti for 10 to 12 minutes, until just barely tender. Drain, rinse under cold running water, and drain again.

3. Meanwhile, in a large skillet, heat the remaining 2 tablespoons olive oil. Add the ground turkey and cook over moderate heat, stirring and breaking up the meat with a wooden spoon, until it loses its pink color, about 3 minutes. In a large bowl, combine the cooked turkey with the ricotta, moz-zarella, Parmesan, egg mixture, parsley, and basil. Stuff the manicotti shells with the ground turkey mixture. Place the shells in the prepared dish and

pour the remaining tomato sauce over the top. (The manicotti can be prepared ahead up to 8 hours before baking, covered, and refrigerated.)

4. Preheat the oven to 350 degrees. Cover the pan with aluminum foil and bake until the sauce is bubbling, about 30 minutes.

Quick Skillet Turkey and Noodles

My mom used to make a hearty ground beef-and-noodle dish with sour cream for her three hungry growing boys. She still cooks it when we all get together, but now with a lighter touch, using ground turkey and yogurt. As the noodles cook right in the sauce, and it's served from the dish, it is a great hurry-up meal.

Makes 4 to 6 servings

2 tablespoons unsalted butter
1 medium onion, chopped
1 pound ground turkey
2 cans (8 ounces each) tomato sauce
2 cups tomato juice
2 teaspoons Worcestershire sauce
½ teaspoon celery seed

½ teaspoon salt
¼ teaspoon pepper
8 ounces egg noodles
¾ cup plain low-fat yogurt
2 tablespoons chopped fresh parsley,
   for garnish

1. In a large skillet, melt the butter over moderate heat. Add the onion and cook, stirring often, until softened, about 3 minutes. Add the ground turkey and cook, breaking up the meat with a wooden spoon, until it loses its pink color, about 3 minutes.

2. Add the tomato sauce, tomato juice, Worcestershire, celery seed, salt, and pepper. Stir in the noodles and cover tightly. Reduce the heat to low and simmer, stirring often, until the noodles are tender, 12 to 15 minutes.

3. Stir in the yogurt and cook just until heated through, about 1 minute. Do not let the sauce boil after adding the yogurt, or it will curdle. Serve, garnished with the parsley.

CHAPTER SEVEN

Turkey for Compliments

W hen company is coming, most of us make an extra effort in the kitchen. I enjoy the luxury of carefully planning out my party menu in advance, poring over cookbooks and food magazines to find just the right dish. With this lead time available, I like to attempt challenging, interesting new recipes. Perhaps the chosen recipe will take a bit more preparation, or maybe I'll have to search out a specialty grocer to buy an ingredient or two, but the prospect of exploring uncharted culinary territory is exciting.

As a caterer in Manhattan for many years, it was my business to create food that sparked life into a celebration. Each of these recipes comes from the menu of my catering business, Cuisine Americaine. They are all spectacular show stoppers; many are for groups of eight or more. These are surefire applause getters for occasions when you are cooking for a crowd.

For an elegant warm-weather buffet (the wedding rehearsal dinner or the anniversary party), a galantine is a beautiful centerpiece. My Galantine of Turkey is a trimmed-down version of the classic French dish, a boned breast filled with sumptuous turkey pâté. For a traditional Mexican Christmas Eve dish, serve the Turkey in Mole Poblano—braised turkey in an elaborately spiced brick-red sauce, or try Daube of Turkey for a relaxed New Year's Day party. Since this hearty

Provençale French stew is marinated and cooked beforehand, it only needs reheating before serving, and the mingling of Mediterranean flavors is incredible. The most successful Super Bowl menu in my past featured Rick's Red, White, and Green Turkey Lasagne with its spinach and turkey filling and two different sauces. And for cocktail parties, there are three bite-size hors d'oeuvres: Moroccan Turkey and Spice Mini-turnovers, Curried Turkey Spring Rolls with Sweet-and-Sour Apricot Sauce, and Grape Leaves Stuffed with Turkey and Rice. All three were constantly requested by my catering clients and are sure to become fixtures at your cocktail parties.

With the exception of the superlative Turkey and Wild Mushroom Risotto, all of these recipes can be made well ahead of time and served at your leisure. When giving a party, it's important to treat yourself like a guest, too!

▶ *"When my mother had to get dinner for eight she'd just make enough for sixteen and serve only half."*

—Gracie Allen

Rick's Red, White, and Green Turkey Lasagne

This refined version of the familiar pasta dish combines cream and tomato sauces with a ravioli-like filling of turkey, spinach, and ricotta cheese. One of the proudest moments of my catering career was when an Italian diplomat told me this was the best pasta he'd tasted since leaving Rome.

Makes 10 to 12 servings

1 pound curly lasagne
2 tablespoons olive oil
Basic Braised Turkey Breast (page 93), finely chopped, or 3 cups chopped cooked turkey
Herbed Marinara Sauce (recipe follows)
6 tablespoons unsalted butter
2 tablespoons all-purpose flour
2½ cups turkey stock, reserved from Basic Braised Turkey Breast, or 1½ cups canned chicken broth mixed with 1 cup water

1 cup heavy (whipping) cream
¾ cup fresh bread crumbs
2 packages (10 ounces each) frozen chopped spinach, thawed
1½ cups part-skim ricotta cheese
½ cup freshly grated Parmesan cheese
2 large eggs, lightly beaten
½ cup chopped fresh parsley
1 garlic clove, minced
¼ teaspoon grated nutmeg
3 cups (about 12 ounces) shredded mozzarella cheese

1. Bring a large pot of salted water to a boil over high heat. Add the lasagne and cook until just barely tender, 10 to 12 minutes. Drain, rinse well under cold running water, and drain again. Drizzle the olive oil over the noodles and toss lightly with your hands until coated to prevent them from sticking together. Transfer the lasagne to a bowl, cover tightly with plastic wrap, and refrigerate for up to 1 day before using.

2. Make the braised turkey breast and the marinara sauce up to a day in advance, if desired.

3. In a heavy medium saucepan, melt the butter over moderately low heat. Whisk in the flour and cook, stirring, for 2 minutes without letting the mixture brown. Whisk in the stock from braising the turkey or the broth and bring to a boil, whisking until thickened and smooth. Reduce the heat to low and simmer, whisking often, for 2 minutes. Blend in ½ cup of the cream. (This cream sauce can be made up to a day ahead. To prevent a skin

(continued)

from forming, press a piece of plastic wrap directly on the sauce and pierce with a knife to allow the steam to escape. Let cool completely, then refrigerate. Reheat over low heat, stirring until smooth, to make the sauce easier to spread.)

4. In a large bowl, combine the bread crumbs and the remaining ½ cup cream. Stir to moisten the crumbs. Squeeze the spinach to remove as much moisture as possible and add to the crumbs. Add the ricotta, Parmesan, eggs, parsley, garlic, and nutmeg. Mix to blend the spinach filling well.

5. Cover the bottom of a lightly oiled 9-by-13-inch baking dish with a thin layer of the cream sauce. Arrange a single layer of the lasagne noodles over it. Spread about half of the cream sauce over the noodles. Cover with half of the spinach filling. Sprinkle on 1 cup of the mozzarella cheese. Then spoon on half the marinara sauce, covering evenly. Arrange another layer of lasagne noodles in the dish. Spread with the remaining cream sauce. Cover with the rest of the spinach filling, another 1 cup mozzarella cheese, and a final layer of lasagne noodles. Spoon the remaining marinara sauce over the top. (The lasagne can be assembled up to 8 hours ahead, covered, and refrigerated. Remove from the refrigerator about 1 hour before baking.)

6. To bake the lasagne, preheat the oven to 350 degrees. Bake for 30 minutes. Sprinkle the remaining 1 cup mozzarella over the top and loosely tent with aluminum foil. Continue to bake until the lasagne is bubbling and the cheese is melted, 20 to 30 minutes longer. Let stand for 10 minutes before serving.

Herbed Marinara Sauce

Makes about 3½ cups

2 tablespoons olive oil
1 medium onion, chopped
1 garlic clove, minced
1 can (28 ounces) Italian peeled
   tomatoes, coarsely chopped,
   juice reserved

1 can (15 ounces) tomato
   puree
1 can (6 ounces) tomato paste
2 teaspoons dried basil
½ teaspoon dried thyme
¼ teaspoon freshly ground pepper

1. In a large nonreactive saucepan or flameproof casserole, heat the oil. Add the onion and garlic and cook over moderate heat, stirring often, until the onion is softened and light golden, about 5 minutes.

2. Add the tomatoes with their juice, the puree, paste, basil, thyme, and pepper. Bring to a boil, reduce the heat to low, and simmer, stirring occasionally, until slightly thickened, about 1 hour. (The sauce can be prepared up to 3 days ahead, cooled, covered, and refrigerated, or it can be frozen for up to 2 months.)

▶ *The celebration of Thanksgiving as a national holiday is due to the efforts of Philadelphia ladies' magazine editor Sara Josepha Hale. From 1846, every year, her November edition of* Godey's Lady's Book *lobbied to establish the holiday. As her magazine was very popular and influential, President Lincoln signed the holiday into effect in 1863.*

Moroccan Turkey and Spice Mini-Turnovers

Allow me to present another of my favorite hors d'oeuvre recipes, one that helped put my catering business on the map. It's really an appetizer version of the classic Moroccan pie, *bastilla*. These tiny filo-wrapped turnovers filled with chopped turkey, eggs, and Moroccan spices, garnished with powdered sugar and cinnamon, may sound unfamiliar to Western ears and palates, but I have *never* served these without entrancing the recipients.

Makes about 40

¼ cup plus 1 tablespoon olive oil
2 turkey thighs (about 1 pound each)
3 cups water
1 large onion, finely chopped
½ cup coarsely chopped fresh parsley
2 garlic cloves, minced
1 teaspoon salt
½ teaspoon ground ginger
¼ teaspoon ground cumin
1¼ teaspoons ground cinnamon

¼ teaspoon freshly ground black pepper
⅛ teaspoon cayenne pepper
6 large eggs
2 tablespoons lemon juice
1 cup slivered almonds, toasted (see page 229)
¼ cup confectioners' sugar
1 stick unsalted butter
½ pound filo dough

1. In a large saucepan, heat 1 tablespoon of the oil. Add the turkey thighs, skin-side down, and cook over moderately high heat, turning once, until lightly browned, about 8 minutes. Add the water, onion, parsley, garlic, ½ teaspoon of the salt, the ginger, cumin, ¼ teaspoon of the cinnamon, black pepper, and cayenne. Bring to a boil, reduce the heat to low, cover, and simmer until the thighs are tender, about 1¼ hours. Transfer the thighs to a plate and reserve the cooking liquid. Remove and discard the skin and bones; finely chop the turkey meat. Place in a large bowl.

2. Measure out 1½ cups of the reserved cooking liquid and set aside. Pour the remaining cooking liquid into a medium skillet and cook over high heat until the liquid is reduced to about ½ cup of thick glaze. Scrape the glaze into the bowl with the chopped turkey.

3. In a medium bowl, beat the eggs and the remaining ½ teaspoon salt until foamy. In a large skillet, bring the reserved 1½ cups cooking liquid and the

lemon juice to a simmer over moderate heat. Stir in the egg mixture and cook, stirring often, until the eggs have formed soft curds, about 2 minutes. Drain the egg curds into a colander. Stir into the turkey filling.

4. In a food processor, pulse the almonds with 1 tablespoon of the confectioners' sugar until very finely chopped. Stir into the turkey mixture.

5. Melt the butter with the remaining ¼ cup oil. Place 1 sheet of filo dough, long side facing you, on a work surface. (Keep the remaining dough under a moist, clean kitchen towel.) Lightly brush the entire surface of the dough with the butter and oil. Using a sharp knife or a pastry wheel, cut the dough top to bottom into thirds. In the bottom left corner of each pastry column, place about 1 tablespoon of the turkey filling. Fold the bottom right corner of the dough diagonally up so that the bottom edge meets the left-hand edge and encloses the filling. Continue folding the filling and dough up and over on themselves (as if you were folding a flag), finishing with a tiny, plump triangle. Transfer the triangles to baking sheets, arranging them in single layers. Repeat the procedure with the remaining pastry leaves and filling. (The triangles can be prepared up to 8 hours ahead, covered tightly with plastic wrap, and refrigerated. They can also be frozen for up to 1 month. The triangles do not have to be defrosted before baking, but if using them frozen, increase the baking time slightly.)

6. Preheat the oven to 375 degrees. Brush the tops of the triangles lightly with the butter-and-oil mixture just before baking. Bake for 20 minutes, turning once, until golden brown on both sides. Remove the turnovers from the oven; reduce the oven temperature to 200 degrees.

7. In a small bowl, combine the remaining 3 tablespoons confectioners' sugar and the remaining 1 teaspoon cinnamon. Just before serving, place the sugar-and-cinnamon mixture in a wire-mesh sieve and sprinkle the tops of the turnovers *lightly* with the mixture. Serve the turnovers while still hot, keeping the remaining turnovers warm in the oven, if necessary.

Curried Turkey Spring Rolls
with Sweet-and-Sour Apricot Sauce

La Petite Chaya, an innovative California restaurant, gave me a similar recipe for a party I catered a few years ago. While any *dim sum* recipe is a little time-consuming, the results are superlative, and these were one of the most popular hors d'oeuvres on my catering menu.

Makes about 50 spring rolls

4 tablespoons unsalted butter
2 tart green apples, such as Granny
    Smith, peeled, cored, and finely
    chopped
1 medium onion, finely chopped
2 garlic cloves, minced
2 teaspoons minced fresh ginger
1 pound ground turkey
1 tablespoon curry powder

1 tablespoon all-purpose flour
½ cup heavy cream
1 pound won ton skins
Vegetable oil,
    for deep-frying
1 cup apricot preserves
1 tablespoon rice vinegar or white
    wine vinegar
2 teaspoons soy sauce

1. In a large skillet, melt the butter over moderate heat. Add the apples, onion, garlic, and ginger and cook over moderate heat, stirring often, until the onions are softened, about 3 minutes. Add the turkey and cook, stirring and breaking up the meat with a wooden spoon, until it loses its pink color, about 3 minutes. Sprinkle on the curry powder and flour and cook, stirring, for 1 minute. Add the heavy cream and bring to a boil, stirring, until thickened, about 1 minute. Let the filling cool completely.

2. Place a won ton skin on a flat work surface, with the points at twelve, three, six, and nine o'clock. Place about 1½ teaspoons of the cooled filling in the center of the won ton skin. Fold in the points at three and nine o'clock, then roll up the skin to form a cylinder. Repeat the procedure with the remaining filling and skins.

3. Preheat the oven to 200 degrees. Line a baking sheet with paper towels. In a large skillet, heat enough vegetable oil to reach 1 inch up the sides of the skillet until very hot but not smoking, 350 degrees. Deep-fry the spring rolls in batches, turning once, until golden brown, about 1 minute per batch. With a slotted spoon, transfer the fried spring rolls to the prepared baking

sheet to drain and keep warm in the oven. (The spring rolls can also be baked, rather than deep-fried, in a preheated 375-degree oven until golden brown, about 15 minutes.)

4. In a small nonreactive saucepan, cook the preserves, vinegar, and soy sauce over low heat, stirring until melted and smooth, 1 to 2 minutes. Serve the spring rolls with the warm sauce for dipping.

▶ *"Contemplation makes a rare turkey-cock of him; How he jets under his advanced plumes!"*

—Shakespeare

Grape Leaves Stuffed with Turkey, Rice, and Mint

Stuffed grape leaves can be a component in a Mediterranean-style buffet, but at cocktail parties, I pass them on a platter as an appetizer with a small bowl of yogurt for dipping.

Makes about 36 dozen

1 jar (16 ounces) prepared grape leaves, drained
4 cups water
1½ teaspoons salt
¾ cup long-grain rice
¼ cup pine nuts
¼ cup olive oil
1 medium onion, finely chopped

3 medium scallions, chopped
¾ pound ground turkey
⅓ cup chopped fresh mint, or 1 tablespoon dried
¼ cup currants or raisins
3 tablespoons lemon juice
¼ teaspoon freshly ground pepper

1. In a large saucepan of boiling water, cook the grape leaves for 1 minute. Drain, rinse well under cold running water, and drain again. Sort through the leaves, choosing the largest ones for stuffing; reserve the smaller ones for lining the saucepan.

2. In a medium saucepan, bring 3 cups of the water and 1 teaspoon of the salt to a boil over high heat. Add the rice, bring to a simmer, reduce the heat to moderately low, and simmer until the rice is just barely tender, about 8 minutes. Drain, rinse well under cold running water, and drain again. Set the rice aside.

3. In a medium skillet, cook the pine nuts over moderate heat, stirring often, until lightly browned, about 2 minutes. Transfer to a plate and reserve. In the same skillet, heat 2 tablespoons of the oil. Add the onion and scallions. Cook over moderate heat, stirring often, until the onions are softened, about 3 minutes. Add the turkey and cook, stirring and breaking up the meat with a wooden spoon, until it loses its pink color, about 3 minutes. Off heat, stir in the reserved rice, the toasted pine nuts, the mint, currants, 1 tablespoon of the lemon juice, the remaining ½ teaspoon salt, and the pepper.

4. Line the bottom of a large saucepan with about 10 of the smaller grape leaves. Place a large grape leaf, veined-side facing up, on a work surface.

Place about 1 tablespoon of the filling in the center of it. Fold in the sides, then roll it up to form a cylinder. Repeat the procedure with the remaining grape leaves and filling. Arrange the grape leaves, packed closely together, in layers in the prepared saucepan, separating the layers with a few of the remaining small leaves. In a measuring cup, combine the remaining 1 cup water and 2 tablespoons lemon juice; pour over the stuffed grape leaves.

5. Bring the saucepan to a simmer over moderate heat, reduce the heat to low, cover tightly, and simmer for 45 minutes. Let cool to room temperature before serving.

Herbed Turkey and Cognac Pâté

This mouth-watering pâté is accented with the green of spinach and herbs, making it a lovely choice for a buffet table. I serve it in many ways—on tiny toast as passed hors d'oeuvres, as a first course in a formal setting, and, perhaps best, as part of an outdoor picnic with crusty French bread, light red wine, and cheeses.

Makes 12 to 16 servings

¼ pound firm white pork fatback, cubed
12 slices of bacon
1 package (10 ounces) frozen chopped spinach, defrosted
2 tablespoons unsalted butter
1 small onion, finely chopped
1 garlic clove, minced
¾ cup fresh bread crumbs
¼ cup Cognac or brandy

1 pound ground turkey
1 pound ground pork
2 large eggs, lightly beaten
¼ cup chopped fresh parsley
2 teaspoons salt
½ teaspoon dried thyme
¼ teaspoon ground allspice
¼ teaspoon freshly ground pepper
Pinch of cloves
2 bay leaves

1. Preheat the oven to 350 degrees. Place the fat on a baking sheet and place in the freezer until partially frozen, about 30 minutes. In a food processor, process the fatback until pureed. Set aside.

2. In a large saucepan, cover the bacon with cold water, bring to a boil over moderate heat, and cook for 5 minutes. Drain, rinse under cold running water, and drain again. Line the bottom and sides of a 9-by-5-by-3-inch loaf pan with 6 of the bacon slices.

3. A handful at a time, squeeze the spinach between your hands to remove as much moisture as possible. In a large skillet, melt the butter over moderate heat. Add the onion and garlic and cook, stirring often, until the vegetables are softened, about 3 minutes. Add the spinach and cook, stirring constantly, until the spinach is dry, 1 to 2 minutes.

4. In a large bowl, combine the bread crumbs and Cognac. Add the pureed fat, turkey, pork, the spinach mixture, eggs, parsley, salt, thyme, allspice, pepper, and cloves. Mix well to blend. Spoon the pâté mixture into the

bacon-lined loaf pan. Place the bay leaves and remaining bacon strips, trimming if necessary, on the top of the pâté. Cover the pâté tightly with a double thickness of aluminum foil and place in a baking pan large enough to hold the loaf pan.

5. Place the baking pan in the oven and add enough boiling water to reach 1 inch up the sides of the loaf pan. Bake until a meat thermometer inserted in the center of the pâté (through the foil) reads 160 degrees, 1 to 1¼ hours. Remove the pâté from the roasting pan and let cool completely with the foil still in place.

6. Place the loaf pan on a baking sheet. Place another loaf pan of the same size filled with heavy cans on top of the pâté to weight it down. Refrigerate overnight. Before serving, remove the foil and bay leaves. Serve, cut into ⅜- to ½-inch slices, directly from the loaf pan, or unmold and wipe away any congealed juices before slicing. (This pâté can be prepared up to 5 days before serving, if unmolded and tightly wrapped in aluminum foil.)

Turkey and Wild Mushroom Risotto

One of the glories of Italian cooking, true risotto was practically un-known on these shores until the recent availability of Arborio rice, which lends a distinct creaminess to the dish. If you can get dried porcini mushrooms, so much the better, but Polish mushrooms will suffice. (Stir an egg into leftovers, form into patties, and fry in a little butter to make an enticing lunch.) This recipe is from my friend chef Steve Evasew of New York City's Indian Market.

Makes 8 servings

1 to 2 ounces dried mushrooms, such as porcini or Polish, more is better (see Note)
1⅓ cups boiling water
8 cups Homemade Turkey Stock (see page 246), or 4 cups canned chicken broth and 4 cups water
1 teaspoon salt
4 tablespoons unsalted butter
1 small onion, finely chopped

2 cups Arborio rice (see note)
2 teaspoons chopped fresh rosemary, or ½ teaspoon dried
½ teaspoon freshly ground pepper
2 cups sliced fresh mushrooms (preferably shiitake, tough stems discarded)
2 cups chopped cooked turkey (about 10 ounces)
1 cup freshly grated Parmesan cheese, for garnish

1. In a small bowl, soak the mushrooms in the boiling water until softened, about 20 minutes. Lift out the mushrooms and strain the liquid through a paper towel–lined sieve; reserve the soaking liquid. Rinse the soaked mush-rooms well under cold running water to remove any hidden grit. Chop coarsely.

2. In a large saucepan, bring the stock and salt to a simmer; keep at a low simmer throughout the cooking period.

3. In another large saucepan, melt the butter over moderate heat. Add the onion and cook, stirring, until golden brown, about 5 minutes. Add the rice, rosemary, and pepper. Cook, stirring, until the rice turns opaque, about 2 minutes. Add the fresh mushrooms, soaked mushrooms, and soaking liq-uid. Cook, stirring often, until the fresh mushrooms soften, about 2 minutes.

4. Reduce the heat to low, stir in 1 cup of the simmering stock, and cook,

stirring often, until the rice has almost absorbed all of the stock, about 2 minutes. Add another cup of stock and repeat the procedure. Continue adding stock as the rice has almost absorbed the previous addition, about every 2 minutes. You will use 6 to 8 cups of stock in all. The risotto is done when the rice is al dente and the sauce is liquid and creamy, not dry. When you estimate that the risotto is about 3 minutes from being done, add the chopped turkey to let it heat through. Season with additional freshly ground pepper to taste.

5. Divide the risotto among 8 warm serving dishes and pass Parmesan to sprinkle on each serving.

> *Note: Arborio rice and porcini mushrooms are available by mail order from Dean and Deluca, 800-221-7714; 212-431-1691.*

Turkey Company Casserole
with Zucchini and Potatoes

This is really a moussaka made with zucchini and turkey instead of lamb and eggplant. Thanks to my cousin Elizabeth for her innovative recipe.

Makes 8 to 12 servings

2 tablespoons olive oil
1 medium onion, chopped
2 garlic cloves, minced
2 pounds ground turkey
1 can (28 ounces) Italian peeled
   tomatoes, drained and coarsely
   chopped
1 can (6 ounces) tomato paste
½ cup dry red wine
2 teaspoons dried oregano

¼ teaspoon freshly ground pepper
4 tablespoons unsalted butter
¼ cup all-purpose flour
2 cups milk, scalded
3 large eggs
1 cup grated Parmesan cheese
   (about 4 ounces)
3 large russet potatoes, peeled
3 medium zucchini
½ teaspoon salt

1. In a large skillet, heat the oil. Add the onion and garlic and cook over moderate heat, stirring often, until the onion is softened, about 3 minutes. Add the ground turkey and cook, stirring and breaking up the meat with a wooden spoon, until it loses its pink color, about 3 minutes. Add the tomatoes, tomato paste, red wine, oregano, and pepper. Bring to a boil, reduce the heat to low, and cook, stirring often, until the sauce is thickened, about 20 minutes.

2. In a heavy medium saucepan, melt the butter over moderately low heat. Whisk in the flour and cook, whisking often, for 2 minutes, without letting the mixture brown. Whisk in the milk and bring to a boil. Reduce the heat to low and simmer, whisking often, until thickened, about 2 minutes. In a large bowl, beat the eggs well. Gradually whisk the sauce into the eggs. Stir in ½ cup of the grated cheese. Set the cheese sauce aside.

3. Preheat the oven to 350 degrees. Lightly oil a 9-by-13-inch baking dish. Using the thin-slicing blade of a food processor or a sharp knife, very thinly slice the potatoes. Cut the zucchini lengthwise into ¼-inch-thick slices. Arrange the potatoes in an even layer in the bottom of the prepared baking dish and season with the salt. Spread the ground turkey mixture evenly over

the potatoes. Arrange the zucchini slices, slightly overlapping, over the turkey filling. Spread the cheese sauce evenly over the top of the zucchini and sprinkle with the remaining ½ cup of grated cheese.

4. Bake for 50 minutes to 1 hour, until the casserole is bubbling and the top is golden brown. Let stand 10 minutes before cutting into squares to serve.

▶ *In 1939, President Franklin D. Roosevelt changed the date of Thanksgiving from the last Thursday in November to the third Thursday, hoping to lengthen the Christmas season and spur sales during the Depression. After two dismal years, the tradition was changed back to its original date.*

Turkey in Mole Poblano

Christmas in Mexico means a special dish to fit the occasion—Turkey in Mole Poblano. Bitter chocolate and sweet raisins and spices have been combined with chilies and nuts since the days of the Aztecs to make this unique sauce. It may take a little extra effort to obtain a couple of the authentic ingredients in this recipe, but it's worth it.

The mole sauce is made a day ahead to allow it to mellow, so be sure to begin this recipe two days before you plan to serve it.

Makes 10 to 12 servings

¼ cup sesame seeds
½ teaspoon coriander seeds
½ teaspoon aniseed
1⅓ cups lard or vegetable oil
¾ cup blanched almonds
1 corn tortilla, torn into eighths
14 dried ancho chilies, stemmed, seeded, and deribbed (see Note)
4 cups Homemade Turkey Stock (page 246), or 2 cups canned chicken broth mixed with 2 cups water
½ cup raisins

1 medium onion, coarsely chopped
2 garlic cloves, crushed
1 cup drained and rinsed canned tomatillos (see Note)
½ teaspoon ground cinnamon
½ teaspoon ground cloves
2 tablespoons plus 1 teaspoon salt
1½ ounces unsweetened chocolate, chopped
1 hen turkey (12 pounds), cut into 8 serving pieces, back discarded
4 quarts water

1. In a large dry skillet, toast the sesame seeds over moderately high heat, stirring, until fragrant, about 1 minute. Transfer to a plate and let cool completely. Remove 2 tablespoons of the sesame seeds and reserve for garnish. Repeat the procedure two more times, first with the coriander seeds and then with the aniseed.

2. Add ½ cup of the lard to the skillet and heat over moderately high heat until hot but not smoking. Add the almonds and fry, stirring often, until golden brown, about 1 minute. With a slotted spoon, transfer the nuts to the plate with the toasted seeds. Add the tortilla pieces and fry, turning once, until golden brown, about 1 minute; transfer to the same plate.

3. Add the chilies to the hot lard and cook, turning once with tongs, until pliable, 20 to 30 seconds; do not burn. Transfer the chilies to a large bowl.

In a small saucepan, bring 2 cups of the stock to a boil; pour over the chilies. Let soak for 30 minutes to soften. Discard the lard.

4. In a food processor, combine the chilies with their soaking liquid, the toasted seeds and almonds, tortilla pieces, raisins, onion, garlic, tomatillos, cinnamon, cloves, and 1 teaspoon of the salt. Puree until the mole is very smooth.

5. In a large flameproof casserole, heat ⅓ cup of the lard over moderate heat. Add the mole sauce, averting your face to avoid splatters, and cook, stirring often, for 5 minutes. Add the chocolate and cook, stirring, until melted, about 2 minutes. Stir in the remaining 2 cups stock. Remove the mole sauce from the heat and let cool, then cover and refrigerate at least 1 and up to 2 days before completing the recipe.

6. In a large stockpot, bring the turkey, water, and 2 tablespoons salt to a boil over high heat, skimming off any foam that rises to the surface. Reduce the heat to low and simmer 1 hour; the turkey will be only partially cooked. Using tongs, transfer the turkey to a colander and let drain, then pat dry thoroughly with paper towels. Discard the cooking liquid.

7. In a large skillet, heat the remaining ½ cup lard over moderately high heat until hot but not smoking. In batches, fry the turkey, turning often and adjusting the heat as necessary to avoid burning, until the pieces are nicely browned all over, about 10 minutes per batch. Remove with tongs and drain on paper towels.

8. Preheat the oven to 350 degrees. In a large flameproof casserole, bring the mole sauce to a simmer, stirring, over moderately low heat. Add the turkey and transfer to the oven. Bake, covered, until the turkey shows no sign of pink when pierced with the tip of a knife, 30 to 45 minutes. If the sauce seems too thick at this point, thin with a little additional stock or water. If it is too thin, boil to reduce on top of the stove, stirring often to avoid scorching. Transfer the turkey to a large serving platter, pour the mole sauce on top, and garnish with the reserved 2 tablespoons sesame seeds.

Note: Dried ancho chilies and canned tomatillos can be ordered from Dean and Deluca, 800-221-7714; 212-431-1691.

Turkey with Mole Verde Sauce

The first time I enjoyed this dish, it was served cold on a beautiful buffet at Beringer Vineyards in St. Helena, California. My fellow diners and I were so impressed by the enticing combination of flavors that we stormed the kitchen to search out the recipe from the sous chef, Joseph Costanzo. Turkey in Mole Verde (green mole, made so by the cilantro, tomatillos, and lettuce) is also excellent served hot, even over cooked pasta.

Makes 6 to 8 servings

6 cups water
1¾ cups canned chicken broth (14-ounce can)
1 large onion, sliced, plus 1 small onion, quartered
1 medium celery rib, chopped
2 garlic cloves, crushed
4 sprigs of parsley
1½ teaspoons salt
¼ teaspoon peppercorns
1 whole turkey breast (4½ pounds), bone in, skin on, halved lengthwise (see page 93)

1 can (13 ounces) tomatillos, drained and rinsed
½ cup blanched slivered almonds, toasted (see page 229)
8 large romaine lettuce leaves
1 jalapeño pepper, seeded, or 2 tablespoons canned green chilies
2 tablespoons chopped fresh cilantro
¼ teaspoon ground cinnamon
¼ teaspoon ground cloves

1. In a large saucepan or flameproof casserole, combine the water, chicken broth, sliced onion, celery, 1 garlic clove, the parsley, 1 teaspoon of the salt, and the peppercorns. Bring to a simmer over moderately high heat. Cook for 15 minutes. Add the turkey breast halves and return to a simmer. Reduce the heat to low, cover, and simmer until a meat thermometer inserted in the thickest part of the meat reads 160 to 165 degrees, 40 to 45 minutes. Let the breast cool completely in the cooking liquid. Remove the turkey; reserve ½ cup of the cooking liquid. Remove and discard the skin and bones and cut the turkey into 1-inch chunks.

2. In a food processor or blender, combine the tomatillos, almonds, 3 romaine leaves, the quartered onion, jalapeño pepper, cilantro, remaining garlic, remaining ½ teaspoon salt, cinnamon, and cloves. With the machine on,

add the reserved ½ cup cooking liquid. Transfer to a large nonreactive skillet and simmer over moderately low heat for 5 minutes. Let cool completely.

3. In a large bowl, toss the turkey breast cubes and about half of the mole verde. On a large platter, arrange the remaining lettuce leaves. Place the turkey on the lettuce leaves and pour the remaining sauce on top. (To serve warm, add the turkey chunks to the simmering sauce and cook for about 5 minutes, stirring often, until the turkey is heated through.)

Daube of Turkey

Daube is to stew what caviar is to fish eggs. They are what they are, but in a class by themselves. Cut up the turkey as you would a chicken to end up with 2 drumsticks, 2 thighs, 2 wings, and 2 breast halves. Start by marinating turkey pieces in a marinade of white wine, olive oil, and brandy with aromatic herbs and vegetables. Braise the turkey in this same marinade, and quickly boil the resulting juices down to concentrate the essences. If you have the time and the self-control, refrigerate the daube overnight and reheat slowly; you'll be rewarded for your patience.

Makes 10 to 14 servings

1 hen turkey (12 pounds), cut into 8
    pieces, back discarded
¾ cup plus 2 tablespoons olive oil
6 cups dry white wine
½ cup Cognac or brandy
2 medium onions, chopped
2 large carrots, cut into ½-inch dice
2 shallots, minced
1 head of garlic, halved
    crosswise
1 teaspoon dried thyme

½ teaspoon freshly ground pepper
2 bay leaves
½ pound pork rind (see Note)
½ pound salt pork, rind removed
2 pigs' feet, split (optional)
1 can (14 ounces) Italian peeled
    tomatoes, drained and coarsely
    chopped
10 ounces medium mushrooms,
    quartered
Salt

1. Rinse the turkey pieces under cold running water and pat dry with paper towels. With a heavy cleaver or sharp knife, cut the breasts crosswise into two pieces each. In a large skillet, heat ¼ cup of the oil. In batches, add the turkey pieces and cook, turning often, until browned, about 10 minutes per batch. Transfer the browned turkey pieces to a baking sheet and reserve.

2. In a large flameproof casserole or a dark blue enameled roaster, combine ½ cup of olive oil, the wine, Cognac, onions, carrots, shallots, garlic, thyme, pepper, and bay leaves. Add the browned turkey pieces, cover, and refrigerate, turning the turkey occasionally in the marinade, for at least 4 hours or overnight.

3. Meanwhile, place the pork rind, salt pork, and pigs' feet in a large stock-

pot or very large saucepan. Fill with cold water and bring to a boil over moderately high heat. Cook 5 minutes, drain, and rinse.

4. Cut the pork rind into ½-inch squares and reserve. Cut the salt pork into ½-by-½-by-2-inch pieces. In a skillet, heat the remaining 2 tablespoons olive oil. Add the salt pork and cook over moderate heat, stirring often, until the pieces are browned, about 10 minutes. With a slotted spoon, transfer to paper towels to drain. (The daube can be prepared up to this point 1 day ahead. Cover all ingredients separately and refrigerate.)

5. Preheat the oven to 325 degrees. Remove the turkey pieces from the marinade. Place the pigs' feet in the marinade. Stir the pork rind, salt pork pieces, tomatoes, and mushrooms into the marinade. Return the turkey pieces to the marinade, placing the dark meat on the bottom and the white meat on top. Bring the daube to a simmer on top of the stove over moderate heat.

6. Transfer to the oven and bake, covered, until a meat thermometer inserted in the meatiest part of a breast piece registers 170 degrees, about 1¼ hours. With tongs, transfer the breast pieces to a baking sheet and cover with aluminum foil to keep warm. Continue cooking the dark meat until a meat thermometer inserted in the meatiest part of the thigh registers 180 degrees, 20 to 30 additional minutes. Remove and discard the pigs' feet. Transfer the dark pieces to the platter and cover with aluminum foil.

7. On top of the stove, boil the cooking juices over high heat until reduced by half, about 20 minutes. Season with additional pepper and salt to taste. Return the turkey pieces to the casserole and cook, turning the pieces in the sauce, until heated through, about 5 minutes. Transfer the turkey pieces to a warmed, very large serving platter and pour the sauce over them.

Note: Pork rind can be specially ordered from butchers or found in many ethnic markets. The rind from salt pork or salt fatback can be used if it is covered with cold water, brought to a boil, cooked for 5 minutes, drained, and rinsed well.

Old-Fashioned French Turkey Confit

For all of the low-fat benefits of turkey, sometimes a recipe just isn't right without the flavor of good ol' lard. I know, because I've tried to make *confit* the new-fashioned way, using "healthier" vegetable shortening, and it was a pale substitute for the real thing. Besides, the fat isn't actually consumed, so relax a little. Originally, *confit* (pronounced "cone-*fee*"), a French stew in which the poultry is cooked in rendered fat, was a time-honored method of preserving meat. Today we enjoy it (usually at a high price at expensive French restaurants) for its unsurpassable taste—complex, yet comforting, simple, and straightforward. Nothing goes better with *confit* than thinly sliced potatoes fried in a little of the cooking lard, sprinkled with minced parsley and garlic. Be sure to allow 24 hours for the turkey thighs to marinate and at least 3 days for the *confit* to cure.

Makes 4 servings

4 turkey thighs (about 12 ounces each)	1 teaspoon coarsely cracked peppercorns
2 tablespoons kosher (coarse) salt	1 bay leaf, crumbled
2 tablespoons minced shallots	1/8 teaspoon dried thyme
2 tablespoons minced fresh parsley	Pinch of ground cloves or allspice
1 garlic clove, minced	6 cups pork lard (see Note)
	Vegetable shortening (optional)

1. Rinse the turkey thighs under cold running water and pat dry with paper towels. In a medium bowl, combine the salt, shallots, parsley, garlic, peppercorns, bay leaf, thyme, and cloves. Rub the thighs well with the seasoned salt, place in the bowl, cover, and refrigerate for at least 16 and up to 24 hours. Using a clean kitchen towel or paper towels, brush the seasoned salt off the thighs and wipe them dry.

2. In a large saucepan, slowly melt the lard over very low heat. Add the thighs, making sure they are submerged in the lard. (If necessary, add enough vegetable shortening to cover.) Cook until the thighs are tender enough to be pierced easily with a toothpick, about 1½ hours. With tongs, transfer the thighs to a plate and reserve.

3. Increase the heat to moderately high and cook, skimming often, until the lard stops sputtering and is clear yellow, and the bubbles on the surface decrease in size from quite large to small, 15 to 20 minutes. Strain the lard through a fine sieve into a bowl. Pour about 1 inch of the lard into the bottom of a medium bowl and freeze until the lard is solid, about 30 minutes. Place the reserved thighs in the bowl and cover completely with the remaining lard. (If necessary, add additional vegetable shortening, melted, to cover the thighs.) Let cool, cover tightly, and refrigerate for at least 3 days and up to 1 week. (The *confit* will improve in flavor as it ages but should not be stored longer than 1 week.) When ready to serve, place the bowl of *confit* in a larger bowl of hot water and let stand for about 1 hour, until the lard has softened enough to allow for easy removal of the thighs.

4. Heat 2 tablespoons of the lard in a skillet over moderate heat. Place the thighs, skin down, in the skillet. Cover tightly and cook for 2 minutes. Rotate the thighs slightly to prevent sticking, cover, and cook for 3 minutes. Reduce the heat to low, turn the thighs over, and cook until the meat is completely heated through, about 10 minutes. Drain on paper towels to remove as much fat as possible before serving.

Note: Please try not to use packaged supermarket lard for this recipe. Freshly rendered lard can often be purchased from some butchers; it is also easy to make your own. Coarsely chop 6 pounds of fresh, firm white pork fat in a food processor or by hand. Place the chopped fat in a large saucepan with 2 cups of cold water. Slowly bring to a simmer over low heat. Cook very slowly for 2½ to 3 hours, until the fat has all melted, the liquid fat is clear yellow, and the fat solids have turned into crisp brown cracklings. Strain the lard, cool, cover, and refrigerate for up to 3 months. Reserve the cracklings to use sprinkled on salads, in omelets, or as a snack.

Galantine of Turkey

An elegant showstopper, a turkey galantine is a poached boned breast that has been stuffed and rolled so that when sliced, it reveals a colorful mosaic of green pistachio nuts, black olives, and pink ham strips. It is picture perfect for a wedding buffet. Because the galantine must be made ahead of time, serving is effortless.

A turkey-stock glaze lightly coats each slice. Decorate with simple carved vegetables, such as radish roses or tomato curls, or use my time-saving trick: garnish the platter with loads of splashy fresh flowers, such as mums and zinnias.

Makes 12 to 15 servings

1 whole turkey breast (about 5 pounds), bone in, skin on
2 cups dry white wine
2 tablespoons Cognac or brandy
1 medium shallot or white of scallion, minced
8 sprigs of parsley
½ teaspoon peppercorns
1 teaspoon dried thyme
1 teaspoon salt
1 bay leaf
¼ pound boiled ham, in a single thick slice, cut into strips ½ inch wide
2 ounces pork fatback, cut into ½-inch cubes and chilled (see Note)

¾ pound ground turkey
¼ cup fresh bread crumbs
1 large egg, lightly beaten
½ teaspoon ground allspice
¼ teaspoon freshly ground pepper
Pinch of ground cloves
½ cup shelled pistachios
12 pitted black olives
4 cups Homemade Turkey Stock (page 246), or 2 cups canned chicken broth mixed with 2 cups water
1 cup water
1 envelope unflavored gelatin
¼ cup cold water

1. Ask your butcher to bone out the turkey breast or do it yourself as follows: Using a sharp, thin-bladed knife, cut down one side of the backbone. Using short strokes with the tip of the knife pointing toward the bone, scrape down the bone, pulling the meat and skin back as you work down the breast. Repeat on the other side. Then carefully cut the meat away from the center of the breastbone, taking care not to cut through the skin.

2. Locate the tenderloins on the breast, thin lobes of meat that run along each side. Separate them and cut away and discard the white tendon that runs down each tenderloin. Cut the tenderloins lengthwise into strips ½ inch wide. (The breast can be boned up to 2 days ahead, wrapped well, and refrigerated.)

3. In a large bowl, combine 1 cup of the wine, the Cognac, shallot, parsley, peppercorns, ½ teaspoon of the thyme, ¼ teaspoon of the salt, and the bay leaf. Add the boned turkey breast, the cubed tenderloin, and the ham strips. Cover and marinate in the refrigerator, turning the meats occasionally, at least 8 hours or overnight.

4. Shortly before assembling the galantine, remove the meats from the marinade and wipe away the seasonings. Strain and reserve ¼ cup of the marinade. In a food processor, finely chop the chilled fatback. Add the ground turkey, bread crumbs, egg, reserved marinade, ¾ teaspoon salt, ½ teaspoon thyme, the allspice, pepper, and cloves; pulse to combine. Transfer to a medium bowl and stir in the pistachios.

5. To assemble the galantine, rinse a large double thickness of cheesecloth under cold running water; squeeze dry. Lay the cheesecloth on a flat work surface. Place the turkey breast, long sides running horizontally, on the cheesecloth. Spread the filling evenly over the turkey, leaving a 1-inch border around all four sides. Alternately arrange the turkey tenderloin and ham strips perpendicular to the long sides over the filling. Trim the ends of the strips, if necessary, to fit. Place the olives in a row parallel to the ham and tenderloin strips down the middle of the breast. Using the cheesecloth as an aid and starting at a short end, roll the breast firmly into a snug cylinder, keeping the cheesecloth as an outside wrap. Twist the ends of the cheesecloth to enclose the rolled turkey securely and tie with white kitchen string. Tie the galantine crosswise in four or five places to help it hold its shape during cooking.

6. In an oval flameproof casserole or a large saucepan, heat the oil. Add the galantine and cook over moderate heat, turning often, until browned all over, about 10 minutes. Add the stock, remaining 1 cup wine, and the 1 cup water. Bring to a simmer, skimming off any foam. Reduce the heat to low and simmer, partially covered, turning the breast over after 40 minutes, until a meat thermometer inserted in the center of the galantine reads 160 degrees, about 1¼ hours. Let the galantine cool in the stock for 2 hours.

7. Remove the galantine from the stock and wrap tightly in aluminum foil. Place in a large loaf pan or on a baking sheet. Cover with another loaf pan of the same size or a board and weight down with heavy cans; refrigerate overnight. (The weighting is an optional step, but it packs down the stuffing

(continued)

and ensures easy slicing.) Let the stock cool to room temperature and refrigerate overnight.

8. Up to 6 hours before serving, in a large saucepan, boil the turkey stock over high heat until reduced to 2 cups, 20 to 30 minutes. Meanwhile, sprinkle the gelatin over the ¼ cup cold water, and let stand for 5 minutes to soften. Stir the softened gelatin into the stock. Cook, stirring, until the gelatin dissolves, 2 to 3 minutes. Pour into a medium bowl set in a larger bowl half filled with ice and water. Let the stock cool, stirring occasionally and adding more ice cubes as necessary, until the stock is syrupy but not set.

9. While the stock is chilling, unwrap the galantine, discarding the foil, string, and cheesecloth. Use a long sharp knife to cut the galantine into ½-inch-thick slices. Arrange them, overlapping, on a large platter. Brush the syrupy stock over the galantine slices and refrigerate, uncovered, for 5 minutes to set the glaze. (If the stock sets while you're working, warm briefly over low heat to melt, stirring until smooth; repeat the cooling process until syrupy.) The galantine can be sliced and glazed up to 6 hours ahead, loosely covered with wax paper, and refrigerated. Remove from the refrigerator about 30 minutes before serving.

> *Note: Fresh pork fatback is available at many supermarkets and most butchers. If your butcher doesn't carry it, ask for the fat trimmings from pork loins. Salted pork fatback can be substituted, but it must be simmered first in water for about 5 minutes to reduce the saltiness.*

CHAPTER EIGHT

Turkey on the Grill

I was raised in northern California, where outdoor grilling was an everyday occasion. Many Californians even cook their Thanksgiving turkey on the grill, somewhat in the style of my Spice-Rubbed Smoked Turkey with Bourbon Soppin' Sauce (page 222). Now that I live on the East Coast, I am constantly trying to devise ways to use my covered kettle grill year-round.

When the weather is cooperating, outdoor grilling is one of the most interesting ways to cook. Turkey is the perfect meat for outdoor cooks, especially those who are watching their fat intake.

The most important aspect of outdoor grilling is heat control. It is important to know how hot your coals are in order to avoid overcooked turkey. As in other methods of cooking turkey, *moderate* heat is the key to successful results. I build a charcoal fire, estimating about 5 pounds of briquets for a standard grill, and then let it burn down until the coals are covered with white ash and the fire is moderately hot. In order to test the heat, hold your hand palm-side down over the coals at cooking height. If you can hold it there for 1 to 2 seconds, the coals are hot; 3 means they are moderate, 5 seconds, low. If you are in a hurry and can't wait, spread the coals out in an even layer. The coals in the center of the grill will be hot, but you can arrange your turkey on the outside of the coals for moderate heat. Open vents fan the fire and make more intense heat, and closed vents make a slower fire.

There are three cooking procedures for basic grilling: *direct heat, foil-wrapped,* and *indirect heat.*

Direct heat is used for turkey products that will cook in less than 25 minutes, such as Grilled Turkey Fajitas and Turkey Thighs and Summer Vegetable Kebabs. Cook over moderate coals, 4 to 6 inches away from the heat source, turning the meat and basting with some of the marinade often. You can cover the grill for quicker cooking and to discourage flare-ups.

For less tender cuts that need a longer cooking time, use the foil-wrap technique. Guadalajara Grilled Drumsticks and Grilled Turkey Teriyaki with Mushrooms and Scallions use this method. Wrap the meat (with some of its marinade, if desired) in heavy-duty aluminum foil, dull side out. Grill until almost done, then remove the foil and place the turkey directly on the grill to encourage browning.

Indirect heat is used for slower cooking of large turkey parts or whole turkeys. A covered grill is needed for this kind of cooking, because it traps the hot air needed to create a proper cooking environment. A moderate-heat fire is built and banked on one side of the grill. Center a flameproof drip pan (I use a disposable aluminum pan) on the bottom of the grill. Bank two mounds of charcoal on either side of the pan, and let them burn down to moderately hot. The turkey is placed over the drip pan, covered, and cooked slowly to juicy perfection. Do not open the grill often, as the heat will be released. You may have to stoke the fire with additional coals to maintain a constant temperature. I have an inexpensive hibachi to keep the extra coals going on the side. Alternatively, you can add raw coals to the two fires' outside edges, but I don't like to expose my food directly to the carbon gases and smoke released. Never add "instant-light" briquets to a covered grill fire, or your meat will taste like lighter fluid.

For indirect cooking on a gas grill, simply turn one side of the burners off, set a drip pan on the turned-off burners, and set the other to Medium. If you don't have dual control, cover one side with a double thickness of aluminum foil to effectively block the direct heat from this side.

Smoking is also possible in a covered grill, using a variation on the indirect method. Sprinkle well-soaked and drained wood chips (available at hardware and outdoor living stores) over a small fire of low-burning coals to create an aromatic smoke that will flavor the meat.

Mesquite, hickory, and apple smoke enhance turkey nicely, but experiment with other woods, too.

To maintain steady, low heat and a smoky cooking atmosphere under the hood, add 10 to 12 additional hot coals and a handful of chips about every 45 minutes and keep the vents closed. The temperature should range from 190 to 225 degrees. To check the temperature, place an oven thermometer over the drip pan. Home-smoked meats should be stored in the refrigerator for no longer than 3 days.

For rotisseries and water smokers, follow the manufacturers' instructions.

Here are some other grilling hints:

▶ Weather will often affect grilling times, so take account of cool temperatures and windy or damp conditions.

▶ Never turn your turkey with a pronged barbeque fork, since piercing the meat will release precious juices. Turn with tongs, instead.

▶ If you are using a tomato-based or sweet basting sauce, use it toward the end of the grilling period, or else the sauce will scorch. If you marinate your turkey in such a sauce, cook it by the foil-wrapped method. Remove the turkey from the foil and grill briefly over direct heat at the end to allow the skin to crisp.

▶ Lightly grease the grill rack before use, and use an oil-based marinade to reduce the chances of the turkey meat sticking.

Guadalajara Grilled Drumsticks

Mexicans perfected the *barbacoa*—a grilling party that became our barbeque. This marinade is based on a recipe I learned many years ago at a backyard party in Guadalajara. I've lightened it with low-fat yogurt in place of the traditional sour cream. The double-cooking technique works wonders on large, tougher pieces of turkey such as drumsticks, wings, and thighs.

Makes 4 servings

4 turkey drumsticks
  (about 12 ounces each)
1 cup low-fat plain yogurt
2 tablespoons lime juice
1 small onion, finely chopped

2 garlic cloves, minced
1 teaspoon ground cumin
1 teaspoon dried oregano
1 teaspoon salt

1. Using the tip of a sharp knife, pierce the turkey drumsticks all over. In a medium bowl, mix the yogurt, lime juice, onion, garlic, cumin, oregano, and salt. Add the drumsticks and toss to coat. Cover tightly and refrigerate for at least 6 hours or overnight.

2. Remove the drumsticks from the marinade; reserve the marinade. Place 1 drumstick with 3 tablespoons of the marinade on the bottom half of a 12-inch square of heavy-duty aluminum foil. Fold the foil over to enclose the drumstick, then tightly crimp the 3 open sides to seal. Repeat with the remaining 3 drumsticks and marinade.

3. In a covered grill, light a hot charcoal fire. (You should be able to hold your hand over the fire for only 1 or 2 seconds.) Grill the drumsticks in their foil packets 6 inches from the coals, covered, turning often, until the drumsticks are almost tender, 45 minutes to 1 hour. (Unwrap a packet to check for doneness.)

4. Unwrap the drumsticks, pouring the juices from the packet into a bowl. Return the unwrapped drumsticks to the grill and continue to cook, covered, turning and basting often with the reserved juices, until browned outside, with no sign of pink when the drumsticks are pierced with the tip of a sharp knife, about 15 minutes.

Turkey Thighs and Summer Vegetable Kebabs

Barbeque enthusiasts jealously guard their secret recipes for "dry rub," a heady blend of dried herbs and spices. This five-alarm seasoning is rubbed onto the meat and left to stand as a "dry" marinade. Dark meat stands up well to this treatment, making these colorful kebabs—with chunks of corn, zucchini, red pepper, and onion—irresistible.

Makes 6 servings

3 turkey thighs (about 12 ounces each), skinned and boned
5 teaspoons chili powder
1½ teaspoons garlic salt
1½ teaspoons paprika
¼ teaspoon cayenne pepper
1 large red bell pepper, cut into 12 chunks

1 large zucchini, cut crosswise into 6 chunks
1 large ear of corn, cut crosswise into 6 chunks
2 medium onions, cut into 6 wedges each
⅓ cup olive oil
2 tablespoons lime juice

1. Pound the turkey thighs to flatten slightly. Cut each thigh into 8 cubes about 1½ inches square. In a medium bowl, combine the chili powder, garlic salt, paprika, and cayenne. Add the turkey cubes and toss to coat. Cover tightly and refrigerate at least 4 hours or overnight.

2. Thread the turkey cubes onto metal skewers alternately with the red pepper, zucchini, corn, and onions. (Wooden skewers may not pierce the corn cobs.) In a small bowl, whisk the olive oil and lime juice, and brush the kebabs with some of the mixture.

3. Light a charcoal fire. Let the coals burn down until the fire is moderately hot. (You should be able to hold your hand over the fire for 3 seconds.) Grill the kebabs 6 inches from the coals, turning and basting with the remaining oil and lime juice, until the turkey shows no sign of pink when pierced with the tip of a knife, 8 to 10 minutes.

Turkey Fajitas

Fajitas, grilled turkey cutlets and onions tucked into tortillas and served with dollops of guacamole, salsa, or sour cream, are definitely fun food, just the thing for a family get-together. This recipe extends easily, the cutlets cook quite quickly, even in large numbers, and all of the side dishes can be prepared well ahead of time.

Makes 4 servings

1¼ cups olive oil
⅓ cup lime juice
3 tablespoons Worcestershire sauce
1 garlic clove, minced
2 jalapeño peppers, seeded and minced, or ¼ cup canned chopped green chilies
2 teaspoons dried oregano
1 teaspoon ground cumin

½ teaspoon salt
¼ teaspoon freshly ground pepper
6 turkey breast cutlets
  (about 4 ounces each)
2 medium onions
12 flour tortillas
Guacamole (see below)
Fresh Tomato Salsa (page 57)
1½ cups sour cream

1. In a large bowl, combine 1 cup of the olive oil, the lime juice, Worcestershire, garlic, jalapeño peppers, oregano, cumin, salt, and pepper. Add the turkey cutlets and mix to combine. Cover tightly and refrigerate for 2 to 4 hours. Do not overmarinate.

2. Cut the onions into ½-inch rounds. Do not separate the rings. Marinate the onion rounds in the remaining ¼ cup olive oil until ready to grill.

3. Light a charcoal fire. Let the coals burn down until the fire is moderately hot. (You should be able to hold your hand over the fire for 3 seconds.) Stack the tortillas and wrap them in a double thickness of aluminum foil. Heat the tortillas on the outside edge of the grill, turning the packet often, until the tortillas are warmed through, about 15 minutes.

4. Remove the turkey cutlets from the marinade; reserve the marinade. Grill the turkey cutlets and onions 6 inches over the coals, turning and basting with the reserved marinade often, until the turkey is cooked through, 6 to 8 minutes. Transfer the cutlers and onion rounds to a serving platter. Cut the turkey vertically into ¼-inch-wide strips.

5. Unwrap the tortillas. To serve, put a few slices of turkey and some cooked onions onto each tortilla. Garnish with the salsa, guacamole, and sour cream to taste. Roll up the tortilla and eat.

REDUCED-FAT VARIATION: Reduce oil to ½ cup. Use ⅓ cup for marinade. Marinate for 1 hour only. Brush onion rounds with remaining oil. Substitute imitation sour cream or low-fat yogurt for the sour cream. Omit guacamole and use extra salsa.

▶ *For a quick Guacamole, mash together with a fork 2 ripe avocados, pitted and skinned (preferably the black-skinned Hass variety); 1 ripe tomato, seeded and chopped; 2 tablespoons chopped onion; 1 jalapeño pepper, seeded and minced; 1 garlic clove, minced; 1 tablespoon lime juice; and 1 teaspoon salt. To store overnight, press plastic wrap directly on the surface of the guacamole and refrigerate.*

Indonesian Turkey Satés with Peanut Dip

Whether grilled outdoors or popped into the broiler, these marinated strips of turkey with a gingery peanut dip never fail to please. Be sure to use unsalted and unsweetened peanut butter, available in supermarkets or health-food stores, or your seasoning will be thrown off.

Makes about 24 satés

¼ cup plus 1 teaspoon lime juice
¼ cup low-sodium soy sauce
1 tablespoon brown sugar
2 tablespoons minced onion
1 tablespoon plus one teaspoon
  minced fresh ginger
3 garlic cloves, minced
½ teaspoon crushed hot pepper flakes
4 turkey cutlets (about 4 ounces each),
  cut into 1-by-3-inch strips

24 wooden skewers, soaked in water
  for 1 hour to prevent burning
1 tablespoon unsalted butter
2 medium shallots, minced
1 teaspoon curry powder
½ cup *unsalted* peanut butter, stirred
  well
½ cup heavy (whipping) cream
¼ cup canned chicken broth

1. In a medium bowl, combine ¼ cup lime juice, 3 tablespoons soy sauce, 2 teaspoons brown sugar, the onion, 2 teaspoons ginger, 2 garlic cloves, and ¼ teaspoon hot pepper flakes. Add the turkey strips and toss to coat. Cover and refrigerate, stirring often, for at least 1 and up to 4 hours. Thread the strips onto the wooden skewers.

2. In a small saucepan, melt the butter over moderately low heat. Add the shallots, curry powder, and the remaining 2 teaspoons ginger and 1 garlic clove, and cook, stirring, until the shallots are softened, about 1 minute. Transfer the vegetables to a blender or food processor. Add the peanut butter and the remaining 1 teaspoon lime juice, 1 tablespoon soy sauce, 1 teaspoon brown sugar, and ¼ teaspoon hot pepper flakes. With the machine on, add the heavy cream and chicken broth; blend until smooth. Transfer the sauce to a small saucepan and bring to a simmer over low heat, stirring; keep the sauce warm.

3. Light a charcoal fire, letting the coals burn down until it is moderately hot. (You should be able to hold your hand over the fire for 3 seconds.) Lightly oil the grilling rack. Grill the satés, with the skewers hanging over the edge of the grill to prevent scorching, turning often, until the turkey is

cooked through, about 5 to 7 minutes. To broil, adjust the broiler rack about 4 inches from the heat and preheat. Wrap the handle of each skewer in aluminum foil, if desired, to prevent scorching. Broil, turning often, until cooked through, 4 to 6 minutes. Serve the satés immediately with the warm peanut dipping sauce.

▶ *The first department store–sponsored Thanksgiving day parade was presented in 1923 by Gimbel's in Philadelphia. Macy's in New York copied the tradition in 1924.*

Grilled Turkey Teriyaki
with Mushrooms and Scallions

A sweet-and-sour teriyaki marinade is always popular on grilled poultry. The mushrooms and scallions are cooked alongside during the last minutes, making for a nearly instant side dish.

Makes 4 servings

½ cup soy sauce
¼ cup dry sherry
2 tablespoons fresh lemon
  juice
1 tablespoon minced fresh
  ginger
2 teaspoons brown sugar

⅛ teaspoon hot pepper sauce, or more
  to taste
1 garlic clove, minced
1 turkey breast half (about 2 pounds),
  bone in, skin on
12 medium mushrooms
12 medium scallions

1. In a large bowl, combine the soy sauce, sherry, lemon juice, ginger, brown sugar, hot pepper sauce, and garlic. Pour ¼ cup of the marinade into a small bowl and set aside. Add the turkey breast to the large bowl; turn to coat. Cover tightly and refrigerate, turning occasionally, for at least 1 and up to 4 hours.

2. Remove the turkey breast from the marinade; reserve the marinade. Place the turkey breast on the lower half of a large sheet of heavy-duty aluminum foil. Crimp up the edges to form a low border. Pour in ⅓ cup of the marinade. Fold the foil over to enclose the breast, then tightly crimp the 3 open sides.

3. Thread the mushroom caps on skewers. Trim the scallions, leaving only about 2 inches of the green tops.

4. Light a hot charcoal fire. (You should only be able to hold your hand over the fire for 1 to 2 seconds.) Grill the breast in the foil packet 6 inches from the coals, turning once, for 20 minutes. Unwrap the turkey breast, pouring the juices from the packet into a bowl. Grill the unwrapped turkey breast, turning and basting often with the reserved juices, until browned outside with no sign of pink when pierced with the tip of a sharp knife, 10 to 15 minutes. A meat thermometer inserted in the meatiest part of the breast will register 165 degrees. During the last 10 minutes of cooking, add

the mushrooms to the grill, turning and basting often with the reserved ¼ cup marinade. During the last 5 minutes of cooking, add the scallions to the grill, also turning and basting often with the reserved marinade.

Grilled Turkey Steaks Romano

Turkey steaks are cut a bit thicker than cutlets. They are just the thing to serve to hungry guys who want something they can really tear into. These herbed steaks are quickly grilled over a charcoal fire, then topped with a thin slice of low-fat mozzarella. While delicious on their own, you may want to serve a dab of pesto or salsa on the side as a quick sauce.

Makes 2 to 3 servings

¼ cup olive oil
2 tablespoons chopped fresh basil, or
    2 teaspoons dried
1 tablespoon chopped fresh rosemary,
    or 1 teaspoon dried
2 garlic cloves, minced
½ teaspoon salt

¼ teaspoon freshly ground pepper
2 turkey steaks
    (about 8 ounces each)
2 slices low-fat mozzarella cheese, cut
    to fit turkey steaks
Fresh whole large basil leaves, for
    garnish (optional)

1. In a large bowl, combine the olive oil, basil, rosemary, garlic, salt, and pepper. Add the turkey steaks and turn to coat. Cover and refrigerate for at least 1 and up to 4 hours.

2. In a covered grill, light a charcoal fire. Let the coals burn down to moderately hot. (You should be able to hold your hand over the fire for 3 seconds.) Remove the turkey steaks from the marinade. Grill them 6 inches above the coals for 4 minutes. Turn and place the cheese on the steaks, cover the grill, and continue grilling until the turkey is cooked through and the cheese is melted, 3 to 4 minutes. Top each steak with several fresh basil leaves, if you have them.

Lucky's Turkey Pizza with Fresh Tomato Sauce, Olives, and Jalapeños

Johanne Killeen and George Germon have become justifiably famous for their Providence, Rhode Island, restaurants, Al Forno and Lucky's. One of their most spectacular creations is a smoky "BBQ'd" pizza, cooked over glowing hardwood coals directly on the grill. They were inspired to re-create an intriguing pizza recipe that a friend brought back from Italy, but it wasn't until they perfected their unusual grill-top method that they found out that the original instructions called for a wood-burning oven and not a grill. My adaptation of this sensational dish is not as difficult as it sounds, and the compliments you'll garner from incredulous guests will make any tentative moments worth the trouble.

Makes two 12-inch pizzas, 4 to 6 servings

¼ teaspoon sugar
1 cup warm (100 to 110 degrees) water
1 envelope (¼ ounce) active dry yeast
¼ cup plus 3 tablespoons olive oil
2½ cups all-purpose flour
¼ cup whole wheat flour
¼ cup jonnycake meal (see Note)
2½ teaspoons salt
4 turkey breast cutlets
  (about 4 ounces each)

¼ teaspoon freshly ground
  pepper
2 garlic cloves, finely chopped
1 cup grated Bel Paese or Fontina
  cheese (about 4 ounces)
Fresh Tomato Sauce (recipe follows)
2 fresh jalapeño peppers, minced
¼ cup coarsely chopped Kalamata
  black olives

1. In a glass measuring cup, dissolve the sugar in the warm water. Add the yeast and let stand until foamy, about 10 minutes. Stir to dissolve the yeast. Add 1 tablespoon of the olive oil to the yeast mixture.

2. In a food processor, pulse the flour, whole wheat flour, jonnycake meal, and 2¼ teaspoons of the salt to combine. With the machine on, add the yeast mixture through the feed tube in a steady stream. Process until the dough forms a ball on top of the blade. (If the dough is too wet or too dry, it will not form a ball. Feel the dough, and if it is sticky and wet, add additional flour, 2 tablespoons at a time, processing after each addition, until the dough forms a ball. If the dough is crumbly and dry, follow the same

procedure, adding additional water, 1 tablespoon at a time.) To knead, process the ball of dough for 45 seconds. (To make the dough by hand, in a large bowl, combine the flours, jonnycake meal, and salt. Make a well in the center and add the yeast mixture. Blend the flour into the well to make a stiff dough. Turn out onto a lightly floured surface and knead until smooth and elastic, about 10 minutes.)

3. Pour 2 tablespoons of the oil into a large bowl. Gather up the dough into a neat ball, place it in the bowl, and turn to coat completely with oil. Cover with a kitchen towel and set aside to rise in a warm draft-free spot until the dough is doubled in bulk, about 1 hour. Punch down the dough, cover, and let rise again until doubled in bulk.

4. In a covered grill, build a hardwood fire, using oak or mesquite, for example (though regular charcoal is also acceptable), banking the fire on one-half of the bottom of the grill, leaving the other side empty. Let the fire burn down until it is medium-hot. (You should be able to hold your hand over the fire for 3 to 4 seconds.) Lightly oil the grill rack. Brush both sides of the turkey cutlets lightly with some of the remaining olive oil and season with the remaining ¼ teaspoon salt and the pepper. Grill the turkey cutlets 6 inches over the coals, turning 2 or 3 times, until the turkey is just cooked through, about 6 to 8 minutes. Cut the cutlets into ¼-inch-wide strips.

5. Meanwhile, prepare the pizzas. Punch down the dough again. Divide the dough in half. On a lightly floured surface, roll out one-half of the dough into a 12-inch circle. Transfer the dough to a baking sheet dusted with cornmeal. Repeat the procedure with the remaining dough.

6. Place the garlic, cheese, tomato sauce, peppers, olives, and remaining olive oil in separate bowls and have them ready at the side of the grill. Brush one circle of dough with some of the olive oil. Slide it off the baking sheet onto the grill so only about one-third of it is over the coals. Cook, covered with the grill cover, for about 2 minutes, until the bottom of the dough is firm. With tongs, rotate the dough so another third is over the coals and cook for about 2 minutes, covered, until that portion is firm on the bottom. Rotate again, and cook, covered, until the last third is firm. Transfer the partially cooked pizza crust to a baking sheet, cover with foil, and repeat the procedure with the remaining dough.

7. Place both crusts, grilled-side up, over the empty side of the grill. Brush with the remaining olive oil. Sprinkle with the garlic, then the cheese. Spread the tomato sauce over the pies, then arrange the turkey slices in a spoke pattern over the sauce. Sprinkle the peppers and olives over the pizzas.

(continued)

Cover the grill and cook the pizzas, shifting the positions of the pizzas occasionally to be sure the bottoms do not scorch, until the cheese is melted and the sauce is hot, about 5 minutes. Transfer the pizzas to serving plates, cut into wedges, and serve immediately.

Note: If jonnycake meal is unavailable, process ¼ cup white cornmeal in a blender until finely ground.

Fresh Tomato Sauce

Italian plum tomatoes make the best tomato sauce, as they contain less water and seeds than the larger beefsteak varieties. Substitute canned Italian tomatoes, drained, for fresh plum tomatoes, rather than trying to use another variety of fresh tomato that may only give you a thin, tasteless sauce.

Makes 3 cups

3 tablespoons olive oil
2 garlic cloves, minced

2 pounds fresh Italian plum tomatoes, peeled, seeded, and chopped (see Note), or 1 can (35 ounces) Italian peeled tomatoes, drained
Salt

1. In a medium nonreactive saucepan, heat the olive oil. Add the garlic and cook over moderate heat, stirring constantly, until golden but not browned, about 1 minute.

2. Add the tomatoes and cook over high heat, stirring often, until the sauce begins to thicken, about 10 minutes. Season with salt to taste.

Note: To peel tomatoes easily, plunge them into boiling water for 1 minute, drain, rinse under cold running water, and drain well. Peel off loosened skin with a small, sharp knife. To remove seeds, cut tomatoes crosswise in half, and squeeze gently.

Marinated Turkey and Sausage Chunks on Skewers

Lemon juice, olive oil, bay leaf, spicy sausage—all ingredients that my Portuguese relatives use with abandon whenever they grill. As the skewers sizzle away, the sausages' juices baste and flavor the other ingredients. Use the most assertive sausage you can find.

Makes 6 servings

¾ cup olive oil
¼ cup lemon juice
1 teaspoon chopped fresh thyme,
   or ½ teaspoon dried
1 garlic clove, minced
13 bay leaves, 1 crumbled, 12 left
   whole
¾ teaspoon salt
¼ teaspoon freshly ground pepper

1 boneless turkey breast roast
   (about 1½ pounds), skin discarded,
   cut into 24 pieces about 1½ inches
   square
3 medium red bell peppers, cut into
   1½-inch squares (18, total)
12 chunks of spicy sausage (about
   1 inch thick), preferably linguiça,
   chorizo, or kielbasa

1. In a large bowl, combine the olive oil, lemon juice, thyme, garlic, crumbled bay leaf, salt, and pepper. Add the turkey chunks, cover, and refrigerate, stirring occasionally, for 2 to 4 hours.

2. On 6 metal skewers (or long bamboo skewers that have been soaked for 30 minutes and drained), thread alternating ingredients in the following order: turkey, red pepper, sausage chunk, whole bay leaf, repeating until all ingredients are used and finishing off each skewer with a piece of turkey. Reserve the turkey marinade. (The skewers can be prepared, covered, and refrigerated, for up to 2 hours before grilling.)

3. In a grill, prepare a charcoal fire, letting the fire burn down to moderate heat. (You should be able to hold your hand over the fire for 3 to 4 seconds.) Lightly oil the grilling rack. Grill the skewers, basting often with the reserved marinade, for 12 to 15 minutes, turning often, until the turkey pieces are cooked through. Serve the turkey-sausage skewers immediately.

> ▶ *Do not marinate poultry in marinades with a high proportion of acid ingredients, such as vinegar, lemon juice, or wine, for too long. The acids can give the cooked meat a mushy texture.*

Spice-Rubbed Smoked Turkey
with Bourbon Soppin' Sauce

Put a few long-necked beers in the cooler, set up a chaise longue in the shade, and get ready to spend a spell smoking a whole turkey, rubbed with zippy spices and slathered with a down-home firewater sauce. You will be rewarded with a gorgeous, crisp-skinned bird delicately flavored with hickory, mesquite, oak, or whatever wood you choose. Remember, smoking is an imprecise skill. Always give yourself a little leeway in timing. If the turkey is done ahead of schedule, no matter—it is fantastic served at room temperature, and no one will know the difference.

Makes 10 to 14 servings

1 whole hen turkey
  (10 to 12 pounds),
  giblets removed
¼ cup vegetable oil
2 tablespoons chili powder
1 tablespoon paprika, preferably
  Hungarian sweet
1 tablespoon freshly ground black
  pepper
1 tablespoon garlic salt
1 teaspoon cayenne pepper
2 large onions

4 to 6 cups hickory, mesquite, or oak
  chips, soaked in water for at least
  30 minutes, drained
6 tablespoons unsalted butter
2 garlic cloves, minced
2 cups ketchup
⅓ cup honey
⅓ cup lemon juice
⅓ cup bourbon
1 tablespoon plus 2 teaspoons
  Worcestershire sauce
1½ teaspoons hot pepper sauce

1. Rinse the turkey well inside and out with cold running water. Pat dry with paper towels. Remove the pop-up thermometer, if inserted. Fold the turkey wings akimbo behind its back. Place the drumsticks in the hock lock or tie together with kitchen string. Brush the turkey all over with some of the vegetable oil. In a small bowl, combine the chili powder, paprika, pepper, garlic salt, and cayenne. Rub the turkey, inside and out, with the spice mixture. Slice 1 of the onions and place the slices in the neck and body cavities of the turkey. Using a thin metal skewer or wooden toothpicks, pin the turkey's neck skin to the back. Cover the turkey with plastic wrap and refrigerate for at least 2 and up to 24 hours. Remove the turkey from the refrigerator 1 hour before smoking.

2. If you have a smoker, use it according to the manufacturer's instructions. To smoke in a covered grill, center a heatproof pan, approximately the same length and width as the turkey (disposable aluminum foil pans work well), on the bottom of the grill. Fill the pan halfway with water. Build charcoal fires on both sides of the pan, letting the fires burn down to moderate heat. (You should be able to hold your hand over the coals for 3 seconds.) Place the turkey on the grill over the pan. Sprinkle the coals with a handful of the drained wood chips and cover the grill immediately. Smoke the turkey until a thermometer inserted in the meatiest part of the thigh, not touching a bone, registers 180 degrees, about 5 to 6½ hours, allowing 30 to 40 minutes per pound. Maintain an average temperature of 225 degrees by adding more hot coals, wood chips, and water as necessary.

3. Meanwhile, chop the second onion. In a heavy medium saucepan, melt the butter over moderate heat. Add the onion and garlic and cook, stirring often, until the vegetables are softened, about 3 minutes. Add the remaining ingredients and simmer over low heat, stirring often to avoid scorching, until the sauce is slightly thickened, 40 to 50 minutes. Remove the sauce from the heat and let cool completely.

4. Let the smoked turkey stand for 20 minutes before carving, and serve, either hot or at room temperature, with the sauce on the side.

Tea-Smoked Oriental Turkey

Imagine the enticing aroma of jasmine tea leaves infusing a smoked turkey breast. The breast is marinated in a Far Eastern mixture of soy sauce, pineapple juice, ginger, sherry, and honey before it is slowly smoked. Serve this dish as part of a summer buffet, accompanied by a cold rice–and–sweet pepper salad, using as many colors of peppers as you can find.

Makes 4 to 6 servings

1 cup unsweetened pineapple juice
½ cup low-sodium soy sauce
¼ cup vegetable oil
2 tablespoons Oriental sesame oil (optional)
2 tablespoons honey
2 tablespoons coarsely chopped fresh ginger

2 tablespoons dry sherry
1 garlic clove, minced
½ teaspoon black peppercorns
1 whole turkey breast (5 pounds), bone in, skin on
½ cup jasmine tea leaves
½ cup rice
½ cup packed brown sugar

1. In a medium nonreactive saucepan, bring the pineapple juice, soy sauce, vegetable and sesame oils, honey, ginger, sherry, garlic, and peppercorns to a simmer over medium heat. Pour into large bowl and let cool completely.

2. Add the turkey breast to the cooled soy-sauce mixture and turn to coat. Cover and refrigerate, turning occasionally, for at least 8 hours or overnight. Remove the breast from the soy mixture and pat dry with paper towels, reserving the marinade.

3. To smoke the turkey breast in a covered grill, center a heatproof pan (disposable aluminum foil pans work well), approximately the same length and width as the breast, on the bottom of the grill. Place the reserved marinade in the pan and fill with enough water to reach halfway up the sides. Build charcoal fires on both sides of the pan, letting the fires burn down to moderate heat. (You should be able to hold your hand over the coals for about 3 seconds.) Place the breast over the pan.

4. Cook the breast until a thermometer inserted in the meatiest part, not touching a bone, registers 155 degrees, 1 to 1½ hours. Add more hot coals

and water as necessary. In a small bowl, combine the tea leaves, rice, and brown sugar. Sprinkle the tea mixture onto the coals, cover the grill immediately, and smoke until the thermometer registers 170 degrees, 30 to 45 minutes.

5. Let the turkey breast stand for 10 to 15 minutes before carving and serve either hot or at room temperature.

CHAPTER NINE

On the Side: Stuffings, Sauces, Relishes, and Side Dishes

A s fond as I am of Thanksgiving roast turkey, for me the meal comes as a complete package: tangy cranberry sauce, unctuous sweet potatoes, smooth gravy, and herbed stuffing all play major parts in the scheme. The only problem is deciding which recipes to make. A tableful of friends and family can only eat so much food.

How to choose which cranberry dish to make, when there's a choice of Gingery Lemon-Cranberry Chutney, Vermont Maple Cranberry Conserve, and Citrus-Cranberry Relish? It's easy. I just make all three. They are easy to make ahead and keep for days, if not weeks, in the refrigerator. Of course there are leftovers, which I pack up and send home with my delighted guests.

The real dilemma comes in picking a stuffing. In addition to those already detailed in the first chapter of this book, I have a recipe file crammed with delicious alternatives. This year should it be Oyster and Sausage Gumbo Dressing; Wild Rice, Cranberry, and Pecan Dressing; or Julie's Fancy Pâté Stuffing? (By the way, *dressing* is simply the Southern regional term for *stuffing*.) Or will everyone want a traditional filling, such as Basic Bread Stuffing 101, or one of its many alternative guises? I narrow down the problem by making two stuffings.

Stuffing must reach 165 degrees to be safely cooked, especially if it includes liver, raw meat, or eggs. With larger birds, the center of the stuffing can still be undercooked when the turkey is done. Consequently, if the turkey is stuffed, an extra 30 to 60 minutes must be added to the roasting time.

Therefore, my first choice is to fill the turkey with aromatics and seasonings and bake the stuffing separately. If your oven is big enough, although few are, you can bake your stuffing alongside the turkey during the last 30 or so minutes that the turkey roasts. Normally, I wait until my turkey is done and remove it to a sideboard, covered in foil, to rest before carving. (The turkey will stay warm up to 1 hour). My oven now empty, I use it to bake my stuffing, basting the stuffing with some of the bird's drippings to add extra turkey flavor.

Here are a few tips for stuffing turkey:

▶ Always stuff turkey just before roasting, never ahead of time. Harmful bacteria can develop inside the warm cavity.

▶ Never prepare stuffing the night before. To save time, cube the bread and let it sit out overnight. Prepare all the other ingredients and refrigerate them. Toss the stuffing together in the morning.

▶ Allow ½ to ¾ cup stuffing per person. Fill both the small neck and the large body cavities loosely to allow for expansion. While exact capacities vary depending on the individual bird, a turkey will generally hold about ½ cup stuffing per pound. Any extra can be baked in a pan on the side.

▶ To bake stuffing on the side, mix it with an extra ½ cup stock, water, or wine to keep it moist. Spoon it into a buttered casserole, cover with a lid or foil, and bake at 350 degrees until the stuffing is completely heated through and any raw ingredients are cooked, usually about 30 minutes. For a crusty top, remove the cover halfway through.

▶ To my taste, Italian or French bread make the best old-fashioned stuffings, though a firm-textured white sandwich bread can be used. I do not trim off the crust, because I like the extra bit of texture it adds. Stale bread makes the best-textured stuffing. Either use bread that has been sitting out for a day, or bake the bread cubes on baking sheets in a preheated 200-degree oven until dry, about 30 minutes.

▶ Remove all stuffing from the turkey before serving. Refrigerate left-over stuffing separately from the meat and use within 2 days. Or freeze it and use within 1 month. Reheat leftover stuffing thoroughly before serving.

In this chapter, you will also find my detailed recipe for Classic Pan Gravy. I find that many cooks, both experienced and novice, become nervous when it's time to make the gravy. So I have outlined a step-by-step technique that's guaranteed to work. As an extra fillip, a glaze, such as Honey-Lemon-Bourbon or Cranberry-Port, can be brushed over the turkey during the last hour of roasting for a glistening mahogany skin.

And for you sweet-potato fans, I offer a choice of flavors and styles: creamy Scalloped Sweet Potatoes with Streusel Topping, savory Gratinéed Stuffed Sweet Potatoes, topped with cheese, and an incredibly simple and subtle Sweet Potato and Pear Puree.

Many recipes in this book call for toasted nuts. To toast almonds, walnuts, and hazelnuts, place in a single layer on a baking sheet and bake in a 350-degree oven, stirring occasionally, until the nuts are fragrant, about 10 minutes. To skin hazelnuts, wrap the warm nuts in a kitchen towel and let stand 20 minutes. Using the towel, rub the nuts between your hands to remove the skins.

Gingery Lemon-Cranberry Chutney

Once you've offered this sweet-and-sour chutney to your guests, they will never want canned cranberry sauce again. I know, because it's happened to me and has even made converts of staunch traditionalists. This condiment's sweetness makes it a welcome addition to the breakfast table on toasted English muffins, especially with cream cheese.

Makes about 3 cups

1 medium lemon
1 package (12 ounces) fresh
   cranberries, rinsed and picked over
2 cups sugar
½ cup diced (¼-inch) crystallized
   ginger (2½ ounces)
½ small onion, finely chopped

1 garlic clove, minced
1 jalapeño pepper, seeded
   and minced, or ¼ teaspoon
   cayenne pepper
½ teaspoon ground cinnamon
½ teaspoon dry mustard
½ teaspoon salt

1. Using a vegetable peeler, remove the lemon zest and finely mince. Using a sharp paring knife, cut away the entire white pith. Cut the lemon into pieces about ¼ inch square, discarding the seeds.

2. In a medium nonreactive saucepan, combine the cranberries, minced lemon zest, diced lemon, sugar, ginger, onion, garlic, jalapeño, cinnamon, mustard, and salt. Cook over moderate heat, stirring constantly, until the sugar dissolves and the mixture comes to a simmer.

3. Reduce the heat to low and cook, stirring often, until the cranberries pop and the chutney is slightly thickened, about 3 minutes. Let cool completely. Serve at room temperature. (The chutney can be prepared up to 1 week ahead, covered tightly, and refrigerated.)

Vermont Maple Cranberry Conserve

Native New Englanders (by this I mean the "Indians") have long appreciated the combination of mellow-tasting, subtly sweet maple syrup and tart cranberries. I have added pecans and pears to make a refreshing, crunchy "no-cook" conserve.

Makes about 2½ cups

1 package (12 ounces) fresh
  cranberries, rinsed and picked over
1 ripe medium pear, peeled and
  quartered

½ cup plus 2 tablespoons
  maple syrup
3 tablespoons sugar
½ cup finely chopped pecans

Process the cranberries, pear, maple syrup, and sugar in a food processor until coarsely chopped. (You can also pass these ingredients through a meat grinder fitted with the coarse blade or chop them in batches in a blender.) Taste, and add additional sugar, if desired. Stir in the pecans. Transfer to a bowl, cover, and refrigerate for at least 4 hours or overnight. (The conserve can be prepared up to 1 week in advance.) Remove from the refrigerator 1 hour before serving.

▶ *If you use supermarket pancake syrup, which is a blend of maple and corn syrups plus flavorings, expect a sweeter maple flavor. The delicate flavor of 100-percent maple syrup, while superb, is, in my opinion, best where it can be appreciated alone, such as on pancakes and waffles.*

Citrus-Cranberry Relish

Whole tangerines, orange marmalade, and a good hit of Grand Marnier add a strong citrus character to this scrumptious side dish. It can be made quickly, and well ahead, with no loss in flavor or quality.

Makes about 3½ cups

2 medium tangerines, rinsed and dried
1 package (12 ounces) cranberries,
   rinsed and picked over
¾ cup orange marmalade

2 tablespoons sugar
2 tablespoons Grand Marnier or other
   orange-flavored liqueur

1. Halve the tangerines horizontally. Pick out the seeds with the tip of a small, sharp knife.

2. Coarsely chop the tangerines with skins on in a food processor. Add the cranberries, marmalade, sugar, and Grand Marnier. Process until the entire mixture is coarsely chopped. (You can also pass the mixture through a meat grinder fitted with the coarse blade or puree it in batches in a blender.) Taste, and add the additional sugar, if desired.

3. Transfer the relish to a bowl, cover, and refrigerate for at least 4 hours or overnight. (This recipe can be prepared up to 3 days ahead.) Remove from the refrigerator 1 hour before serving.

Basic Bread Stuffing 101

Here's my rendition of a familiar Thanksgiving tune, bread-and-herb stuffing, with a whole songbook full of variations on the theme. Stuffing is something that should be personal, so have fun when composing your own riff, using my basic structure as a guide.

Makes about 10 cups

1 stick unsalted butter
1 medium onion, finely chopped
2 celery ribs with leaves, finely chopped
2 teaspoons salt
1 teaspoon dried thyme
1 teaspoon dried rosemary
1 teaspoon crumbled dried sage

1 teaspoon freshly ground pepper
½ teaspoon dried savory
8 cups stale Italian or French bread, cut into 1-inch cubes
⅓ chopped fresh parsley
½ to 1 cup Homemade Turkey Stock (see page 246) or canned chicken broth

1. In a large skillet, melt the butter. Add the onion, celery, salt, thyme, rosemary, sage, pepper, and savory. Cook over moderate heat, stirring often, until the onion is softened, 4 to 5 minutes. Transfer the vegetables to a large bowl.

2. Add the bread cubes, parsley, and ½ cup stock and mix well. Either use to stuff a turkey or bake separately.

3. To bake separately, preheat the oven to 350 degrees. Place the stuffing in a buttered 9-by-13-inch baking dish. Drizzle another ½ cup of stock over the stuffing and cover the dish with aluminum foil. Bake until heated through, 35 to 45 minutes. (For a crusty top, remove the foil halfway through the baking time.)

CORN BREAD AND HAM STUFFING: Substitute Rick's Melt-in-Your-Mouth Corn Bread (see page 252), cut into 1-inch cubes and toasted, for either half or all of the bread cubes. Cook 1 red bell pepper, finely chopped, and 1 cup defrosted frozen corn kernels with the vegetables. Add 2 cups diced smoked or boiled ham (without a sweet glaze). Follow the recipe as directed.

(continued)

WHOLE WHEAT AND MUSHROOM STUFFING: Substitute stale or lightly toasted whole wheat bread for the Italian bread. Substitute 1 pound sliced fresh mushrooms for the celery. Follow the recipe as directed.

SAUSAGE AND PEAR STUFFING: Before cooking the vegetables in step 1, cook 1 pound mild bulk pork or turkey breakfast sausage in only 4 tablespoons butter, stirring and breaking up the meat with a wooden spoon, until it loses its pink color, about 5 minutes. Using a slotted spoon, transfer the sausage to a large bowl. Pour off all but ¼ cup of the drippings from the pan. Add 2 medium pears, cored and chopped, to the drippings in the skillet along with the vegetables, and continue with the recipe as directed.

WINTER VEGETABLE STUFFING: Peel and cut 1 medium celery root, 2 carrots, and 2 parsnips into ½-inch cubes. Cook with the vegetables in the butter for 2 minutes, add ½ cup stock or broth at this point, cover, and simmer until the vegetables are crisp-tender, about 10 minutes. Continue with the recipe as directed.

MEDITERRANEAN MEAT STUFFING: Cook 1½ pounds ground beef in the butter, stirring and breaking up with a wooden spoon, until it loses its pink color, about 5 minutes. Using a slotted spoon, transfer the beef to a large bowl. Substitute 1 teaspoon dried oregano for the sage. Add 1 cup pitted and coarsely chopped green olives to the stuffing. Continue with the recipe as directed, cooking the vegetables in the beef drippings.

CHESTNUT AND COGNAC DRESSING: Add 2 pounds chestnuts—roasted, peeled, and coarsely chopped—to the stuffing. Replace half of the chicken broth with ¼ cup Cognac or brandy. Continue with the recipe as directed.

ORANGE AND WALNUT DRESSING: Substitute 4 scallions for the onion. Use 4 navel oranges: grate the zest of 1 orange, remove the skin, pith, seeds, and tough center membranes from all 4 oranges; coarsely chop them. Add the oranges, zest, and 1½ cups toasted coarsely chopped walnuts to the stuffing. Continue with the recipe as directed.

Oyster and Sausage Gumbo Dressing

Simple herbed oyster dressing is standard holiday fare in many households, but when asked to create a heartier seafood stuffing for food-loving friends, I came up with this Cajun-inspired bulls'-eye. Plump shucked oysters are complemented by cubes of spicy sausage, chopped celery, red bell pepper, scallions, onions, and a host of bayou spices. Ask your fishmonger to shuck the oysters for you.

Makes about 10 cups

6 tablespoons unsalted butter
¾ pound smoked turkey or pork
    kielbasa, cut into ½-inch pieces
1 large onion, finely chopped
4 medium scallions, finely chopped
2 celery ribs with leaves, finely
    chopped
1 small red bell pepper, finely chopped
2 garlic cloves, minced
1 teaspoon dried oregano

1 teaspoon dried thyme
1 teaspoon salt
½ teaspoon freshly ground pepper
½ cup finely chopped fresh parsley
1 tablespoon Worcestershire sauce
6 cups cubed (1-inch) stale Italian or
    French bread
2 dozen oysters, shucked, oyster
    liquor reserved
2 large eggs, lightly beaten

1. In a large skillet, melt the butter. Add the kielbasa and cook over moderately high heat, stirring often, until the sausage is lightly browned, about 3 minutes. Using a slotted spoon, transfer the sausage to a large bowl. Add the onion, scallions, celery, red pepper, garlic, oregano, thyme, salt, and pepper to the fat remaining in the skillet. Cook, stirring often, until the onion is softened, 3 to 4 minutes. Stir in the parsley and Worcestershire; transfer to the bowl with the sausage.

2. Add the bread cubes, oysters with their liquor, and eggs to the bowl. Toss to mix well. (This dressing will be moist.) Either use as a stuffing or bake separately.

3. To bake separately, preheat the oven to 350 degrees. Place the stuffing in a buttered 9-by-13-inch baking dish and cover with aluminum foil. Bake until heated through, 35 to 45 minutes.

Wild Rice, Cranberry, and Pecan Dressing

Pair this exceptional dressing with a roast wild turkey and you will have a match made in heaven.

Makes about 8 cups

1 cup sugar
1 cup water
1 package (12 ounces) fresh cranberries
4 tablespoons unsalted butter
1 large onion, finely chopped
2 large celery ribs, finely chopped
2 cups wild rice, well rinsed

5 cups Homemade Turkey Stock (see page 246), or 2½ cups canned chicken broth mixed with 2½ cups water
1 teaspoon salt
1 teaspoon dried thyme
½ teaspoon freshly ground pepper
1 cup coarsely chopped pecans, toasted

1. In a medium saucepan, combine the sugar and water over moderate heat. Bring to a simmer, stirring constantly until the sugar is dissolved. Add the cranberries and cook just until all of the cranberries are popped, about 3 minutes. (Do not overcook; you want the cranberries to stay relatively whole.) Using a slotted spoon, transfer the cranberries to a medium bowl, leaving the cranberry syrup in the saucepan.

2. In a large saucepan, melt the butter over moderate heat. Add the onion and celery and cook, stirring often, until the vegetables are softened, about 4 minutes. Add the wild rice and cook, stirring, for 1 minute. Add the stock, salt, thyme, and pepper. Bring to a boil, reduce the heat to low, cover, and simmer until the wild rice is tender but pleasantly chewy, about 45 minutes.

3. Remove from the heat and let stand, covered, for 15 minutes. (Drain the wild rice of excess cooking liquid, if necessary.) Add the wild-rice mixture and the toasted pecans to the cranberries. Toss to mix well. Either use as a turkey stuffing or bake separately.

4. To bake separately, preheat the oven to 350 degrees. Place in a buttered 9-by-13-inch baking dish and bake, covered, until heated through, 30 to 40 minutes.

▶ *The delectable syrup left in the saucepan can be used to create "Thanksgiving Kirs": Stir a bit into a glass of champagne or dry white wine.*

Lancaster County Dressing

Imagine chunks of tender potatoes, dotted with bits of celery, scented with caraway, and blended with buttery bread cubes. This is for those of us who can't decide which we like better—potatoes or stuffing.

Makes about 12 cups

4 medium boiling potatoes (about 2 pounds), well scrubbed
1 stick unsalted butter
1 medium onion, finely chopped
2 medium celery ribs, finely chopped
6 cups stale Italian or French bread, cut into 1-inch cubes

2 large eggs, lightly beaten
⅓ cup chopped fresh parsley
1 tablespoon caraway seed
¾ teaspoon salt
½ teaspoon freshly ground pepper
½ cup Homemade Turkey Stock (see page 246) or canned chicken broth (optional)

1. In a large saucepan of boiling salted water, cook the potatoes until just tender, about 25 minutes. Drain, rinse under cold running water, peel, and cut into 1-inch cubes.

2. In a large skillet, melt the butter over moderate heat. Add the onion and celery and cook, stirring often, until the vegetables are softened, 3 to 4 minutes.

3. In a large bowl, combine the bread and potato cubes, the onions and celery, eggs, parsley, caraway, salt, and pepper. Either use as a turkey stuffing or bake separately.

4. To bake separately, preheat the oven to 350 degrees. Place in a buttered 9-by-13-inch baking dish. Drizzle the stock over the stuffing and cover the dish with aluminum foil. Bake until heated through, about 30 minutes.

Rick's Kitchen Sink Stuffing

This is the stuffing I prepare most often, because it has something for everyone. We call it my "kitchen sink" stuffing, because that's about the only thing that isn't an ingredient! Moist, herby, chunky, meaty—it has it all.

Makes about 12 cups

2 tablespoons unsalted butter
1½ pounds ground bulk breakfast sausage, pork or turkey (not spicy)
2 medium onions, chopped
2 medium celery ribs, chopped
2 medium carrots, chopped
2 medium green apples, such as Granny Smith or Pippin, cored and chopped
8 cups stale Italian or French bread, cut into 1-inch cubes

1½ pounds roasted and peeled chestnuts, coarsely chopped
½ cup dry white wine
½ cup chopped fresh parsley
2 tablespoons poultry seasoning
2 teaspoons salt
½ teaspoon freshly ground pepper
1 cup Homemade Turkey Stock (see page 246) or canned chicken broth (optional)

1. In a large skillet, melt the butter over moderate heat, Add the sausage and cook, stirring often and breaking up the meat with a wooden spoon, until the sausage loses its pink color, about 8 minutes. Do not brown the sausage. Using a slotted spoon, transfer the sausage to a large bowl. Pour off all but ¼ cup of the drippings.

2. Add the onions, celery, carrots, and apples to the skillet. Cook over moderate heat, stirring often, until the onions are softened, 8 to 10 minutes; add to the sausage. Add the bread cubes, chestnuts, wine, parsley, poultry seasoning, salt, and pepper, and mix well. Either use to stuff a turkey or bake separately.

3. If baking separately, preheat the oven to 350 degrees. Divide the stuffing between two buttered 9-by-13-inch baking dishes. Drizzle the stock over the stuffing and cover with aluminum foil. Bake until heated through, about 30 minutes.

Pumpernickel and Autumn Fruit Stuffing

The robust, slightly sour taste of dark rye bread is balanced by the sweet flavors of dried pears, apples, prunes, and apricots. I use supermarket packages of mixed dried fruit, but you can use 3 cups of any combination of dried fruit that is available. When you make a gravy to go with this stuffing, add 2 tablespoons of brandy or applejack to every 2 cups of poultry stock to strike a complementary note.

Makes about 9 cups

2 packages (8 ounces each) mixed dried fruit, coarsely chopped (about 3 cups loosely packed)
2 cups water
1 stick unsalted butter
1 medium onion, chopped
2 celery ribs with leaves, chopped

7 cups (about 1 pound) pumpernickel bread cubes
½ cup Homemade Turkey Stock (see page 246) or canned chicken broth
¼ cup brandy or applejack
1 teaspoon salt
½ teaspoon freshly ground pepper

1. In a medium saucepan, combine the fruit with the water. Simmer over low heat until the fruit is plumped, about 3 minutes. Drain, reserving ½ cup of the cooking liquid.

2. In a large skillet, melt the butter. Add the onion and celery and cook over moderate heat, stirring often, until the vegetables are softened, about 7 minutes.

3. In a large bowl, combine the bread cubes, cooked vegetables with their butter, cooked fruit, stock, the reserved fruit-cooking liquid, and the brandy. Season with the salt and pepper. Either use to stuff a turkey or bake separately.

4. To bake separately, preheat the oven to 350 degrees. Place the stuffing in a buttered 9-by-13-inch baking dish and cover with foil. Bake until heated through, 30 to 40 minutes.

Corn Bread and Chorizo Stuffing

My friend Nelson made this incredible concoction one year for a table full of spice-loving guests. Actually, it is too good to save for only once a year, and I often make it for dinner parties as a side dish for Texas Turkey with Chili-Onion Rub (see page 9).

Makes about 12 cups

1 tablespoon olive oil
1 pound pork chorizo, casings removed, coarsely crumbled (see Note)
2 medium onions, finely chopped
4 medium celery ribs, finely chopped
1 small red bell pepper, finely chopped
1 small green bell pepper, finely chopped
2 garlic cloves, minced

Cheddar and Chili Corn Bread (see page 252), either a day old or dried in the oven
¾ cup Homemade Turkey Stock (see page 246) or canned chicken broth
4 tablespoons unsalted butter, melted
¼ cup chopped fresh parsley
2 teaspoons crumbled dried sage
½ teaspoon salt
¼ teaspoon freshly ground pepper

1. In a large skillet, heat the oil. Add the chorizo and cook over moderate heat, stirring often, until lightly browned, about 5 minutes. Add the onions, celery, red and green peppers, and garlic. Cook, stirring often, until the vegetables are softened, about 5 minutes.

2. In a large bowl, mix together the chorizo and vegetables with the corn bread, stock, melted butter, parsley, sage, salt, and pepper. (The dressing can be prepared up to 4 hours ahead, covered, and refrigerated.) Either use as a stuffing for turkey or bake separately.

3. To bake separately, preheat the oven to 350 degrees. Place the stuffing in a buttered 9-by-13-inch baking dish, and cover with foil. Bake until heated through, 30 to 40 minutes.

Note: Low-Fat Turkey Chorizo (see page 119) can be substituted for the pork chorizo. If using turkey chorizo, do not brown first in oil, but cook with vegetables until the vegetables are softened, about 10 minutes.

Julie's Fancy Pâté Stuffing

One day, while swapping recipes, my neighbor, Paul Buhtanic, told me of his mother Julie's traditional Slavic meat stuffing, which is a close cousin to pâté. I immediately jotted down the instructions and tested it the next day. Serve alongside a gorgeous roast turkey with plenty of your best gravy. If you can't fit all of your dressing in the turkey, you can either bake it separately or roll it into little meatballs and fry them on top of the stove.

Makes about 8 cups

4 tablespoons unsalted butter
2 medium onions, chopped
2 celery ribs, chopped
2 garlic cloves, minced
2 cups fresh bread crumbs
3 large eggs, lightly beaten
¼ cup brandy or Cognac
2 pounds ground beef

1½ pounds ground turkey
1 pound ground pork
½ cup chopped fresh parsley
1 tablespoon salt
2 teaspoons dried thyme
½ teaspoon ground allspice
½ teaspoon dried savory
1 teaspoon freshly ground pepper

1. In a large skillet, melt the butter over moderate heat. Add the onions, celery, and garlic. Cook, stirring often, until the vegetables are softened, about 5 minutes.

2. In a large bowl, combine the bread crumbs, eggs, and brandy. Add the ground meats, cooked vegetable mixture, parsley, salt, thyme, allspice, savory, and pepper. Mix well with your hands to combine. Use as a turkey stuffing and bake excess separately.

3. To bake separately, preheat the oven to 375 degrees. Place the excess stuffing in a 9-by-5-by-3-inch loaf pan. Bake until a meat thermometer inserted in the center of the dressing reads 160 degrees, about 1 hour.

Wild, Wild Stuffing

Wild rice and wild mushrooms are luxurious ingredients, so I save this special stuffing for my toniest affairs. If you have access to fresh shiitake mushrooms, substitute them for the white. Do try to find the *pancetta* (an unsmoked rolled Italian bacon), but slab bacon, cooked first for 5 minutes in boiling water to remove the salt and the smoky flavor, would work in a pinch.

Makes about 12 cups

2 ounces dried porcini mushrooms (see Note)
1 cup boiling water
4 tablespoons unsalted butter
2 pounds fresh white button mushrooms, thickly sliced
½ pound *pancetta*, cut into ¼-inch dice (see Note)
4 shallots, minced

3 cups wild rice, well rinsed
7 cups Homemade Turkey Stock (see page 246), or 3½ cups canned chicken broth mixed with 3½ cups water
1 tablespoon chopped fresh rosemary, or 1 teaspoon dried
1½ teaspoons salt
½ teaspoon freshly ground pepper

1. In a small bowl, cover the porcini with the boiling water. Let stand until softened, 20 to 30 minutes. Lift out the porcini; reserve the liquid. Rinse the porcini well to remove any hidden grit and chop coarsely. Strain the liquid through a paper coffee filter or a double layer of cheesecloth and reserve.

2. In a large skillet, melt 2 tablespoons of the butter over moderately high heat. Add the fresh mushrooms and cook, stirring often, until the mushrooms give up their liquid, about 3 minutes. Add the chopped porcini and the soaking liquid, and cook until almost all of the liquid is evaporated, about 5 minutes. Remove from the heat.

3. In a large saucepan, melt the remaining 2 tablespoons of butter over moderate heat. Add the *pancetta* and cook, stirring often, until the cubes are lightly browned, about 5 minutes. Add the shallots and cook until softened, about 1 minute. Add the wild rice, cooked mushrooms, stock or broth, rosemary, salt, and pepper. Bring to a boil, reduce the heat to low, cover, and simmer until the wild rice is tender but pleasantly chewy, about 45 minutes. Remove from heat and let stand, covered, until all of the liquid is

absorbed, about 15 minutes. (Drain the wild rice of excess cooking liquid, if necessary). Either use as a stuffing for turkey or serve separately. (The dressing can be made up to 1 day ahead, covered, and refrigerated.)

4. If baking separately, preheat the oven to 350 degrees. Place the stuffing in a buttered 9-by-13-inch baking dish and cover with foil. Bake until heated through, 30 to 40 minutes.

Note: Porcini mushrooms are available at Italian delicatessens and specialty grocers, or by mail order from Dean and Deluca, 800-221-7714; 212-431-1691. Pancetta is available at Italian delicatessens and specialty grocers, and by mail order from Rapelli of California, 1090 West Church, Fresno, California, 93706; 800-232-3354, in California, 800-628-2633.

Classic Pan Gravy

Although there is a pan gravy included in the recipe for Perfect Roast Turkey (see page 8), I have separated these instructions with details so you will have them handy during a possible "gravy crisis." Everyone has their own way of making gravy—thickening with a flour-water paste or cornstarch, cooking the gravy in a saucepan or in the roasting pan, and so on. I would like to give you my recipe for possibly the best giblet pan gravy you'll ever have, with suggestions you can apply that may be useful with whatever gravy recipe you may use.

▶ Delicious pan drippings are the secret to an excellent gravy. Don't let your drippings burn during roasting. If the drippings look like they are turning too dark, add water, wine, or stock to the bottom of the pan to keep the drippings moist.

▶ Always degrease your drippings, stock, or broth before using to make gravy.

▶ The proportions for any gravy are 1 tablespoon each butter and all-purpose flour to each cup of liquid, part of which should be the pan drippings. Use these proportions for any size turkey and any amount of gravy. For example, for about 4 cups of gravy, use 4 cups of liquid and 4 tablespoons each of butter and flour. This makes a beautiful gravy that pours well. If you want a thicker gravy, you may increase the butter and flour up to 2 tablespoons each for each 1 cup of liquid.

▶ Invest in a wire whisk. It is your best bet for avoiding lumps.

▶ Up to one-fourth of your gravy-cooking liquid can be dry red or white wine. You may use 1 to 2 tablespoons of sherry, port, Madeira, or brandy per cup of gravy cooking liquid. A higher proportion of alcohol may make the gravy too strong.

Makes about 3½ cups

Cooked giblets and neck from
   Homemade Turkey Stock
   (see page 246)
Pan drippings from roast
   turkey

About 3½ cups Homemade Turkey
   Stock (see page 246), or 2 cups
   canned chicken broth mixed with
   1½ cups water (see Note)
4 tablespoons unsalted butter
¼ cup all-purpose flour
Salt and freshly ground pepper

1. Remove the heart, gizzard, and neck from the turkey stock. Remove the neck meat in strips; finely chop neck meat and giblets.

2. As soon as your turkey is done, set it aside on a carving board, loosely covered with foil to keep warm. Pour the pan drippings into a 1-quart measuring cup or medium bowl. Leave any browned bits in the bottom of the pan. Let stand for 5 minutes and skim the clear yellow fat that rises to the top. Add enough turkey stock to make 4 cups total cooking liquid.

3. Set the roasting pan on top of the stove over 2 burners, add the butter, and melt over moderately low heat. Sprinkle on the flour and cook, whisking constantly, until the mixture is beige, 1 to 2 minutes. Whisk in the cooking liquid and bring to a boil, scraping up the brown bits from the bottom and sides of the pan. Add the giblets and simmer for 2 to 3 minutes, whisking occasionally. Season the gravy with salt and pepper to taste. Pour the gravy into a warmed sauceboat and serve hot.

> *Note: Instead of making stock, cook the giblets in 4 cups of canned chicken broth and 2 cups of water until tender, about 2 hours. Strain the cooking liquid and add additional water to make 4 cups, if necessary. Use this liquid in place of the Homemade Turkey Stock.*

Homemade Turkey Stock

Every Thanksgiving, I make a double batch of turkey stock, and it's amazing how fast the whole pot goes. First I dip into the pot for a little stock to moisten my dressing. Next I measure out a quart or two for my first course, usually a light, appetite-teasing soup. Then a good amount is turned into cream sauce for baby onions. And at least 3 cups are used in the gravy. Any leftover stock is utilized the next day when I cook up the carcass for soup, or frozen for future use. Obviously, a tasty turkey stock is an important component of the holiday celebrations, but try to have some on hand in the freezer year-round to add character to everyday meals.

Tips for Perfect Turkey Stock

Don't let my long list of tips throw you off—turkey stock is *easy to make*. But even simple chores have their little secrets to make things go more smoothly.

▶ If you are cooking up a large batch of stock, purchase turkey backs, wings, or necks separately, rather than gathering up the giblets of 2 or 3 turkeys. Double the ingredients in the recipe below for every 2 pounds of turkey parts. Turkey wings, because of their large proportions of skin and bone, make especially good stock.

▶ Never let stock come to a rolling boil, or it will get cloudy and have a less refined flavor. I use my ancient college crockpot (which I thought was permanently retired) to make foolproof stock. The night before I need the stock, I brown the turkey pieces in the broiler for about 20 minutes, turning often, then transfer them, with the other ingredients, to the crockpot. The stock barely simmers all night long, creating the clearest, most delicious stock imaginable.

▶ I find that there just isn't enough meat on a single turkey's neck and giblets to make a full-flavored stock. So I add a *small amount* of canned chicken broth to underline the poultry flavor. (Too much canned chicken broth will overwhelm the turkey.) If you are a purist, add a few chicken wings or additional turkey parts to the stock to strengthen the flavor instead.

- ▶ Always salt your stock at the end of the cooking time, not the beginning. Canned chicken broth is salty, and the salt flavor will intensify as the liquid in the stock evaporates.

- ▶ Don't add herbs and spices to a stock until after you've skimmed it. If you add the seasonings at the beginning, they will float to the top of the stock in the foam with the impurities and be removed along with the foam when skimming.

To store turkey broth, cool it to room temperature before refrigerating. The best and quickest way is to strain the stock into a large bowl set in a larger bowl of ice water, then stir often to cool. Change the ice water as it melts. Degrease the stock, transfer to a covered container, and refrigerate for up to 3 days.

Freeze the stock, if desired. Transfer the cooled stock to 1- or 2-cup plastic containers for ease in defrosting and measuring, cover, and freeze for up to 3 months.

Makes about 1 quart

Neck and giblets from 1 turkey
1 tablespoon vegetable oil
1 small onion, chopped
1 small carrot, chopped
1 small rib celery, chopped
5 cups cold water
1¾ cups canned chicken broth

¾ cup dry white wine or additional water
4 sprigs of parsley
¼ teaspoon dried thyme
¼ teaspoon peppercorns
1 small bay leaf
½ teaspoon salt

1. Using a heavy meat cleaver or a large knife, chop the neck into 1- to 1½-inch pieces. Using a sharp knife, trim away any membranes from the giblets, especially the gizzard. In a medium saucepan, heat the oil. Add the neck and giblet pieces and cook over moderate heat, stirring often, until the turkey is browned all over, about 10 minutes.

2. Add the onion, carrot, and celery; cook, stirring often, until the vegetables are lightly browned, about 5 minutes. Add the water, chicken broth, and wine. Bring to a simmer over moderately high heat, skimming off the foam. Reduce the heat to low and add the parsley, thyme, peppercorns, and bay leaf. Simmer for 2 to 3 hours, the longer the better.

3. Strain the stock into a large bowl. Let stand for 5 minutes and skim off the clear yellow fat that rises to the surface. If desired, reserve the giblets,

(continued)

cool, and chop finely for use in gravy. (The neck meat may be removed in strips, chopped, and reserved, as well.) Cool the stock completely before refrigerating or freezing.

MICROWAVE INSTRUCTIONS: Place all ingredients except the oil in a large microwave-safe bowl, and cover tightly with microwave-safe plastic wrap. Microwave on Medium (50 percent) for 60 minutes. (Try not to let the stock come to a full boil.) Strain and skim off the fat. For a brown stock, broil the turkey parts, turning often, until browned, then proceed.

▶ *Turkeys are not stupid. They are very curious birds and will investigate any unusual objects. However, when visiting a turkey farm, I was warned that they are so curious they can crush each other in attempting to check out any disruption.*

Honey-Lemon-Bourbon Glaze

Every now and then, you want to add a little fillip to your turkey. This glaze adds both color and flavor.

Makes about 1 cup

6 tablespoons unsalted
  butter

½ cup honey
2 tablespoons bourbon

In a small saucepan, melt the butter. Stir in the honey and bourbon. To use as a glaze, brush on the turkey every 20 minutes during the last hour of estimated roasting time. If the turkey begins to get too brown, tent loosely with aluminum foil.

Cranberry-Port Glaze

Don't worry if you have some of this fruity glaze, with its hints of orange and port wine, left over. Simply offer it on the side as a smooth sauce to drizzle onto sliced turkey along with your gravy.

Makes enough for a 12- to 18-pound turkey

2 cups fresh cranberries
1 cup water
1 cup sugar

½ cup port wine
Grated zest of 1 large orange
⅓ cup fresh orange juice

1. In a medium nonreactive saucepan, combine all of the ingredients and cook over moderate heat, stirring frequently, until the cranberries pop and the sugar is dissolved, 3 to 5 minutes. Reduce the heat to low and simmer for 2 minutes. Transfer the mixture to a food processor and puree. (The glaze can be prepared up to 3 days ahead, covered, and refrigerated. Reheat gently just before using.)

2. To use the glaze, 1 hour before the end of the estimated cooking time, baste the turkey with some of the warm glaze. If the glaze cools and firms, reheat gently until viscous again. Baste the turkey every 20 minutes, a total of 3 times. (Do not start basting earlier or the glaze may scorch.) If the turkey is not cooked through by the end of the glazing period, tent the turkey with aluminum foil until the turkey is done.

Harriet's Secret Glaze

Practically every chef has a favorite family recipe that they secretly crave, regardless of how unsophisticated or mismatched the ingredients may seem. My pal, Harriet Bell, who just happens to be one of the best cookbook editors in the business, swears by this unusual concoction. It creates the darkest, crispest, most delicious turkey skin ever—as well as adding succulence to the meat inside the tasty covering.

Makes enough glaze for an 18- to 24-pound turkey

1 stick unsalted butter
1 jar (12 ounces) red currant jelly
1 cup dry red wine

1 can (8 ounces) tomato sauce
2 teaspoons Worcestershire sauce

1. In a medium nonreactive saucepan, melt the butter. Add the jelly, wine, tomato sauce, and Worcestershire. Bring to a simmer over moderately low heat, stirring to dissolve the jelly. (The glaze can be prepared up to 3 days ahead, covered, and refrigerated. Reheat gently just before using.)

2. To use the glaze, baste the turkey, loosely tented with aluminum foil, with the glaze mixture every 30 minutes. (It is important to tent the entire turkey when using this glaze, or the glaze may scorch.) During the last hour of the estimated roasting time, remove the aluminum foil, allowing the turkey skin to brown.

Scalloped Sweet Potatoes with Streusel Topping

In their typical holiday guises, sweet potatoes are just *too* sweet for me. But even I ask for seconds then they're topped with just the right amount of brown-sugar streusel.

Makes 8 servings

6 medium (about 3 pounds) sweet potatoes, peeled and cut into ¼-inch-thick slices
1½ cups heavy cream

2 tablespoons unsalted butter, softened
2 tablespoons all-purpose flour
¼ cup packed light brown sugar

1. Cook the sliced sweet potatoes in a large pot of boiling salted water for 2 minutes. Drain, rinse under cold running water, and drain well. (The sweet potatoes can be prepared up to this point 8 hours ahead, covered, and refrigerated.)

2. Preheat the oven to 375 degrees. Lightly butter a 9-by-13-inch baking dish. Place the sweet-potato slices, slightly overlapping in rows, in the prepared dish. Pour the cream over the sweet potatoes. In a small bowl, using your fingers, work the butter, flour, and brown sugar together until well combined. Sprinkle the streusel mixture over the top of the sweet potatoes.

3. Bake until the sweet potatoes are tender and the topping is browned, 40 to 50 minutes. Serve hot.

Rick's Melt-in-Your-Mouth Corn Bread

While I am nuts about corn bread, I am persnickety about its fine points. I don't like it dry, crumbly, or overly sweet. (Many a good corn-bread stuffing recipe has been ruined by a sweet-as-cake commercial instant corn-bread mix.) And packaged corn-bread stuffing is too salty. My recipe is so moist and tender it barely needs to be buttered.

Makes two 9-inch round loaves, 8 servings each

2 cups yellow cornmeal
2 cups all-purpose flour
2 tablespoons sugar
1½ teaspoons salt
1½ teaspoons baking soda

3 cups buttermilk, at room
  temperature
1½ sticks unsalted butter, melted and
  cooled
3 large eggs, lightly beaten

1. Preheat the oven to 375 degrees. In a large bowl, whisk the cornmeal, flour, salt, and baking soda to combine. Make a well in the center of the dry ingredients and pour in the buttermilk, 6 tablespoons of the melted butter, and the beaten eggs; whisk just until smooth.

2. Divide the remaining melted butter between two 9-inch round cake pans. Place in the oven and bake until the butter is hot but not browned, about 2 minutes. Divide the batter between the 2 pans and bake until the corn bread begins to shrink from the sides of the pan and a toothpick inserted in the centers comes out clean, 25 to 30 minutes. Cool the loaves in the pans on wire cake racks for 5 minutes. Cut into wedges; remove wedges with a spatula and serve while warm, or cool and use for dressing.

CHEESE AND CHILI CORN BREAD: Stir 1 cup grated sharp Cheddar cheese (4 ounces) and 2 cans chopped green chilies, rinsed and drained (or 2 to 4 tablespoons minced fresh green chilies), into the batter. Sprinkle another 1 cup grated sharp Cheddar cheese over tops of the unbaked corn bread and bake as above.

Note: To use for stuffing, cool the corn bread to room temperature. Crumble it into 2- to 3-inch pieces, place on 2 baking sheets, and let stand overnight at room temperature. Alternatively, bake the corn bread in a preheated 250-degree oven until dried, about 30 minutes.

Gratinéed Stuffed Sweet Potatoes

Here's another sweet potato recipe that is practically effortless. The chewy roasted skins are a treat, and the slight saltiness of the cheese cuts the sweetness of the potatoes.

Makes 8 servings

4 large sweet potatoes (about 2 pounds), well scrubbed
3 tablespoons unsalted butter, softened

1 cup grated Swiss or Gruyère cheese (about 4 ounces)

1. Preheat the oven to 375 degrees. On a baking sheet, bake the sweet potatoes until tender, 50 to 60 minutes. Cool slightly, then cut in half lengthwise. Using a spoon, scoop out and reserve the insides of the sweet potatoes, leaving a ¼-inch shell with the skin.

2. In a medium bowl, using a fork, mash the sweet potatoes with the butter. Fill the skin shells with the mashed sweet potatoes and place on a baking sheet. Sprinkle the top of each potato half with the grated cheese. (The potatoes can be prepared up to this point 8 hours ahead, covered, and refrigerated.)

3. Increase the oven temperature to 400 degrees. Bake the potatoes until the cheese is melted and bubbling, 5 to 10 minutes. Serve hot.

Sweet Potato and Pear Puree

Sweet potatoes and pears—that's it. No amount of butter, cream, or sugar will make it any more delicious, so why gild the lily?

Makes 6 to 8 servings

6 large sweet potatoes (about 3 pounds), peeled and cut into 2-inch chunks

4 medium ripe pears, peeled, quartered, and cored

In a large saucepan of lightly salted boiling water, cook the sweet potatoes until almost tender, 20 to 25 minutes. Add the pears and cook until both are tender, about 5 minutes. Drain well; transfer to a large bowl. Using an electric hand mixer, mash the sweet potatoes and pears to desired consistency. Serve immediately. (The puree can be prepared up to 1 day ahead, refrigerated, and reheated slowly over low heat, stirring often.)

INDEX

Dilled yogurt sauce, Scandinavian meatballs
in, 160
reduced-fat, 160
Dip
blue cheese, Buffalo turkey wings with,
121
peanut, Indonesian turkey satés with, 214
Dirty rice dressing, 16
Bayou roast turkey with, 14
Dressing. *See* Salad dressing; Stuffing
Drumsticks
about, 112
braised, with olives over pasta, 114
microwave instructions, 115
reduced-fat and -calorie, 115
Guadalajara grilled, 210
and hominy soup, Mexican, 118
minestrone, 120
reduced-fat, 121
osso buco–style, 113
sauerkraut-smothered smoked, 125
and smoked turkey sausage gumbo, 126
spinach-and-feta-stuffed, 116
Dumplings
ricotta, Nonni's turkey vegetable soup
with, 66
scallion, Beulah's turkey fricassee with, 84
and turkey casserole, "take it easy," 47

Enchiladas, turkey and olive, with red
sauce, 50

Fajitas, turkey, 212
reduced-fat, 213
Farmer's turkey potpie with mashed potato
crust, 165
Feta cheese, drumsticks stuffed with
spinach and, 116
Flaky chive crust, 92
turkey potpie with, 90
Fontina cheese, turkey cutlets with
asparagus and, 152
Four seasons corn and turkey chowder, 109
Fragrant rice stuffing, roast turkey with, 22
French-style dishes
burgers au poivre, 167
confit, old-fashioned turkey, 202
daube of turkey, 200
galatine of turkey, 204
herbed turkey and Cognac pâté, 190

Fresh turkey, about, xi
Fricassee with scallion dumplings, Beulah's
turkey, 84
Frozen turkey, about, xii
Fruit(s)
autumn, and pumpernickel stuffing,
239
and pork stuffing, rich, roast turkey
Lombardy style with, 10
quick turkey curry with nuts and, 46

Garlic
cream, pasta with turkey and artichokes
in, 144
Italian lemon-rosemary turkey with
roasted potatoes and, 26
Giblet gravy, perfect roast turkey with
gorgeous, 7
Ginger
lemon-cranberry chutney, gingery, 230
sauce, Cantonese turkey and vegetable
stir-fry with, 132
-and-soy-braised turkey breast, 76
Glaze(d)
chestnut stuffing, wild turkey with, 36
cranberry-port, 249
Harriet's secret, 250
honey-lemon-bourbon, 248
peachy plantation, turkey breast roast
with bourbon gravy and, 82
sweet-and-sour, 29
Grapefruit and turkey salad, with poppy
seed dressing, 95
Grape leaves stuffed with turkey, rice, and
mint, 188
Gravy
bourbon, turkey breast roast with peachy
plantation glaze and, 82
classic pan, 244
giblet, perfect roast turkey with gorgeous,
7
loaf, all-in-one, 42
ranch-house milk, chicken-fried turkey
steaks with, 153
Greek-style dishes
burgers, turkey, 175
company casserole with zucchini and
potatoes, 194
grape leaves stuffed with rice, mint, and,
188

Indonesian turkey satés with peanut dip, 214

Italian-style dishes. *See also* Pasta
antipasti roulade, turkey breast, 98
breaded turkey cutlets with Parmesan cheese, 140
burgers, turkey, 175
cold turkey breast with tuna sauce, 96
drumsticks osso buco–style, 113
grilled turkey steaks Romano, 217
lemon-rosemary turkey with roasted potatoes and garlic, 26
marinara sauce, herbed, 183
minestrone, turkey, 120
reduced-fat, 121
pizza
dough, food processor, 151
heartland, 150
Lucky's turkey, with fresh tomato sauce, olives, and jalapeños, 218
risotto, turkey and wild mushroom, 192
roast turkey with rich pork and fruit stuffing, Lombardy style, 10
saltimbocca, 139
sausage-stuffed turkey rollatini, 138
scallopini Marsala with mushrooms, turkey, 148
tetrazzini, Luisa's turkey, 54
thighs in herbed tomato sauce with polenta, 124
turkey cutlets with prosciutto and Parmesan, 142

Jalapeños, Lucky's turkey pizza with fresh tomato sauce, olives, and, 218
Julie's fancy pâté stuffing, 241

Kebabs, turkey thighs and summer vegetable, 211
Kielbasa
in dirty rice dressing, 16
turkey, sources for, 16
and turkey gumbo, 126
and turkey on skewers, marinated, 221
Kosher turkeys, xiii

Lancaster County dressing, 237
Lard, to make, 203
Lazy day turkey potpie, 44

Leftover turkey, 39–69
all-in-one gravy loaf, 42
and bacon, and tomato club sandwiches with blue cheese mayonnaise, 62
cheesy tomato and turkey bake, 43
chilaquiles, 51
and corn croquettes with fresh tomato salsa, 56
and corn spoon bread, 45
curry with fruits and nuts, quick, 46
divan, zippy, 53
and dumpling casserole, "take it easy," 47
hash pancakes O'Brien, 59
hints on, 39–40
à la king
new wave, 58
traditional, 59
-noodle supper, Pennsylvania Dutch, 48
and olive enchiladas with red sauce, 50
potpie, lazy day, 44
sandwiches
Cheddar, apple, and, toasted, 63
Monte Cristo, 65
smoked, pasta bow ties with sun-dried tomatoes, basil, and, 64
soup
cream of, 69
noodle, 69
vegetable, old-fashioned, 68
southwestern stir-fry with peppers, corn, and, 61
to store, 5–6
-Swiss soufflé, nutted, 55
tetrazzini, Luisa's, 54
tostadas mañana, 67
turnovers, tearoom, 60
vegetable soup, Nonni's, with ricotta dumplings, 66
and wild mushroom risotto, 192
Lemon
-cranberry chutney, gingery, 230
-honey-bourbon glaze, 248
-rosemary turkey with roasted potatoes and garlic, Italian, 26
sauce, roast turkey with Greek stuffing and, 30
-tarragon turkey cutlets, 131
Linguiça and turkey on skewers, marinated, 221